Thomas Brayshaw

Churchwardens of Giggleswick, 1683-1883

Thomas Brayshaw

Churchwardens of Giggleswick, 1683-1883

ISBN/EAN: 9783337162276

Printed in Europe, USA, Canada, Australia, Japan

Cover: Foto ©ninafisch / pixelio.de

More available books at **www.hansebooks.com**

CHURCHWARDENS

OF

GIGGLESWICK.

1638—1883.

COMPILED BY

THOS. BRAYSHAW.

STACKHOUSE,
NEAR SETTLE,
MARCH 13TH, 1884.

Amongst the books deposited in the safe at Giggleswick Church is a very old one, much worn and tattered, but recently touched up and rebound in vellum; and in this book have been recorded, year by year, the names of the Churchwardens, and in many cases, those of the overseers and other parochial officers.

Thinking that this is a matter of general interest, I have extracted the list of churchwardens and arranged them in tabulated form.

It may be as well to state that from time immemorial, there have been four wardens at Giggleswick, one each for Giggleswick, Settle, and Stainforth, and (until the year 1851,) one for the townships of Rathmell and Langcliffe alternately. In 1851 however, Langcliffe was created a Vicarage, (Settle and Stainforth remaining perpetual curacies,) and from that date the fourth warden has represented Rathmell only.

A few items from other Church books, in connection with the Churchwardens or their accounts, are added.

THOS. BRAYSHAW.

Six large and fifty small paper copies printed for private circulation.

Churchwardens of the Parish Church of Giggleswick.

Year	Giggleswick.	Settle.	Stainforth.	Rathmell and Langcliffe.
1638	Richd. Preston	Robert Carr	Richd. Carr	Wm. Foster, junr.
1639	Thos. Lawson	Brian Cookeson	Chris. Foster	Edmond Carr
1640	Thos. Foster	Thos. Cockman	Jas. Armitstead	Wm. Armitstead
1641	Robt. Carr	Wm. Hall	Richd. Paley	William Kidd
1642	Hugh Stackhouse	Wm. Lawson	Richd. Clapham	Stephen Armitstead
1643	Hugh Stackhouse	Wm. Lawson	Richd. Clapham	Stephen Armitstead
1644				
1645				
1646	Wm. Banks	Thos. Lawson, jun.	Thos. Foster	Thos. Paley
1647	Robt. Armitstead	Wm. Newhouse	Chris. Dawson	John Foster
1648	Wm. Bateman	Anthony Hall	Thos. Foster	Roger Carr
1649	Thos. Bankes, Eldr.	Thos. Knowles	Richd. Armitstead	Richd. Lawson
1650	Hy. Taylor	Jas. Cookeson	Thos. Armitstead	John Bankes
1651	Thos. Paley	Robt. Preston	Robert Twisleton	Charles Nowell
1652	Thos. Taylor	Richd. Coulton	Robert Brown	Thos. Geldart
1653	Richd. Preston	John Carr	Thos. Clapham	Geo. Benson
1654	Thos. Banks	Robt. Armitstead	Thos. Clapham	Josias Dawson
1655	Thos. Carr	Thos. Wright	James Foster	Jas. Swinlehurst
1656	Wm. Armitstead	John Howson	John Paley	John Armitstead
1657	Robt. H. Overend	Thos. Cook	Robt. Lawkland	Anthony Armitstead
1658	Thos. Carr	Hy. Knowles	John Brayshey	James Houghton

Year	Giggleswick.	Settle.	Stainforth.	Rathmell and Langcliffe.
1659	George Bonde	Brian Cookson	Wm. Foster	Wm. Kidd
1660	Lawrence Lawson	Hugh Hall	Wm. Paley, jun.	Thos. Carr
1661	Thos. Paley	Richd. Preston	Jeffrey Fish	Wm. ———*
1662	Wm. Preston	Wm. Taylor	Thos. Carr	J. Armitstead
1663	Thos. Brayshey, sen.	Richd. Wright	Richd. Foster	Law. Swainson
1664	Wm. Sigswick	Anthony Eylin	Richd. Halthropp	Hugh Cost
1665	Robt. Claphamson	Roger Armitstead	Richd. Berry	Hy. Clarke
1666	Richd. Roome	Wm. Preston	Wm. Foster	John Browne
1667	Richd. Burton	John Lawson	Wm. Redmaine	Mr. Bank
1668	John Cote	Thos. Kidd	Wm. Browne	John Paley
1669	Thos. Brayshey	Anthony Procter	Wm. Swainson	Richd. Armitstead
1670	John Foster	Robt. Moorhouse	Thos. Armitstead	John Swainson
1671	James Fawsit	Robt. Windsor	Wm. Wildman	Richd. Armitstead
1672	Thos. Watkinson	Rowld. Greenwood	Richd. Armitstead	James Carr
1673	Wm. Bankes	Anthony Knowles	Robt. Twistleton	Wm. Carr, sen.
1674	Wm. Armitstead	John Cookeson	John Green	Richd. Lawson
1675	Wm. Paley	Adam Lawson	Wm. Armitstead	Wm. Bankes
1676	Wm. Wildman	Lawrence Knowles	Thos. Armitstead	Thos. Settle
1677	Thos. Carr, jun.	Wm. Paley	Wm. Paley	Thos. Knowles
1678	Thos. Sorey	Robt. Chamberlaine	Roger Craven	Wm. Carr
1679	Richd. Frankland	Chris. Lawson	Thos. Clapham	Thos. Geldard
1680	Lawrence Lawson	Robt. Carr	Thos. Clapham	Wm. Knipe

* Qy. Craven.

7

Year	Giggleswick.	Settle.	Stainforth.	Rathmell and Langcliffe.
1681	Thos. Stackhouse	Jas. Armitstead	Chris. Browne	Char. Nowell
1682	John Harrison	Thos. Carr	John Brayshay	Francis Foster
1683	John Lister	Richd. Preston	Bryan Dawson	Chris. Dawson
1684	Roger Crumleholm	John Richardson	Robt. Foster	Anthony Armitstead
1685	Thos. Carr	Hugh Hall	Francis Buck	Stephen Woodworth
1686	Roger Carr	John Skirrow	Thos. Armitstead	Miles Close
1687	Richd. Wagsden	John Battie	Robert Foster	Francis Duckett
1688	Wm. Foster	Robt. Towler	Stephen Fish	Wm. Taylor
1689	Josias Dawson	Thos. Reynoldson	Wm. Bankes	Lawrence Swainson
1690	Anthony Wetherall	Jas. Baines	Thos. Foster	Chas. Abbotson
1691	Rowld. Carr	Hugh Lawson	Hy. Knowles	Thos. Bradley
1692	Thos. Brayshaw, sen.	John Wildman	Thos. Carr	Stephen Carr
1693	Wm. Carr	Wm. Shaikleton	John Lawkland	John Paley
1694	Thos. Brayshaw, jun.	Josias Dawson	Robt. Clapman	Richd. Lawson
1695	Wm. Lawson, jun.	Leond. Bowland	Wm. Hartley, jun.	Richd. Carr
1696	Thos. Wilson	Jer. Lawson	Chris. Metcalfe	Hy. Bullock
1697	Robt. Fawset	Bryan Cookson	Hy. Brown	Robt. Swainson
1698	Wm. Bradley	Roger Armitstead	John. Armitstead	Richd. Lawson
1699	Thos. Frankland	Thos. Paley	Thos. Pearson	Wm. Carr
1700	Wm. Paley	John Windsor	Richd. Clapham	Wm. Banks
1701	Richd. Atkinson	Thos. Carr, jun.	Wm. Stackhouse	Hy. Nowell
1702	Richd. Atkinson	Robt. Towler	Jas. Brown.	John Brown
1703	Matt. Wilkinson	John Skirrow	W. Weatherheard	John Waidson

Year	Giggleswick.	Settle.	Stainforth.	Rathmell and Langcliffe.
1704	Robt. Young	Wm. Carr, sen.	Robt. Twisleton	Wm. Sailsbury
1705	Thos. Frankland	Jas. Cookson	Robt. Gibson	Robt. Clarke
1706	Hy. Claphamson	Jas. Hall	Wm. Banks	Hy. Nowell
1707	Hy. Claphamson	Wm. Shackleton	Thos. Pearson	Robt. Settle
1708	Thos. Carr	Wm. Carr, jun.	Richd. Lawkland	Wm. Taylor
1709	John Wadson	Thos. Paley	Wm. Clapham	Thos. Swainson
1710	Thos. Carr	Hy. Knowles	Richd. Clapham	Wm. Banks, jun.
1711	John Wadson	John Camne	Gilbert Farbridge	Hy. Brown
1712	Thos. Lawson	Robt. Armitstead	Jas Hargraves	Thos. Procter
1713	Hy. Newhouse	Leonard Kidd	Ralph Buck	Robt. Rudd
1714	Robt. Watkinson	Thomas Pearson	Anthony Paley	Thos. Paley
1715	Anthony Lister	Richd. Chamberlaine	Anthony Scambler	Mr. Chute
1716	Matt. Wetherhead	Richd. Chamberlaine	Robt. Twisleton	Richd. Houghton
1717	Wm. Frankland	Hugh Hall	Jas. Foster.	John Walker
1718	Richd. Brayshaw	John Armitstead	Francis Clapham	Richd. Lawson
1719	Chas. Harris	Wm. Hall	John Brown	Wm. Carr
1720	John Foster	Wm. Dawson	John Brown	Stephen Carr
1721	Thos. Brayshaw	Robt. Carr	H. Coate	Stephen Haryson
1722	Thos. Lawson	Richd. Procter	Jas. Armitstead	Thos. Jackson
1723	Robt. Carr	M. Lawson	Thos. Foster	Thos. Geldard
1724	Geo. Whaley	John Batty	Wm. Duckit	John Bins
1725	Geo. Whaley	John Batty	Joh.n Bank	Thos. Cark
1726	Hy. Taylor	Richd. Balderston	Jas. Foster	Richd. Knowles

Year	Giggleswick.	Settle.	Stainforth.	Rathmell and Langcliffe.
1727	Wm. Bradley	Richd. Chamberlaine	Thos. Stackhouse	Chas. Settles
1728	Matt. Weatherhead	John Shackelton	Wm. Iveson	Richd. Balderston
1729	Robert Carr	Matt. Hargraves	Ed. Saunders	Wm. Bradley
1730	Henry Carr	Roger Armistead	John Armistead	Richd. Carr
1731	Mr. Lister	Allen Carr	Mr. Wetherhead	John Brown
1732	Wm. Frankland	John Lister	Richd. Foster	Chas. Nowell
1733	Robert Airton	Edw. Maud	John Twisleton	Chas. Heward
1734	Jas. Jackson	John Windsor	Edm. Saunders	John Binns
1735	Wm. Carr	Chas. Albison	Thos. Rawson	Stephen Harrison
1736	Matt. Watkinson	Allen Carr	Geo. Howson	Henry Coare
1737	Thos. Carr	Robt. Brown	Wm. Brown	Edw. Eglinn
1738	Thos. Redman	M. Elershaw	Wm. Foster Smith	Mr. Lister
1739	Wm. Paley	John Thompson	John Binns	Geo. Paley,
1740	Wm. Birkit	Mr. Pearte	Anthony Clapham	Mr. Bank, jun.
1741	Geo. Jackson	Wm. Paley	Sam. Lucas	James Carr
1742	Edm. Wilson	Hy. Town	John Tunstill	Wm. Birkit
1743	Bryan Waller	Jno. Tatham	Thos. Clapham	Richd. Lawson
1744	John Foster	Roger Armistead	Chris. Brown	Robert Roberts
1745	Thos. Brayshaw	Wm. Hall	Jas. Pearson	John Settle
1746	Thos. Lawson	Hy. Town	Robert Bank	John Foster
1747	Geo. Carr	Thos. Williams	Robert Brown	Craven Bacon
1748	John Foster	Robt. Procter	Thos. Williams	Wm. Bradley
1749	Thos. Williams	Robt. Procter	Thos. Clapham	Thos. Lister

Year	Giggleswick.	Settle.	Stainforth.	Rathmell and Langcliffe.
1750	Thos. Clapham	John Preston	Robt. Bank	Thos. Williams
1751	Wm. Bradley	Thos. Williams	Jas. Pearson	John Cundell
1752	Thos. Carr	Thos. Williams	Thos. Carr	John Cundell
1753	Thos. Brayshaw	Thos. Williams	Thos. Carr	Thos. Geldart
1754	Geo. Carr	Robt. Roberts	Richd. Clapham	Thos. Williams
1755	Mr. Hardacker	Thos. Williams	Chr. Stackhouse	Wm. Buck
1756	Richd. Frankland	Thos. Williams	Michael Williams	Wm. Bradley
1757	Wm. Bradley	Wm. Hall	Chr. Brown	Wm. Paley
1758	John Willman	Thos. Williams	Oliver Carr	Thos. Hall
1759	John Willman	Wm. Bradley	Thos. Williams	Thos. Hall
1760	Mr. Gaythorn	Thos. Williams	Richd. Ivison	Wm. Parker
1761	Thos. Clapham	Jos. Bell	Lawrence Wharfe	Thos. Maudsley
1762	Robt. Taylor	Thos. Coar	Chr. Armitstead	Thos. Maudsley
1763	Thos. Carr	Thos. Williams	Chr. Armitstead	Robt. Roberts
1764	John Place	Thos. Shacleton	Thos. Batty	Geo. Paley
1765	Wm. Barrows	John Coats	Wm. Foster	Wm. Silverwood
1766	Wm. Barrows	Thos. Settel	Richard Iveson	Wm. Silverwood
1767	Anthony Lister	Thos. Wilson	Wm. Carr	Richd. Iveson
1768	Wm. Foster	Richd. Foster	Richd. Iveson	Wm. Silverwood
1769	Thos. Blackburn	John Preston	Wm. Preston	Wm. Silverwood
1770	Jas. Hunter	Fran. Town	Richd. Iveson	Nic. Geldard
1771	John Frankland	Wm. Bolland	Thos. Hey	Anthony Brown
1772	Wm. Silverwood	Wm. Lawson	Thos. Hey	Thos. Peacock

Year	Giggleswick.	Settle.	Stainforth.	Rathmell and Langcliffe.
1773	Hy. Wood	John Shackelton	Foster Smith	Thos. Hey
1774	Hy. Maudsley	Chris. Procter	Mr. Clapham	Wm. Geldard
1775	Thos. Brayshaw	Richd. Foster	John Lund	Thos. Green
1776	Thos. Brayshaw	Wm. Preston	Stephen Howgate	Thos. Hall
1777	John Bradley	Thos. Hall	Wm. Preston	Chr. Stackhouse
1778	John Bradley	Thos. Hall	Chr. Brown	Fran. Howson
1779	John Bradley	Fran. Howson	Thos. Stackhouse	Hy. Clark
1780	Wm. Lawson	Catterson Paley	Jno. Bradley	Thos. Holden
1781	Thos. Clapham	Catterson Paley	Chris. Pearson	Wm. Kendall
1782	John Moore	Jas. Rawsthorn	Chris. Pearson	Thos. Brayshaw
1783	Wm. Preston	Jas. Rawsthorn	Rd. Iveson	Thos. Paley
1784	John Carr	Jas. Rawsthorn	Jas. Foster	John Armistead
1785	Thos. Maudsley	Jas. Rawsthorn	Jas. Foster	Anthony Brown
1786	John Kendall	Hy. Coor	Wm. Carr	Anthony Brown
1787	Richd. Frankland	Jos. Bell	Chr. Procter	Richd. L. Starkie
1788	Jas. Foster	Jermiah Hartley	Chris. Armitstead	Thos. Paley
1789	Wm. Clapham	Jas. Ellison	Richd. J. Batty	Wm. Buck
1790	John Carr	Thos. Tristram	Richd. Johnson	Wm. Silverwood
1791	Wm. Barrows	Thos. Hargraves	Richd. Redmayne	Thos. Maudsley
1792	Thos. Maudsley	Thos. Wilson	Anthony Stackhouse	R. Redmayne
1793	Wm. Ferinside	Richd. Procter	John Lund	Fran. Howson
1794	Robt. Barker	Robt. Horner	Jas. Foster	Chr. Holgate
1795	Robt. Silverwood.	Wm. Buck	John Stackhouse	Thos. Green

Year	Giggleswick.	Settle.	Stainforth.	Rathmell and Langcliffe.
1796	Thos. Kirkley	John Holden	Robt. Silverwood	Anty. Brown
1797	Thos. Kirkley	John Carr	Robt. Silverwood	Robt. Horner
1798	Thos. Kirkley	Robt. Horner	Thos. Heyes	Fran. Howson
1799	Robt. Horner	John Waddington	John Armitstead	John Geldard
1800	Thos. Maudsley	Thos. Troughton	John Winder	Thos. Holden
1801	John Frankland	Jas. Thornber	Jas. Pearson	Hy. Clarke
1802	Robert Holden	John Duckett	Jas. Pearson	Wm. Holgate
1803	Wm. Lawson	Wm. Holgate	Anty. Stackhouse	Wm. Holgate
1804	Thos. Maudsley	Turner Hardacre	Peter Hargraves	George Kendal
1805	Stephen Dawson	Robt. Redmayne	Peter Hargraves	Hugh Armitstead
1806	Edmd. Armitstead	Wm. Bolland	Wm. Foster	Wm. Carr
1807	Robt. Holden	John Holden	Wm. Moore	Robt. Hill
1808	Wm. Procter	Wm. Whittam	John Parker	Richd. Foster
1809	John Parker	Thos. Windsor	Anty. Stackhouse	John Higson
1810	J. Foster	G. Procter	Matt. Redmayne	H. Butler
1811	Wm. Wildman	John Preston	Chr. Brown	Hy. Kendal
1812	J. Dawson	Robt. Procter	Wm. Hill	C. Banks
1813	H. Maudsley	Robt. Harger	Anty. Holgate	Fran. Howson
1814	Thos. Parker	Thos. Hurtley	Jas. Foster	Thos. Buck
1815	Peter Hargraves	Thos. Hurtley	Jas. Foster	Geo. Wolfenden
1816	John King	Wm. Harger	John Batty	John Geldard
1817	Jas. Ayrton	Anthony Stackhouse	Thos. Brown	Col. Banks
1818	Wm. Stackhouse	Robt. Redmayne	Anty. Holgate	Jas. Redmayne

Year	Giggleswick.	Settle.	Stainforth.	Rathmell and Langcliffe.
1819	Wm. Stackhouse	Robt. Scott	John Metcalfe	Thos. Holden
1820	Wm. Stackhouse	Wm. Bilton	M. Redmayne	Robt. Geldard
1821	Wm. Wildman	Wm. Bilton	Thos. Winder	Ralph H. Brown
1822	John Waller	Vin. Hallpike	Sam. Preston	Richd. Foster
1823	Thos. Hartley	Thos. Ellison	Jos. Brayshaw	Matt. Jackman
1824	Stephen Dawson	John Turner	John Stackhouse	John Clark
1825	Hy. Maudsley	Wm. Redshaw	Matt. P. Slinger	Thos. Parker
1826	John Procter	Jas. Silverwood	Jas. Foster	Hy. Maudsley
1827	Cuth. Parker	Richd. Shepherd	Stepn. Hargraves	Hy. Yeadon
1828	Cuth. Parker	Thos. Procter	Thos. Brown	Fran. Howson
1829	John Taylor	Thos. Hardacre	Jon. Morphet	Wm. Kendal
1830	Geo. Newsholm	John Parker	M. P. Slinger	T. Holden
1831	Wm. Wildman	Peter Skirrow	M. Redmayne	T. Holden
1832	J. Holroyd	Peter Skirrow	Robt. Hill	Chr. Leach
1833	John Maudsley	Peter Skirrow	Thos. Redmayne	Chr. Wright
1834	Wm. Leech	Robt. Lancaster	Jas. Foster	John Armistead
1835	Wm. Leech	Jas. Wilkinson	Thos. Lawson	Jos. Maudsley
1836	Chr. Wildman	Stephen Wilman	Richd. Armitstead	John Kendall
1837	John Fell	Stephen Wilman	Fran. Twisleton	Thos. Yeadon
1838	John Fletcher	John Bland	Fran. Twisleton	Jon. Jackman
1839	John Dixon	Chr. Ratcliffe	John Fletcher	Geo. Towler
1840	John Hartley	John Bullock	Jos. Maudsley	Jas. Taylor
1841	Jas. Pulman	John Thornber	Thos. Winder	Robt. Charnley

Year	Giggleswick.	Settle.	Stainforth.	Rathmell and Langcliffe.
1842	Chas. Jenkinson	Jas. Ellison	John Batty	Matt. Lofthouse
1843	Wm. Carr	John Hayhurst	Chr. Sedgwick	Thos. Preston
1844	John Langhorne	Thos. Nixon	Paul Helm	Robt. Helm
1845	John King	J. Birkbeck	Stephen Wildman	Stephen Airton
1846	Wm. Waller	John Armitstead	Ben. Heseltine	Wm. Standing
1847	John Parker	Henry Snell	Jas. Metcalfe	Chas. Wilson
1848	John Johnson	Wm. Shepherd	M. Armitstead	Hy. Yeadon
1849	John Taylor	John J. Hatley	M. Armitstead	Robt. Clarke
1850	John Pollard	Richd. Greenwood	M. Armitstead	Richd. Knowles
1851	John Johnson, jun.	Geo. W. Newsholme	Thos. Maudsley	Wm. Taylor
1852	Wm. Waller	Wm. Hargraves	Thos. Parker	Wm. Burniston
1853	Thos. Littlefair	Ed. T. Foster	Anty. Stackhouse	John Robinson
1854	John Hartley	Geo. Hartley	Thos. Redmayne	Wm. Kendall
1855	John Hartley	Stepn. Hargreaves	Chris. Brown	Wm. Kendall
1856	John Hartley	Thos. Birkbeck	Thos. Stackhouse	Wm. Kendall
1857	John Hartley	Thos. Birkbeck	Thos. Stackhouse	Wm. Foster
1858	John Hartley	Jos. Birkbeck	Thos. Stackhouse	Wm. Foster
1859	John Hartley	Jos. Birkbeck	Thos. Stackhouse	Wm. Kendall
1860	Wm. Carr	Thos. Procter	Ben. Heselton	Thos. Holden
1861	Henry King	Thos. Holmes	Thos. Maudsley	Richd. Newhouse
1862	Thos. Parker	Robt. Calvert	Wm. Batty	John Garner
1863	Wm. Waller	Thos. Stewart	Jos. Hodgson	Wm. Parsons
1864	John Brown	Wm. Towler	Chr. Sidgeswick	John Bolland

Year	Giggleswick.	Settle.	Stainforth.	Rathmell and Langcliffe.
1865	John Brown	Wm. Towler	Emanuel Johnson	John Bolland
1866	John Brown	Wm. Towler	Emanuel Johnson	Richard Towler
1867	Wm. Procter	Wm. Towler	Foster Metcalfe	Richard Towler
1868	John Clark	John Wilkinson	Thos. Heselton	Chr. Wood
1869	John Clark	John Preston	Wm. Foster	Felix Dawson
1870	John Clark	John Preston	Wm. Foster	John Turner
1871	John Birkbeck, jun.	H. D. Robinson	Wm. Foster	Stephen Robinson
1872	John Birkbeck, jun.	H. D. Robinson	Wm. Foster	Richd. Frankland
1873	John Birkbeck, jun.	John Lister	Wm. Foster	Richd. Frankland
1874	John Birkbeck, jun.	John Lister	Wm. Foster	Geo. Towler
1875	John Birkbeck, jun.	John Lister	Wm. Foster	Geo. Towler
1876	John Birkbeck, jun.	John Lister	Wm. Foster	Geo. Towler
1877	John Birkbeck, jun.	John Lister	Wm. Foster	Geo. Towler
1878	John Birkbeck, jun.	John Lister	Wm. Foster	Geo. Towler
1879	John Maudsley	John Lister	Wm. Foster	Geo. Lewthwaite
1880	Thos. Brayshaw	John Lister	Wm. Foster	Geo. Lewthwaite
1881	Thos. Procter	John Lister	Wm. Foster	Geo. Lewthwaite
1882	Thos. Procter	John Lister	Wm. Foster	Geo. Lewthwaite
1883	Thos. Procter	John Lister	Wm. Foster	Rd. Haythornthwaite

EXTRACTS

FROM THE

CHURCHWARDENS' MINUTE BOOKS, &c.

15TH SEPTEMBER, 1749.

WHEREAS the Churchwardens for this parish have usually been allowed for the several accustomed meetings or attendances yearly as hereafter mentioned, to wit ;—for the Quarterly meetings, sixteen shillings; for their attendance on Easter Mondays, six shillings; for attendance on ringing days, ten shillings; on the perambulation days, eight shillings; and upon stating their accounts, four shillings,—which said several allowances amount unto the sum of two pounds four shillings, which is thought by a majority of the gentlemen called the Four and Twenty, at their meeting this day, too considerable. Therefore it is hereby ordered, that for the said several meetings or attendances the Churchwardens for the time being shall only have allowed the sum of one pound four shillings. And it is further ordered that the said gentlemen for the time being, called the Twenty four, shall at their several meetings pay and bear their own expenses thereof, any order heretofore made notwithstanding.

  WILLM. BANK.   THOS. BRAYSHAW.
  WM. HALL.   WILL. BANKS.
  WM. BRADLEY.   HUGH HALL.
  THOS. SETTLE.

Let it be remembered that the order above was oppos'd and look'd upon as ridiculous and foolish by us whose names are now subscribed.

  JNO. FOSTER.   JON. SETTLE.
  GEO. CARR.   THOS. LISTER.
  HENRY TOWN.
   Cross'd by me.
      A. LISTER,
       Vicar.

 This last note by the Vicar refers to a large cross he had made over the entry, thus cancelling the same.

The " Gentlemen called the Twenty four " seem to have had good times when they met to elect churchwardens. It would appear that they either held their meetings at, or adjourned immediately afterwards to, one of the Inns in Giggleswick. A Mr. Paley kept one inn, a Mr. Waller the other, and the Twenty four patronised each alternately. They had plenty of refreshments, which they duly inserted in the accounts, and for which the parish had to pay. The amount spent on these occasions varied, at times (for instance in 1782,) the average amount spent was three shillings and eightpence for each person who attended, and at other times (1763, &c) the amount came to three shillings each, and yet at the same time these good people were a strange mixture of extravagance and economy, for at one of these same meetings in 1763, the twenty four whilst spending the parish money freely on themselves, resolved " That Thomas Storey shall not be employed in the Church work for the next year, his Bill being thought very extravagant."

The resolution of Sept. 1749, set out before, was aimed at this practice of having refreshments at the public expense, but, as we have seen, this reform was upset by the highhanded action of the Vicar and a minority of the Twenty four.

A favorite method the Churchwardens adopted in order to raise funds to cover their refreshment bill, seems to have been to *sell the bell ropes* and to spend the money so obtained, at the meetings of the Twenty-four. Certain it is that new bell-ropes seem to have been required far oftener than could have been reasonably expected.

Another example of the jealousy with which the Churchwardens guarded the parish expenditure, always excepting that spent on their own enjoyment, is to be found in the following resolution :—

" November the 20th, 1735.

Be it Remembered that it was unanimously agreed upon by the Vicar and Twenty-four men then met together, that Robert Young and Richard Smith of Settle, Glaziers, shall for ever hereafter be discharged for doeing any work or being any further employ'd in any work hereafter to be done, in or about this church, for the gross abuses and ill usage the 24 believe the parish has sustained by the said Robert Young and Richard Smith."

"July 8th, 1742.
Spent by the Twenty-four in taking the accounts of the Churchwardens, and hiring the great Bell carrying to York at the same time £1 7 0

In 1761 the seats in the Church were repaired at a cost of £35 2s. 4d.

In 1788 the Churchwardens' accounts do not seem to have been satisfactory to the Twenty-four, and the meeting accordingly adjourned to another date "when the Churchwardens are requested to exhibit their accounts sufficiently authenticated."

"July 1st, 1795. Whereas the roof of the Chancel is out of repair, and some doubt arises who are to repair, the Churchwardens for the time being are hereby directed to apply to the Spiritual Court or elsewhere, in order to get a copy of any Record or information they can."

In 1815 the church yard was enlarged by taking-in a portion of the Grammar School yard, the Governors of the School giving their consent.

In 1820—21 the Church was repewed and the Churchwardens paid to the Committee appointed to manage such repewing, the sum of £151 4s. 0d. for "public sittings."

1835. It was resolved that the Church be underdrawn and the Churchwardens were empowered to raise £100 for that purpose.

In 1838 there was a strike amongst the bellringers, which was terminated by their demand for an increase of wages from 14s. 8d. to £1 each per annum being agreed to.

About the same time complaints became frequent that the church was cold and damp, and this was remedied at a cost of £142 12s. 9d.

In 1841, James Pulman, one of the Churchwardens, became Bankrupt, and we find the Twenty-four resolved in the year following that "the Churchwardens shall put down in their accounts the sum of £2 3s. 1d. as lost by James Pulman, the late Churchwarden, and shall give credit for the sum of £1 10s, being compensation paid by the said James Pulman for his debt." But this did not cover the loss the parish sustained, as in 1843 we find that the sum of £5 15s. 7d. was retained by the Churchwardens for 1842 "and applied, as stated by them, to the payment of several bills which were passed in their account as paid by Mr. Pulman, but which proved to have been not so paid."

Salaries.

The following item relates to an official whose services are now happily dispensed with.

"March the 21st, 1736. Be it Remembered that it is this day agreed upon by the Twenty-four men then met together that whoever hereafter acts as Dog-whipper to avoid disturbance in the church, shall receive five shillings a year for his pains and noe more, and be subject to the orders given."

This official's salary, as we shall see later on, was afterwards raised to ten shillings.

In 1747 the Twenty-four seem to have had some bother about the wages due to the clerk and sexton, as I find the following entry.

"The Twenty-four present Feb. ye 3rd, do order yt no standing dues for ye Clerk and Sexton be allowed for ye future, being charged in particulars, as appears by some bills that Mr. Wm. Hall has in his keeping."

"What was allowed for Standing during ye year 1707:

	£	s.	d.
Washing Linning	0	6	8
For Register writing and parchment	0	8	6
Sending it to York	0	1	0
For Cleaning ye Church, &c.	0	3	0
For taking care of ye clock	0	8	0
For taking care of ye cloths and dressing ye plate	0	6	6
For dressing leads	0	1	6
For dressing grayte	0	0	6
	£1	15	8"

This does not seem to have worked well, for in the following year we find the following resolution entered:—

"29th June 1748. Agreed by the gentlemen called the Twenty-four that James Jackson is to have thirty shillings for taking care, dressing &c. as under:—

Washing Linning and mending.
Taking care of the Clock.
Candlestick cleaning.
Oil for Bells and Clock.
Cleaning Plate.
Dressing Church and Church Gates.
Stoneing Church yard.
Dressing the Leads.
Attending on the Communion Days, and taking care of the Cloths.
Dressing the Bells.

I promise to take care of things as above for the year ensuing. As witness my hand.

His letter.
JAMES ✚ JACKSON.

Whether Jackson or the Twenty-four rued of their bargain I cannot say, but at a later stage of the same meeting the office was transferred from Jackson to William Paley, who promised to perform the duties for the very moderate sum of twenty-six shillings per year.

This stipend however was increased to two guineas the following year, and the few members of the Twenty-four who attended the meeting called to discuss this weighty matter, seem to have been so exhausted by their deliberations that they consumed sixteen shillings worth of refreshments, duly paid for out of the parish funds.

Fourteen years afterwards, in 1762, William Paley again had his salary raised, this time to £2 10s., but out of this he had to provide fuel.

Aug. 11th, 1772. "Agreed by the Four and Twenty that Thomas Hargraves is to have five shillings per year for keeping the clock in proper repair. Also that John Higson is to have ten shillings per year for whiping the dogs out of the Church and keeping the doors shutt."

Sept. 3rd, 1773. "Mr. Moor to have the sum of five pounds and five shillings allowed for directing the musick for one year."

This Mr. Moor seems to have held his office of choirmaster for five years, as we do not find his name mentioned after 1777, but in 1796 we find the parish again in want of some one to direct the singing, and a committee was appointed "to procure a proper person to instruct such as are disposed to learn to sing in the Church." The salary to be given was five guineas, but for some reason or other the Committee does not seem to have been successful, and in the following year the resolution was rescinded.

In 1804 the "Churchwardens allowance for the perambulation was increased to two guineas. I cannot ascertain what sum had been allowed them up to this time, but, as we saw in the resolution of 15th Sept., 1749, they had an allowance of eight shillings a year at that date. The last occasion on which this payment is entered in the minute book is in 1844.

BRIEFS.

In former times when a Church had to be rebuilt, from

fire or other cause, or a great calamity had befallen a town or body of men, it was customary, (having first obtained the sanction of the Ecclesiastical authorities,) to send a notification to every parish, stating the amount of the loss or damage, and requesting that a collection be made in aid of such rebuilding, or for the relief of the sufferers.

Such intimations were styled "briefs," and I give particulars of such "briefs" for an average year.

"An account of the Briefs collected by the Churchwardens in the year 1746, when read, and how much collected in each.

	£	s.	d.
Rodington Church in Com. Salop.			
Charge, £1007. Collected June 29th	0	2	6½
Garstang Church, in Com. Lancaster.			
Charge, £1910. Collected July 27th	0	3	8
Weston Turvile, in Com. Bucks, Loss by fire,			
£1214. Collected August 24th	0	3	9
Hythe Church, in Com. Kent.			
Charge, £1100. Collected September 28th	0	2	3
Poulton Church, in Com. Lancaster.			
Charge, £1047. Collected October 26th..	0	1	11½
Meole Brace Church, otherwise Brace Meole Church, in Com. Salop.			
Charge, £1000. Collected November 16th	0	3	3
Shillington Church, in Com. Bedford.			
Charge, £2087. Collected December 21st	0	3	7½
Flixton Church, in Com. Lancaster.			
Charge, £1108. Collected February 8th..	0	2	6½
Mold Church, otherwise Mount Alto Church, in Com. Flint.			
Charge, £1959. Collected April 26th	0	2	4½
Wyke, Townhope, &c., in Com. York, Hereford, &c. Loss by fires, £1107, &c. Collected June 14th.......................	0	3	4
	£1	9	3½
Quakers................	0	2	2

The last occasion on which I can find a list of briefs is for the year 1827. Few particulars are given in the account, which is as follows :—

	£	s.	d.
Leck and Heaton. Fire. Lancashire........	1	0	5½
Ingoldmells. Fire. Lincoln.................	0	9	0
Walton on Trent Church, Derby	0	0	6
Weston Beggard Church, Hereford	0	0	6
Uttoxeter Church, Stafford.................	0	0	7
Rushtor Spencer Church, Stafford	0	0	9
Beeley Church, Derby..	0	0	8
Wistaston Church, Chester	0	0	8
	£1	13	1½

The great difference in the amount collected on various occasions is worthy of note.

A memento of the persecution to which members of the Society of Friends were subject to, is to be found in the following Entry :—

"May ye 30th, 1688.
"We whose names are here subscribed do consent and aggree w'th ye present Churchwardens of Gigleswick and yir successors yt charges soever they are at in prosecuting Samuel Watson of Knight Stainforth for non-payment of his Churchgold" (qy. Churchrate) "yt it shall be upon ye parish account, and allow'd them, as witness our hands."

WILLIAM ARMITSTEAD	CHARLES NOWELL
THOMAS CARR	R. PRESTON
THOMAS CLAPHAM	HUGH ST.........
THOMAS ARMITSTEAD	JO. LISTER
THO. CARR	THOS. BRAYSHAW
WILLIAM LAMB	WILLIAM PALEY
ADAM LAWSON	JOHN COOKSON
JOSIAS DAWSON	HUGH HALL
LEONARD CARR	CHR. BROWNE
T. DAWSON	WM. PALEY (Settle)
WILLIAM FOSTER	ROBERT COOKSON

"STRAINGE PARSONS."

There seems to have been a custom at Giggleswick Church to pay any Clergyman who came to preach there the sum of one shilling. A separate account of these payments headed "An Account of the Strainge Parsons" was kept, in which was also entered the name of the Churchwarden who made the payment.

A copy of this account for one year may be interesting, so we will take the year 1741—2 as an example.

	s.	d.
"June ye 21st, 1741, paid Mr. John Carr, of Settle,.... George Jackson	1	0
ye 28th. Mr. John Carr, of Settle .. Wm. Paley	1	0
July ye 5th. Mr. Ward preached........Sam. Lucas	1	0
ye 12th. Mr. Twisleton ....James Carr	1	0
ye 25th. Mr. Chamberlaine .... George Jackson	1	0
September ye 13th. Mr. Bows ....Wm. Paley	1	0
October ye 18th. Mr. Swainson .... Sam. Lucas	1	0
November ye 1st. Mr. Carr ....James Carr	1	0
ye 8th. Mr. Wade........George Jackson	1	0

January ye 3rd. Mr. Carr	Wm. Paley	1	0
January ye 10th. Mr. Sedgwick	Lucas	1	0
ye 17th. Mr. Swainson	James Carr	1	0
March ye 7th. Mr. Weatherherd	Jackson	1	0
March ye 28th. Mr. Swainson	Paley	1	0
April ye 18th. Mr. Sidgwick	Lucas	1	0
Mr. Bows, when Oyster Dredgers.... J. Carr		1	0"

To the last item no date is fixed. It would seem that Mr. Bows had come round collecting for some distressed oyster dredgers.

The second name in each entry is that of the Churchwarden who paid the "strainge parson," and from the above list it would appear that the worshippers at Giggleswick Church had no lack of variety in their preachers.

I cannot say at what date the payment of one shilling was discontinued, but the record of the "strange parsons" ends in 1846.

The following extract is noteworthy as showing that in 1757 the Sacrament of the Holy Communion seems to have only been administered three times a year, in addition to Easter; and that it was, even at that day, an "antient custom" for the Vicar to provide the Bread and Wine at his own cost at Easter.

"Sept. 13th, 1757. This day agreed between the Rev. Mr. Thomson and us whose names are hereunto subscribed for and on behalf of the Parish of Giggleswick, That the Churchwardens for the time being shall and will yearly and every year pay to the said Mr. Thomson the sum of three guineas on condition he shall provide Bread and Wine suficient for three sacrament days, usually bought by the Parish, so long as he the said Mr. Thomson shall conform to the antient custom of procuring Bread and Wine suficient at Easter at his own expense. The first year to comence the week before Easter last."

(Here follow the signatures.)

This allowance was afterwards increased to four guineas, in 1795 to four guineas and a half, and in 1796 to five guineas, in consequence of " the high duty for wine."

CHARTERS

AND OTHER

EARLY DOCUMENTS

RELATING TO

GIGGLESWICK CHURCH.

WITH ILLUSTRATIONS.

EDITED BY

THOS. BRAYSHAW.

* * *

STACKHOUSE,
NEAR SETTLE,
SEPTEMBER 20TH, 1884.

In the year 1837 the Surtees Society issued a volume containing the Charters and Account Rolls of the Priory of Finchale, and in 1872 the same society published The Register, or Rolls, of Walter Gray, Lord Archbishop of York. It is from these two volumes that the documents contained in this pamphlet are extracted, but I have considered myself as justified in reprinting them in the form of one of this series of "Local Tracts" for two reasons, in the first place because the above-named works are very scarce,—the issue being limited,—and in the second place because the Latin documents are untranslated, and are therefore lost on many of us, whose knowledge of that language is very shaky, and as I myself am one of that unhappy number, I have gratefully to record my thanks to the REV. J. J. MILNE, M.A., of Heversham, for the assistance he has rendered to me in the work of translation.

I have contented myself with very few notes on the various documents, and persons mentioned therein, as I propose to issue two further pamphlets with reference to Giggleswick Church.

In sending out this, the third of my series of "Local Tracts," (which, I may here state, I hope to issue quarterly), I take the opportunity of asking my friends to communicate to me, at any time, notes on Local History, biography, antiquities, customs, traditions, family history, folk-lore, place-names, sayings, legends, superstitions, worthies, societies, publications, engravings, or on any other subject of local interest. By so doing they will confer a great favor on me.

THOS. BRAYSHAW.

Twelve large and one hundred small paper copies printed for private circulation.

EARLY CHARTERS AND DOCUMENTS RELATING TO GIGGLESWICK CHURCH.

I.

Carta Henrici de Puteacho* de Ecclesiis de Wictona et Gicheleswic.

UNIVERSIS sanctae matris ecclesiæ filiis ad quos litteræ istæ pervenerint, Henricus de Puteacho salutem in vero salutari. Noverit universitas vestra me concessisse et dedisse, et hac presenti karta mea confirmasse intuitu pietatis Divinæ, et salutis animæ patris mei, et matris meæ, et animæ meæ, et Dionisiae uxoris meae, omniumque parentum meorum, Deo et Beatæ Mariæ et Beato Cuthberto et Sancto Godrico et Monachis Dunelmensibus Deo et Beatæ Mariæ et Sancto Godrico apud Finchale servientibus, ecclesiam de Wictona, cum omnibus ad eum pertinentibus, et ecclesiam de Gichelswic, cum omnibus ad eam pertinentibus, in puram et perpetuam elemosinam, liberam, et quietam ab omni servitio seculari et exactione, cum omnibus libertatibus et liberis consuetudinibus, quascumque unquam praedictæ ecclesiæ de Wicthona and Gicheleswic liberius honorabilius vel quietius tenuerunt et possederunt; scilicet in villa, et extra villam, cum toftis et croftis, in bosco, in plano, in viis, in semitis, in moris, et marasiis, in aquis, in molendinis et stagnis, in pratis, in pasturis, et in omnibus aliis aisiamentis ad predictas ecclesias pertinentibus. Hiis testibus, magistro Henrico camerario, magistro Alano de Richemund, Roberto de Hadigtona, magistro Willielmo de Blais, magistro Ricardo de Haitona, magistro Waltero de Dunelmo, magistro Waltero de Hadigtona, Willielmo de Besewilla et aliis multis.

Seal of Henry de Pudsey (for representation of which see Fig. 1), is appended by a silk label.

---

* This Henry de Pudsey was one of the sons of Hugh Pudsey, who was Bishop of Durham from 1153 to 1196, his mother being Adelis de Percy, and it was through her that Henry acquired his rights in the Parish and advowson of Giggleswick, that place forming part of the Percy Fee.

Translation.

Deed of Henry de Pudsey, concerning the Churches of Wicton and Giggleswick.

TO all the sons of the Holy Mother Church whom this letter shall reach, Henry de Pudsey sends his sincere greeting. Let your community know that I have granted and given, and in this my present deed confirmed with a view to my reverence for God, and the safety of the soul of my father, and my mother, and my own, and that of Dionysia my wife, and those of all my ancestors, to God and the blessed Mary, and the blessed Cuthbert and St. Godric and to the Monks of Durham who minister to God, and the blessed Mary and blessed Cuthbert and St. Godric at Finchale, the Church of Wicton with all things pertaining to it, and the Church of Giggleswick with all things pertaining to it, for a pure and perpetual charitable bequest, free and secure from all secular service and exaction, with all liberties and free customs whichsoever at any time the aforesaid churches of Wicton and Giggleswick more freely, honourably, or securely have held and possessed; that is to say, in villa,* or out of villa, with tofts,† and crofts††, in wood, in the open, in highways, in footpaths, in moors and marshes, in waters, in millstreams and lakes, in meadows, in pastures, and in all other easements pertaining to the aforesaid churches. These persons are witnesses, Master Henry, the chamberlain, Master Allen de Richmond, Robert de Hadigton, Master William de Blais, Master Richard de Haiton, Master Walter de Durham, Master Walter de Hadigton, William de Besewill, and many others.

II.

A.D. 1208.—JOHANNES Dei gratia rex Angliæ, dominus Hyberniæ, dux Normanniæ, Aquitaniæ, et comes Andegaviæ, archiepiscopis, episcopis, abbatibus, comitibus, baronibus, justitiariis, vicecomitibus, præpositis, et omnibus ballivis et fidelibus suis salutem. Sciatis nos concessisse

---

* Villa means a country house or farm.

† Toftum—A messuage, or rather the place where a messuage has stood.

†† Croftum—A small slip of ground near a house.

7

et hac carta nostra confirmasse rationabilem donationem quam Henricus de Puteaco fecit priori et monachis de Finchal de advocatione ecclesiæ de Gycleswik; habendum et tenendum in perpetuum, libere et quiete, integre, plenarie, et honorifice, cum omnibus libertatibus et liberis consuetudinibus, sicut carta prædicti Henrici quam inde habuit rationabiliter testatur. Testibus dominis, W. London., E. Elyensi, P. Wynton., S. Wygorn., et H. Sarr,, episcopis, G. filio Petri comite Essex, Willelmo Briwer, Roberto de Turnham. Data per manum Hugonis de Well', Archidiaconi Well', apud Winton, xix die Octobris, anno regni nostri nono. (Reg. Giffard 77a.)

Translation.

JOHN, by the Grace of God, King of England, Lord of Ireland, Duke of Normandy and Aquitain, and Count of Andegavia, to the archbishops, bishops, abbots, counts, barons, judges, viscounts, wardens, and to all bailiffs and to his faithful subjects, sends greeting. Knew ye that we have granted, and by this our Charter have confirmed, the reasonable gift which Henry de Pudsey hath made to the prior and monks of Finchale concerning the advowson of Giggleswick, to have and to hold in perpetuity, freely and quietly, completely, fully, and honourably, with all its liberties and free customs, as the Charter of the said Henry, which he had at that time, reasonably testifies. Witnessed by W. Lord Bishop of London, E. of Ely, P. of Winton, S. of Wigorn, and H. of Salisbury, G. son of Peter, Earl of Essex, Wm. Brewer, Robert de Turnham. Given by the hand of Hugo de Wells, Archdeacon of Wells, at Winton, the 19th day of October, in the 9th year of our reign.

III.

*Carta Willielmi de Percy.**

UNIVERSIS sanctæ matris ecclesiæ filiis hanc præsentem cartam visuris vel audituris, Willielmus de Percy, salutem. Noverit universitas vestra me, caritatis intuitu, et pro salute animæ Henrici de Percy patris mei, et pro salute animæ meæ, et pro anima Johannæ uxoris meæ, et pro animabus omnium antecessorum, successorum, et heredum meorum, dedisse,

---

* William de Percy, Lord of the Percy Fee in Craven, and immediate ancestor of Percy of Northumberland, died 29 Henry III (A.D. 1244), and was buried in the Monastery of Sallay, founded by his ancestors.

concessisse, et hac presenti carta mea confirmasse Deo, et Beatæ Mariæ, et Sancto Johanni Baptistæ, et Sancto Godrico de Finchal, et Priori et Monachis ibidem Deo servientibus, advocationem ecclesiæ de Gyckeleswic, et omne jus et clamium quod in eadem ecclesia habui, vel habere potui, cum omnibus pentinenciis suis et libertatibus, absque ullo retinemento, inpuram et perpetuam elemosinam. Et ut hæc mea donatio, concessio, et confirmatio, rata, illibata et stabilis perpetuis, temporibus perseveret, presentem cartam sigilli mei impressione munuvi. Hiis testibus, Roberto de Cokefeld, Vicecomite Ebor*, Henrico de Percy fratre meo, Marmeduc de Tweng, Galfrido filio Gafridi, Waltero de Percy, Hugone de Leley, Stephano de Menhil, Roberto de Plumton, Jordano de L'Estre, Willielmo Britone, Simone de Bruntoft, Jordano Hayrun, Willielmo de Hessewell, et multis aliis.

(Seal wanting, but see hereafter.)

Translation.

Deed of William de Percy.

TO all the sons of the Holy Mother Church who shall see or hear read this present deed, William de Percy sends greeting. Let your community know that I, with a regard for my affection for, and for the safety of the soul of, Henry de Percy my father, and for the safety of my own soul, and for the soul of Johanna my wife, and for the souls of all my ancesters, successors, and heirs, I have given, granted, and in this my present deed confirmed to God and the Blessed Mary, and St. John the Baptist, and St. Goderic of Finchal, and to the Prior and Monks who minister unto God at that place, the advowson of the Church of Giggleswick, and every right and claim in the same church which I have had or could have, with all its pertinences and liberties, without any reserve, for a pure and perpetual charitable bequest. And in order that this my gift, grant, and confirmation may remain established, settled and fixed for all times, I have confirmed this deed with the impression of my seal. The following being witnesses, Robert de Cokefeld, Sheriff of Yorkshire, my brother Henry de Percy, Marmaduke de Tweng, Galfrid the son of Galfrid, Walter de Percy, Hugo de Leley, Stephen de Menhill, Robert de Plumton, Jordan de l'Estre, Wm. Britone, Simon de Bruntoft, Jordan Hayrun, William de Hessewell, and many others.

---

* Robert de Cokefeld was Sheriff of Yorkshire from 1226 to 1229 inclusive, the date of this Charter is therefore limited to one of these years.

Fig. 1.
HENRY DE PUDSEY.

Fig. 2.
WILLIAM DE PERCY.

Seals appended to Deeds relating to Giggleswick Church.

IV.

Transactio inter Priorem de Finchale et Laurentium Clericum (pro solucione pensionis de Gigleswik.

HAEC est composicio facta inter Johannem Priorem de Finchall et Laurentium personam de Gykeleswic, in presencia Domini Henrici de Puteaco patroni ipsius Prioris, scilicet quod predictus Laurentius assignavit predicto Priori de Finchall omnes obvenciones et decimas de Setel, magnas et minutas, exceptis oblacionibus, et exquiis mortuorum; et omnes decimas villatæ de Rothemel, exceptis decimis lactis, et oblacionibus, et exequiis mortuorum, pro solucione pensionis ecclesiæ de Gikeleswic: unde prius reddidit viginti marcas eidem Priori, in vita Adæ de Thornhouer qui percipit duodecim marcas in eadem ecclesia. Et cum predictum Adam in fata decessisse, vel habitum mutasse contigerit, idem Laurentius solvet predicto Priori de Finchalle xx Marcas annuas, nomine pensionis de ecclesia de Gykeleswic, vel adcrescet super easdem decimas prenominatas usque ad xx marcas. Et erit in electione predicti Prioris capiendi xx marcas vel incrementum super easdem decimas ad valenciam xx marcarum. Hanc composicionem affidavit predictus Laurentius tenendam in manu Henrici de Puteaco sine frande, et dolo. Quod si quandoque a solucione cessaverit, vel contra factum istud venerit, renuncians omni priviligio, appellacione remota, judicio stabit Decani et Capituli Ebor., et dabit decem marcas, nomine pœnæ, predicto Priori. Hiis testibus, domino S. Decano Ebor., Priore de Bridlington, H. thesaurario Ebor., Henrico de Puteaco, Ada de Novo Mercheto, Hugone de Feritate, Henrico de Nova Mercheto, Rogero de Everley, Radulpho Haranc, Rudulpho filio Ricardi, Roberto de Crave et aliis.

(To this document have been attached three seals: the first is that of the Prior of Finchale of which a representation is given in Fig 3, as far as it is preserved; the second is that of Henry de Puteaco (See Fig. 1); the third is wanting).

Translation.

Transaction between the Prior of Finchale and Lawrentius, Clerk in Holy Orders (for the payment of the stipend of Giggleswick).

THIS is an agreement made between John,* Prior of Finchale, and Lawrentius, parson of Giggleswick, in the presence

---

* This John was the second Prior of Finchale, and ruled the priory about the year 1225.

of Master Henry de Pudsey, patron of the said prior, that is to say, that the aforesaid Lawrentius has assigned to the aforesaid Prior of Finchale all the revenues and tithes of Settle, great and small, except offerings and burial fees, and all tithes of the village of Rathmell, except tithes of milk and offerings and burial fees, for the payment of the stipend of the Church of Giggleswick; first paying thereout the sum of twenty marks to the same Prior during the life of Adam de Thornhouer who has a claim of twelve marks on the same church. And when it shall happen that the aforesaid Adam shall have departed this life or changed his abode, the same Lawrentius shall pay to the aforesaid Prior of Finchale twenty marks a year, under the name of stipend of the Church of Giggleswick, or shall make the said above-mentioned tithes amount to the sum of twenty marks. And the aforesaid Prior shall have the option of taking twenty marks, or an increase over the same tithes up to the value of twenty marks. And the aforesaid Lawrentius has given his word that this agreement shall remain in the possession of Henry de Pudsey without fraud and deceit. But if at any time he shall have stopped payment, or, contrary to the deed this shall have happened, renouncing claim to every privilege, without appeal, he shall stand his trial before the Dean and Chapter of York, and shall pay ten marks, under the name of penalty to the aforesaid Prior. The following are witnesses, The Lord S. Dean of York, the Prior of Bridlington, H. Treasurer of York, Henry de Pudsay, Adam de Novo Mercheto, Henry de Feritate, Henry de Novo Mercheto, Roger de Everley, Radulph Haranc, Radulph son of Richard, Robert de Craven, and others.

V.

A.D. 1230.—UNIVERSIS sanctæ matris ecclesiæ filiis ad quos præsens scriptum pervenerit, Radulphus prior et conventus Dunolm. ecclesiæ salutem in Domino. Noverit universitas vestra nos præcise et absolute commisisse ecclesias de Wilton et de Gykeleswic, et jus patronatus earundem ordinationi venerabilis patris nostræ, domini W. Dei gratia Ebor., archiepiscopi, Angliæ primatis, perpetuo duraturae; ratum et gratum habituri, et inviolabiliter, imperpetuum observaturi, quicquid de illis duxerit ordinandum. Ita tamen quod occasione illius ordinationis monachus noster canonicus non

* fiat, aut nomine canonici censeatur. Actum est hoc anno gratiæ M°cc° tricesimo, iiij. kalendas Junii, anno archiepiscopatus dicti venerabilis patris nostri Walteri quintodecimo. Teste sigillo nostro.

(Reg. Mag. Alb. pars ii, 8, 9; Claudius B. iii. 6; Reg. Giffard, 77.

Translation.

To all the sons of the Holy Mother Church to whom these presents shall come, Ralph the Prior,† and the Convent of the Church of Durham send greeting in the Lord. Let your community know that we have concisely and absolutely entrusted the Churches of Wilton and Giggleswick, and the right of patronage of the same, to the perpetual ordination of our venerable father, Walter, by the grace of God Archbishop of York, Primate of England, who shall exercise it firmly and kindly, and keep inviolate for ever whatever he shall think ought to be ordained concerning them. So also, whatever the monk our prebend [omit to do] let it be considered as done, or else let a note be made in the name of the prebend. This decree was made in the year of grace 1230, on the 29th of May, in the 15th year of office of the said Walter, our Venerable Father. Witness our seal.

VI.

A.D. 1230.—UNIVERSIS sanctæ matris ecclesiæ filiis ad quos præsens scriptum pervenerit, Rudulphus prior et conventus de Finchal salutem in Domino. Noverit universitas vestra nos præcise et absolute commisisse ecclesias de Wilton et de Gykeleswyk et jus patronatus earundem ordinationi venerabilis patris nostri domini Walteri Dei gratia Ebor. archiepiscopi, Angliæ primatis, perpetus duraturæ; ratum et gratum habituri et inviolabiliter imperpetuum observaturi quicquid de illis duxerit ordinandum. Actum est hoc anno gratiæ M°cc°xxx°, iiij., kalendas Junii, anno archiepiscopatus dicti venerabilis patris nostri W. xv°. Testo sigillo nostro. (Reg. Mag. Alb. pars ii., 8, 9, &c.)

Translation.

To all the sons of the Holy Mother Church to whom these presents shall come, Ralph the Prior, and the Convent of Finchale send greeting in the Lord. Let your community

---

* I fancy some word like "faciat" should be inserted here.

† Ralph was the third Prior of Finchale.

know that we have concisely and absolutely entrusted the Churches of Wilton and Giggleswick, and the right of patronage of the same, to the perpetual ordination of our Venerable Father, Walter, by the Grace of God Archbishop of York, Primate of England, who shall exercise it firmly and kindly, and keep inviolate for ever whatever he shall think ought to be ordained concerning them. This decree was made in the year of Grace 1230, on the 29th of May, in the 15th year of office of the said Walter, our Venerable Father. Witness our seal.

VII.

EBOR 5 id. Junii 1230.—THE Prior and Convent of Durham, and the Prior of Finkhal, having submitted the church of Gikeslwik to our ordination, we ordain as follows, with the assent of our Chapter: 'Ob reverentiam beatorum Cudberti et Godricii, domum de Finkhal nostræ provisionis beneficio honorare volentes,' we appropriate the Church of Gikeleswik to the use of the Monks of Finkhal, after the death or cession of Walter, the present rector, reserving a perpetual vicarage therein.

(From Archbishop Gray's Register).

VIII.

Appropriatio Ecclesiæ de Gikelswyk per Archiepiscopum Ebor.

A,D. 1230.—OMNIBUS Christi fidelibus ad quos presens scriptum pervenerit, Walterus Dei gratia Eboracensis Archiepiscopus, Angliæ Primas, salutem in Domino. Noveritis quod cum dilecti filii Prior et Conventus Dunolmensis et Prior de Finkhal ecclesias de Gikeleswik et de Wihton et jus patronatus earundem libere, precise, et absolute, nostræ commisissent ordinationi, perpetuo duraturæ, nos de voluntate es assensu Capituli nostri ita de illis ordinavimus; videlicet, quod, ob reverentiam beatorum Cuthberti et Godricii, Domum de Finkhal nostrae provisionis beneficio honorare volentes, ecclesiam de Gigkeleswik Priori et Conventui Dunelmensi concessimus in usus monachorum Deo et beato Godricio apud Finkhal ministrancium, post decessum, vel qualemcunque cessionem, Walteri ipsius ecclesiæ nunc rectoris, in perpetuum libere convertendam, salva in omnibus auctoritate et dignitate Eboracensis ecclesiæ; salva etiam competenti vicaria perpetua in eadem ecclesia Vicario assignanda, qui in eadem personaliter ministret, et nobis et successoribus nostris de spirituabilus respondeat. Ecclesiam autem de Wihton, quæ cum fuerit Eboracensis Ecclesiæ prebenda, sicut nobis manifestis constitit indiciis eidem hactenus exstitit minus licite subtracta, nobis et ecclesiæ nostræ Eboracensi in perpetuum reservavimus. Ita quod dicti Prior et Conventus Dunolmensis, aut Prior de Finkhal, nichil omnino juris in ipsa, aut in jure patronatus ejusdem, ullo umquam tempore sibi possint vendicare. Et ,ut haec nostra ordinatio perpetuæ firmitatis robur obtineat, presenti scripto tam sigillum nostrum quam sigillum Capituli nostri est appositum. Actum apud Eboracum quinto idus Junii, anno Domini millesimo ducentesimo tricesimo.

(The seal of Archbishop Grey affixed. Reverse:—The heads of St. Peter and St. Paul, with the circumscription ✠ ORATE PRO NOBIS S'CI DEI APO'LI. The Archbishop was Walter Gray, formerly Bishop of Worcester, who was translated to the see of York 27th March 1216, and died 1st May 1255.

Translation.

Appropriation of the Church of Giggleswick through the Archbishop of York.

To all faithful followers of Christ to whom this present writing shall come, Walter, by the Grace of God Archbishop of York, Primate of England, sends his greeting in the Lord. Know ye that when my beloved children the Prior and Convent of Durham and the Prior of Finchal entrusted the Churches of Giggleswick and Wikton and the right of patronage of the same freely precisely and absolutely, to our ordination, which is to last for ever, We, by the will and assent of our Chapter have thus ordained concerning them : that is to say, because of our reverence for the blessed Cuthbert and Godrick, wishing to honour the House of Finkhall with a gift made in our forethought, we have conceded the Church of Giggleswick to the Prior and Convent of Durham, to be freely handed over for ever to the use of the Monks who minister to God and the Blessed Godrick at Finkhal, after the departure, by death or otherwise, of Walter, the present rector of that Church, in all things the authority and dignity of the Church of York being preserved ; there being maintained also in the same Church a perpetual Vicarage to be assigned to a competent Vicar who may personally officiate in the same, and to be answerable in spiritual matters to ourselves and our successors. But the Church of Wikton, which, whilst it has been a prebend of the Church of York, as is evident to us from manifest proofs, but up to the present time has been separated from the same, having been illegally taken away from us, we have reserved in perpetuity for ourselves and our Church at York. So that the said Prior and Convent of Durham, or the Prior of Finchal cannot ever at any time claim to themselves any power whatever over it, or in the right of patronage of the same. And in order that this our ordination may continue in force for ever, to the present writing both our own seal and that of our Chapter is affixed. Written at York on the 9th day of June, 1230.

IX.

THORP, 6 id., Dec. 1231 (1230).—THE Prior and Convent of Durham, the Prior of Finchale, and Walter de Vestiario, having submitted the Church of Gygleswic to the ordination of us and J., sub-dean of York, with the consent of the consent of the said sub-dean, we thus arrange the matter:—The said Walter resigns the Church. He shall receive fifty five marks per ann. from the 'camera' of the Prior and Convent of Durham, through the Prior of Finchale, every year, at York. By the hand, &c.

(From Archbishop Gray's Register).

X.

EBOR., 6 kal. AUG. 1231.—ON the resignation of Walter de Vestiario, we have inducted the prior of Finkehale to the Church of Gygleswic; a proper perpetual vicarage to be ordained therein on the death of the said Walter.

(From Archbishop Gray's Register).

XI.

Carta Walteri Ebor., Archiepiscopi.

A.D. 1232.—OMNIBUS Christi fidelibus ad quos presens scriptum pervenerit, Walterus Dei gratia Eboracensis Archiepiscopus, Angliæ Primas, salutem in Domino. Noveritis nos ad resignacionem Walteri de Vestiario induci fecisse Priorem

Fig. 3.

Fig. 4.

Seals of the Priors of Finchale appended to Deeds relating to Giggleswick Church.

de Finkhall in corporalem possessionem ecclesiæ de Gikeleswyk. Salva competenti vicaria perpetua in eadem ecclesia post decessum dicti Walteri ordinanda. In cujus rei testimonium sigillum nostrum duximus apponendem. Data apud Eboracum, vj^{to} kalendas Augusti, Pontificatus nostri anno sexto decimo.

Translation.
Deed of Walter, Archbishop of York.

To all faithful followers of Christ 'to whom the present writing shall come, Walter, by the Grace of God Archbishop of York, Primate of England, sends greeting in the Lord. Know ye that We, on the resignation of Walter de Vestiario have caused the Prior of Finkhal to be inducted into corporal possession of the Church of Giggleswick. A perpetual vicarage must be appointed in the same church for a competent minister after the decease of the said Walter. In testimony of which circumstance we have caused our seal to be affixed. Given at York, the 27th July, in the 16th year of our Pontificate. [A.D. 1232.]

XII.
Bulla Gregorii Papæ.

A.D. 1232.—GREGORIUS episcopus,* servus servorum Dei, dilectis filiis Priori et Conventui de Finkhall, ordinis Sancti Benedicti, salutem et apostolicam benedictionem. Justis petencium desideriis dignum est nos facilem prebere assenum, et vota, quæ a racionis tramite non discordant, effectu prosequente complere, Ea propter, dilecti in Domino filii, vestris justis postulacionibus grato concurrentes assensu, ecclesiam de Gikeleswyk cum pertinentiis suis, quam de concessione venerabilis fratris nostri Eboracensis Archiepiscopi, capituli sui accedente consensu, canonice proponitis vos adeptos, sicut eam juste ac pacifice possidetis, vobis, et per vos monasterio vestro, auctoritate apostolica confirmamus et presentis scripti patrocinio communimus. Nulli ergo omnine hominum liceat hanc paginam nostræ confirmacionis infringere, vel ei ausu temerario contraire. Si quis autem hoc attemptare presumpserit indignacionem Omnipotentis Dei et beatorum Petri et Pauli Apostolorum ejus se noverit incursurum. Data Lateran' v^{to} idus Marcii, Pontificatus nostri anno iiij^{to}.

---

* Pope Gregory IX. (Ugolino, bishop of Ostia, and a cardinal). Elected and enthroned 19th March, 1227. Died 21st August, 1241.

Translation.

GREGORY, POPE, servant of the servants of God, to his beloved children the Prior and Convent of Finkhall, of the Order of St. Benedict, sends greeting and an apostolical benediction. To the just request of your petitioning it is right that we should give a ready assent, and by putting them into effect should fulfil your wishes, which are not at variance with the dictates of reason. For these reasons, beloved children in the Lord, We, readily complying with your just demands, confirm with apostolic authority to you, and through you to your monastery, the church of Giggleswick with its pertinences, which, according to the concession of our venerable brother, the Archbishop of York, with the additional consent of his Chapter, you assert that you acquired in a manner in accordance with the canon, as also you retain possession of it in accordance with justice and peace, and we furnish you with the additional support of this present writing. Let no man whatever therefore venture to infringe this page of our confirmation, or with rash daring to go contrary to it. But if any one should presume to attempt this, let him know that he will incur the indignation of the Omnipotent God and of the blessed Peter and Paul his Apostles. Given at the Lateran, 11th March, in the 4th year of our Pontificate. [A.D. 1232].

XIII.

CAWAD, 7 id., Sept., 1249.—THE Archbishop appropriates the Church of Horton to the nuns of St. Clement, York, 'inducente nos paupertate et inopia;' the advowson of which has been given to them by 'nobilis mulier' Alicia de Staveley: reserving to the Church of Gikeleswic its pension therefrom.

(From Archbishop Gray's Registers).

XIV.

Ordinatio Vicariæ de Gykleswyk.

A.D. 1259.—OMNIBUS Christi fidelibus presentes literas visuris vel audituris G. * miseracione Divina Ebor. Archiepiscopus, Angliæ Primas, salutem in Domino sempiternam. Noveritis nos, de assensu Prioris et Conventus Dunel-

---

* This is Bishop Godfrey de Ludham, *alias* Kimeton.

mensis ac Prioris de Fynchall, Vicariam perpetuam in ecclesia de Gykleswyk taliter ordinasse, videlicet quod vicarius, qui pro tempore fuerit, habeat decimas garbarum de Lanclyve et de Stainford sub monte, et decimam feni tocius parochiæ, molendinorum, ortorum, albi, ancarum, et etiam gallinarum. Item habeat omnes oblaciones altaris per annum, decimas personales, et mortuaria quæ de vivo non fuerint animali; et mansum de terra ecclesiæ ad inhabitandum, quod tenuit quondam Henricus Thoppan. Vicarius autem contentus in predicta ecclesia se altero presbitero [ita] personaliter residebit, facietque ecclesiæ et parochiæ tam in ministris quam aliis honeste et congrue deserviri ac onera tam Archidiaconalia quam synodalia sustinebit. In cujus rei testamonium presenti scripto sigillum nostrum duximus apponendum. Data apud Cawod, idus Maii anno Domini MCC quinquagesimo nono.

Translation.

Ordination of the Vicarage of Giggleswick.

TO all faithful (servants) of Christ who shall see or hear read these present letters. G[odfrey], by the Divine Grace Archbishop of York, Primate of England, sends eternal greeting in the Lord. Know ye, that we, with the assent of the Prior and Convent of Durham and the Prior of Finchal have ordained a perpetual vicarage in the Church of Giggleswick in the following manner, viz., that the Vicar for the time being shall have tithes of the sheaves of Langclife and of Stainforth-under-the-hill,* and a tithe of all the parish hay, of grist, of garden produce, of wages, of geese, and also of hens. Also he may have all oblations of the altar from year to year, personal tithes, and those mortuaries † which are not paid for a living animal; and the house on the church land to live in, which Henry Thoppan formerly held. Now the Vicar shall be content to reside in the aforesaid church in person, with another priest, and shall take care that the duty is performed to the Church and Parish both in services and other things, both in an honest and fitting manner, and shall perform duties both archidiaconal and synodical. In testimony of which thing we have affixed our seal to this present writing. Given at Cawood, the 15th May, in the year of our Lord 1259.

---

* This was the old name for Stainforth, to distinguish it from Knight Stainforth (now known as Little Stainforth).

† A mortuary was anciently the best animal of a deceased parishioner, which became the property of the Incumbent of the Parish in which he died.

XV.

Dismissio Esclesia Parochialis de Gigleswyk.

A.D. 1439.—HÆC indentura facta inter Johannem permissione Divina Priorem ecclesiæ Cathedralis Dunelm. ex parte una et Rogerum Tempest de Broghton armigerum, Christoferum Alton capellanum, et Johannem Armested yoman, ex parte altera, testatur, quod dictus Prior concessit et ad firmam dismisit dictis Rogero—decimas garbarum ac omnes fructus—ad parochialem ecclesiam de Gigleswike spectantia, exceptis decimis et porcionibus vicario dictæ ecclesiæ—assignatis—Habenda—[for one year's rent £44.] Dat Dunelm. 1 Feb., 1439.*

Translation.

Leasing of the Parish Church of Giggleswick.

THIS Indenture made between John, by devine permission Prior of the Cathedral Church of Durham, on the one part, and Roger Tempest of Broghton, Esquire, Christopher Alton, clerk, and John Armisted, Yeoman, on the other part, bears witness, that the said Prior has granted and leased to the said persons, Roger, &c., the thithes of sheaves and all fruits, things pertaining to the Parish Church of Giggleswick, except the tithes and portions assigned to the Vicar of the said Church, to be held for one year, rent £44. Given at Durham 1st Feb., 1439.

XVI.

Carta Prioris Et Conventus de Fsnkhale Facta Simoni Filio Swani.

UNIVERSIS sanctæ matris ecclesiæ filiis ad quos presens scriptum pervenerit, Radulphus Prior et Conventus de Finkhale, salutem in Domino. Noverit universitas vestra nos dedisse, concessisse, et presenti carta nostra confirmasse Symoni filio Swani unum tofptum cum omnibus pertinenciis suis in Gicleswic in quo dictus Swainus pater suus quondam

---

* There are other Leases of Rectorial Tithes, and parcels of the glebe land. In the latter the lessees are of the family of Carr, afterwards of Stackhouse.

manebat, et totum Briggeholm, habendum et tenendum sibi et heredibus suis de nobis et successoribus in perpetuum, in feodo et hereditate, libere, quiete, pacifice et honorifice, reddendo inde annuatim nobis et successoribus nostris duos solidos ad duos terminos, scilicet, duodecim denarios ad Pentecosten et duodecim denarios ad festum Sancti Martini in hyeme, pro omnibus aliis serviciis. Et ut hæc nostra donacio, concessio et confirmacio futuris temporibus robur optineant presens scriptum sigilli nostri apposicione roboravimus. Hiis testibus, Elya de Gycleswic, Henrico de Stainford, Ricardo de Hortun, David de Setle, Ranulfo filio suo, Symone mercatore de Gycleswic, Richeman, Kallei, Johanne filio Arnaldi de Stainfordei, Waltero Tusard, Willielmo de Routhemelei, et Ada de Palei et aliis.

(The seal of the Prior of Finchale, for a representation of which see Fig. 4, is appended to this Deed).

Translation.

Deed of the Prior and Convent of Finchal made with Symon, son of Swain.

TO all the sons of the Holy Mother Church to whom this present writing shall come, Ralph the Prior and the Convent of Finkhal, send greeting in the Lord. Let your community know that we have granted, conceded, and by this our present deed confirmed, to Symon, son of Swain, the messuage with all its appertenances in Giggleswick, in which the said Swain his father formerly used to live, and the whole of Briggeholme, to have and to hold for himself and his heirs from us and our successors for ever, in fee and perpetuity, freely, quietly, peacefully and honourably, to pay thence every year to us and our successors two shillings at two fixed dates, viz., 12 pence at Pentecost, and 12 pence at the Feast of St. Martin in winter, for all other services. And in order that this our gift, concession, and confirmation may have force for future times, we have confirmed the present writing by the affixing of our seal. These being witnesses :—Elias of Giggleswick, Henry of Stainforth, Richard of Horton, David of Settle, Ranulph his son, Simon the merchant, of Giggleswick, Richeman, Kalley, John the son of Arnold of Stainforth, Walter Tusard, Wm. of Rathmell, and Adam de Paley, and others.

XVII.

Carta Domini Willielmi de Perci (De I Tofto et Crofto cum pertinentiis in Giggleswik reddendo II^s. Ecclesiæ Ibidem).

WILLIELMUS DE PERCY, omnibus hominibus suis, clericis et laicis, Francis et Anglis, presentibus et futuris, salutem. Sciatis me concessisse et presenti carta mea confirmasse Suaino filio Normanni totum toftum cum omnibus pertinenciis suis in Gileswic in quo Gospatricius quondam manebat, per [terras] divisas quæ fuerunt inter ipsum Gospatricium et Willielmum clericum, et totum Brigholme cum omnibus pertinentiis suis illi et heredibus suis, tenenda et habenda de Deo et de ecclesia de Gileswic et de persona ecclesiæ ejusdem et de successoribus suis in perpetunm, in feodo et hereditate, libere et quiete et honorifice. Reddendo inde annuatim Deo et ecclesiæ de Gileswic et personæ ejusdem ecclesiæ et successoribus suis duos solidos pro omni servicio et exactione, scilicet ad Pentecosten duodecim denarios et ad festum Sancti Martini duodecim denarios; sicut carta ejusdem personæ, quam inde habet, testatur et proportat. Hiis testibus testibus, Henrico de Percy fratre meo, Jordano de......stre, Radulfo de Bonevill, Helia de Gileswic, Ricardo de Setel, Roberto de Setel, Richeman, et aliis pluribus.

(The Seal of William de Percy, for representation of which see Fig. 2, is annexed).

Translation.

Deed of William de Percy, concerning the payment of two shillings to the Church of Giggleswick for one toft and croft with its appurtenances there.

WILLIAM DE PERCY, to all his servants, both clerical and lay, French and English, present and future (sends) greeting. Know ye that I have conceded, and with this my present deed have confirmed, to Swain, son of Norman, all the toft with all its appurtenances in Giggleswick in which Gospatric formerly used to dwell, and the land lying between that of the said Gospatric and that of William the clerk, and all Brigholme, with all its appurtenances, to him and his heirs, to be had and held from God and the Church of Giggleswick and the parson of the same church and his successors for ever, in fee and perpetuity, freely and quietly and honourably. He must pay thence annually to God and the Church of Giggleswick and the parson of the same church, and to his successors, two shillings, as payment for all service and exaction, viz., 12 pence at Pentecost, and 12 pence at the Feast St. Martin as the deed of the same parson, which he has from thence, testifies and purports. The following are witnesses—my brother Henry de Percy, Jordan de [L'E]stre, Ralph de Boneville, Helias of Giggleswick, Richard of Settle, Robert of Settle, Richeman, and many others.

XVIII.

Resignacio Symonis filii Swayn [de terra sua vocata Briggeholme cum Pertinenciis Facta Priori et Monachis de Finchall.]

OMNIBUS hoc scriptum visuris vel audituris, Simon filius Swayn de Gykeliswyk, salutem in Domino. Noveritis me resignasse et quictum clamasse de me et heredibus meis totam terram meam quæ vocatur Briggeholme, cum pertinentiis, sine aliquo retenemento, Deo et Beato Godrico et domino Ricardo Priori de Finchehal et suis successoribus et monachis ibidem Deo servientibus, in perpetuum, pro quondam summa pecuniæ quam mihi præ manibus in magna necessitate mea pacavit. Ita, videlicet, quod ego Simon nec heredes mea in predicta terra aliquod jus vel clameum possimus exigere vel vendicare, Et sciendum quod ego Simon filius Swayne cartam quam habui de domino Radulfo quondam Priore de Finchehal cum carta domini Willielmi de Percy predicto Ricardo Priori de Finchehal et monachis ejusuem loci reddidi et quietam clamavi. Et ego vero Simon filius Swayn de Gykeliswic et heredes mei totam illam terram de Briggeholme cum pertinentiis dicto Ricardo Priori de Finchehal et suis successoribus et monachis ibidem Deo servientibus contra omnes homines et feminas warrantizabimus, acquietabimus et defendemus in perpetuum. Hiis testibus, domino Helie [*ita*] de Cnolle, Willielmo Fleming, domino Johanne vicario de Gikeliswik, Thoma de Mallum, Roberto de Stayneford, Radulfo de Berburne et aliis.

Oval seal of the smallest size,—white wax,—a stag couchant ......
SIMON .. LI SWEN ..

Translation.

Surrender by Simon, son of Swayn, of his land called Briggeholme, with its appurtenances, to the Prior and Monks of Finchal.

TO all who shall see or hear read this writing, Simon, son of Swayn of Giggleswick sends greeeting in the Lord. Know ye that I have resigned and renounced all claim on the part of me and my heirs, to the whole of my land which is called Briggeholme with its appurtenances, without any reservation, to God and the Blessed Godrick and Sir Richard,* Prior of Finchal, and his successors, and the monks who serve God at the same place, in perpetuity, in consideration of a certain sum of money, which being forthcoming when I was in a great strait, assisted me. Therefore, neither I, Simon, nor my heirs, can put forth or assume any right or claim over the aforesaid land. And let it be known that I, Simon son of Swayne, have given up and resigned all claim to the deed which I had from Sir Ralph, formerly prior of Finchal, together with the deed of Sir William de Percy, to the aforesaid Richard, Prior of Finchal, and the Monks of the same place. And assuredly I, Simon son of Swayne of Giggleswick, and my heirs will warrant, acquit and maintain in perpetuity, against all men and women, the whole of that land of Briggeholme with its appurtenances to the said Richard, Prior of Finchal and his successors and the monks who at that place perform the service of God. The following are witnesses—Sir Helias de Cnolle [Knowles], William Fleming, Sir John,† Vicar of Giggleswick, Thomas of Mallum, Robert of Stainforth, Ralph de Berburne, and others.

XIX.

Resignacio Agnetis Uxoris Syms .. Swayn [de Terra et Prato in Brigholm.]

A.D.—OMNIBUS Christi fidelibus ad quos presens scriptum pervenerit, Agnes quondam uxor Simonis filii Swayn de Gikelswic, salutem in Domino sempiternam. Noverit universitas vestra me remisisse, et omnino quietam

---

* Prior Richard de Eskerick is said to have made his canonical obedience to the Archbishop of York in May, 1284, doubtless as *Rector* of the Church of Giggleswick.

† It was customary to give the clergy the title of ' Sir.'

clamasse totum jus et clamium quod habui, vel aliquo modo habere potui, racione dotis, in terra et prato de Brigholm, quæ quondam fuerunt Symonis filii Swayn quondam viri mei, pro quatuor solidis argenti michi in tota vita mea annuatim reddendis ad duos anni terminos, medietatem scilicet ad Pentecosten, et aliam medietatem ad festum Sancti Martini in hyeme. In cujus rei testimonium presens scriptum sigilli mei impressione roboravi. Hiis testibus, domino Ada tunc vicario de Gikeswic, Roberto de Stainford Scotan, Nigello de Stanford sub monte, Stefano tunc ballivo de Setel, et multis aliis.

(Small oval seal of white wax: a Fleur-de-Lis).

Translation.

Renunciation by Agnes, wife of Simon, son of Swayn, of the land and meadow called Briggeholm.

TO all faithful servants of Christ to whom this present writing shall come, Agnes formerly wife of Simon, son of Swayn of Giggleswick, sends eternal greeting in the Lord. Let your community know that I have surrendered, and have altogether renounced every right and claim which I had, by reason of my dowry, over the land and meadow of Brigge- holme, which were formerly the property of Symon son of Swayn, my late husband, for four shillings in silver to be paid to me annually for the rest of my life at two fixed dates of the year, that is to say, half at Pentecost, and the other half at the Feast of St. Martin in winter. In testimony of which things I have given force to this writing by the impression of my seal, The following are witnesses—Sir Adam then Vicar of Giggleswick, Robert of Stainforth Scotan, Nigel of Stain- forth-under-the-hill, Stephen then Bailiff of Settle, and many others.

XX.

Resignacio Thomæ filii Henrici Cupman de tribus bovatis thrræ Terræ in Gikliswyk [in Craven facta Priori de Finchal.]

A.D, 1279—UNIVERSIS Christi fidelibus presens scriptum visuris vel audituris, Thomas filius Henrici Coupeman de Gykeliswyke in Craven, salutem in Domino. Noveris me remisisse, resignasse, et omnino pro me et

heredibus meis in perpetuum quietam clamasse Deo et
Beatæ Mariæ et Beato Johanni Baptistæ et Beato Godrico
et Priori de Finkehall, et ejusdem loci Conventui et eorund-
em successoribus omne jus et clameum, quodcumque
habui, vel habere potui, seu potero, in tribus bovatis
terræ cum pertinenciis in villa et territorio de Gikeles-
wyke in Craven, de quibus ipsos, per breve Dimini Regis de
morte antecessoris, corum Justiciarios apud Eboracum itiner-
antes, anno Domini M°cc°.Lxx°. nono inplacitavit [sic] ita
quod nec ego, nec heredes mei, seu aliquis nomine nostro, in
dictis tribus bovatis terræ cum pertinenciis, seu in earumden
aliqua parte jure hereditario aliquid juris vel clamii exigere
vel vendicare possimus in posterum. Et ut hæc mea resignacio, remissio, et quieta clamancia perpetua gaudeant securi-
tate et firmitate presens scriptum pro me et heredibus meis
sigilli mei impressione roboravi. Hiis testibus dominis
Ranulfo de Daker tunc vicecomite Ebor., Willielmo Fleming,
militibus, domino Ada tunc vicario de Gykeleswyke, Nigillo
filio Willielmi de Stayford [ita], Roberto filio Aubray de
Setel, Waltero Hayre de eadem, Laurencio de Gykeleswyke,
Ricardo Rascy de Setel, Raynero de eadem, Roberto de Stayford, Ricardo de Paley, Johanne clerico, hujus scripti notario,
et aliis.

Small oval seal of white wax : a Fleur-de-lis.

Translation.

Renunciation by Thomas, son of Henry Cupman, of three oxgangs of land in Giggleewick (in Craven, made to the Prior of Finchal).

TO all faithful servants of Christ who shall see or hear read this present writing, Thomas son of Henry Coupeman of Giggleswick in Craven, sends greeting in the Lord. Know ye that I have surrendered, resigned, and altogether as far as concerns me and my heirs in perpetuity, have utterly re-nounced in favour of God and the Blessed Mary and the Blessed John the Baptist and the Blessed Godrich and the Prior of Finchall, and the Convent of the same place, and the successors of the same, every right and claim soever which I had, or have been able or shall be able to have, over the three oxgangs* of land with its appurtenances, in the manor and territory of Giggleswick in Craven, concerning

---

* An oxgang of land contained an uncertain number of acres, vary-ing from 13 to 30.

which I brought an action before the travelling justices at York, in the year of our Lord 1279, a short time before the death of our late Lord, the King, so that neither I, nor my heirs, nor any one else in our name, over the said three oxgangs of land with its appurtenances, or over any part of the same can by hereditary right put forth or assume any claim for the future. And in order that this my resignation and perpetual renouncing of all claim may enjoy security and power, I have given force to the present writing as far as concerns me and my heirs by the impression of my seal. These being witnesses:—Lord Ralph de Daker, then Sheriff of Yorkshire, Sir William Fleming, Sir Adam then Vicar of Giggleswick, Nigel son of William of Stainforth, Robert son of Aubrey of Settle, Rayner of the same place, Robert of Stainforth, Richard de Paley, John the Priest, the notary of this Deed, and others.

XXI.

To the Worshipfull Sir and Reverent Fader in God the Priour of Durham.

WORSHIPFULL Sir, and Reverent Fader in God, I commende me to you with all my hert; and ye will undirstond ther is a vicerege in Craven, of Gigilswik, of the which the presentacion longith to you, as of the right of your chirch of Fyncall, wherfor I pray you hertly that ye wold be tender Lord and furtherer to a prest of myn Sir William Hacforth,[*] the which is servant to my ryght wurshippfull Lord and fadir th' Erle of Westm'l', so that he might be preferred to the next avoidaunce of the same vicarege, considerynge that he is on able Prest and virtuous. And this you lik to do att the contemplacion of this my writyng as y may do thyng to your plesaunce en tym to com. And Almyghte God gyf you right gode lyf, graciously to endure for his mercy. Writen at Hert the Monday next eftir Saynt Luke daye.

THOMAS LORD OF CLIFFORDE.

---

[*] This letter of recommendation was attended to. William Hackford was presented to the Vicarage of Giggleswick on the 21st of September 1438, and held the living for two years. The writer of the letter was Thomas Lord Clifford, eight Lord of the Honor of Skipton, the son of John Lord Clifford and Elizabeth, daughter of Henry Lord Percy, who was slain in the battle of St. Alban's in 1455. His father the Earl of Westmoreland, of whom he speaks was the second husband of his mother. Hert, from whence the letter is dated, is Hart, in the County of Durham, which, with its appurtenances, had been granted to the family of Clifford upon the forfeiture of Bruce in 1306.

XXII.
Letter from the Prior of Durham to Thomas Lord Clifford.

RYGHT wirshipfull mayster, I recomend me to yow, besekand God that he evermor will send his blessing apon yowe to kep yow in saule and body to hys plesyre. And like yowe to weet that I haff resavyd yowr full honorabill lettre contenyng two maters. On is to giff our assent to a pension to Sr William Hakforth, yowr prest, to be had of the kirke of Gygleswyk, and to the vicary of the same kirke voide be resignacione of the said Sir William Hakforth to presennt Sr Christofer Altam,* whom ye said Sr William has desyryd theto to be presennt, whilk mater at the reverence of your maystership is fulfillid. The secund mater, in yowr wyrshipfull lettre contenyd, is to graunt the Sr William the first voidance of a prebend in Hemyngburgh, in the whilk mater, likit yowr maystership to undrestand that both the King and my Lord of Durham at diverse times has writyn to my brethir and me for the first voidance of a prebend of owr patronage, and also other diverse Lords, of the whilk some of yowr awen kyn, as my Lord yowr uncle of Northumbrland for his son, and also Sir William Eure for his son, has send lang tyme sythen for thair fortherance till some prebende whilk noon yhett is spede, bod, as I at the reverence of yow fortherid Sir William Hakforth to the vicar of Giglesswik, and now til have a pension therof, so my liste and my will is and sall be to forther hym when itt goodly may be. And Almyghty God haff you evermor in his gracyus keping. Writyn att Durham the ix day of Septembre.—[1440].

* Altam seems to have been presented upon the resignation of Hackforth, but his name does not occur in the list of Vicars given in Whitaker's Craven.

XXIII.
Litera missa Domino De Clifforde.

A.D. 1446.—WIRSHIPFULL and my right goode Lorde, I recommende me to yowe in my most humble wyse, thankyng your goode Lordshippe* whilke yhe haff at all tymez effectually shewide to the kirke of Seynt Cuthbertt and his mynisters, beseking yow of your goode contynuance. And as for the

* Some words seem to be wanting, between the words 'Lordshippe' and 'whilke' in this sentence, but so it is in the copy.

mater concernyng vicar of Gigleswike, for wham your said Lordshipp late by the vicar sennde your letteres to me, please it you to consave that my predecessor and the Chapiter his brether, att the gret instaunce and prayer of the right wirshippfull Sr Thomas Percy knyght, graunted and promyste that thay wald have recommende Sr Richard Fulthorpp, a chapeleyn of his, to the vicary of Gigleswike, what tyme som ever the said vicar att now is incumbent wald resigne or leve his vicary aforsaid, whilke promysse and graunte I and my brether moste of honesty and trewth kepp and fulfill. And wheer your Lordshipp desires that the vicar myght have the kirke aforsaid bounden to hym undre our common seall for oon annuell pension duryng his lyffe, trewly we have noon auctoritee no power by the common law to bynnde the kirke in ony sich pension, bod, att the reverence and contemplacion of your goode Lordshipp, we will, as patrons of the said kirke, giff our consenntt and goode will undre our common seall that our right wirshipfull Lorde cardinall of Yorke by hys auctoritee ordinary assigne to the said vicar a competent porcion yherly to be resavide of the fruites and reveneux of the said kirke and also to bynnde the said kirke and the vicars therof for tyme beyng to the trew and hale payment of the said pension als lang as the vicar aforsaid leves. And if I and my brether myght doo ony moor in this mater, by the common lawe, to the plesaunce of your goode Lordshipp, we wald be full gladde to fulfill your entennt, and that knowes our lorde Jhu', who have you in his gracieux kepying and giff you mykill worshipp lanng to endour for his mercy. Wreten att Durham the vj. day of Decembre [1446].*

XXIV.

To my very good Lord the Priour of Durham be this delyvered.†

MY LORD PRIOR, in my right hartie maner I commend me vnto you. And where it pleasyd you at my last being in Durham to gyve vnto me your tythe in Gygleswyk, the whiche I have gyven vnto my son Thomas Clyfford, and at

---

* This is another letter on the subject of the Vicarage of Giggleswick, with respect to which a strange traffic was carrying on. Sir Thos. Percy's chaplain, Richard Fulthorpe, was presented on the 29th July 1447, and we hear no more of Altam until the year 1461, when, by his will dated in that year, he desires to be buried in the Church of Giggleswick.

† The superscription of the letter.

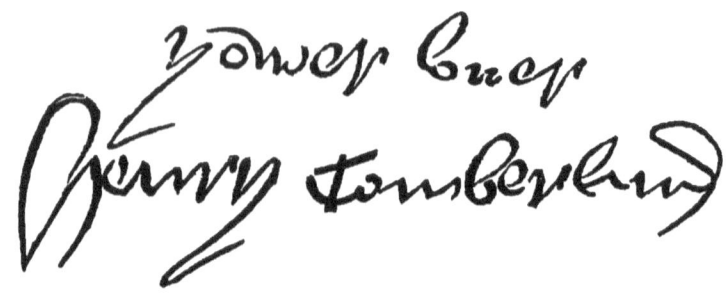

Fig. 5.

Facsimile of Signature of HENRY, EARL OF CUMBERLAND.

Fig. 6.

Facsimile of Signature of SIR ARTHUR DARCY.

suche tyme as he was with yow for the same ye made a steye by reason of Sr Arture Darcye, whose mynd and pleasur therin I trust ye shall know. In consideracion wherof, and according to the graunt ye made before my lord of Westmerland, Henry Evers and me, I disire you to graunt the same tythe under your Convent seale unto my said son; and, ye this doyng, I shalbe glad to sho you lyke pleasure; as knoweth our Lord, who preserve you. From Carlesle the vjth day of December.

Your Lover,*

HENRY CUMBERLAND.

XXV.

To my good Lord Prior off Durhem'.

MY LORD PRIOR, where as ye dyd make a promyze to me y^t I chulld have ye taking off ye parssonage of Gyglsin Craven lyke as my grantfather Sir Ryc. Tempest hadd off yowr grant from ye hows of Dureme, my lord so ytt is y^t my good lord ye erlle of Cumberland & my good frend Sr Thomas Clyfford hath soe intrettyd me y^t I gyff to them my tenant right oft ye same & allso I doo requyre yow to lett them have ytt & ye promyze y^t yow dyd make to me I clerly releas to them & God send you & yowr hows virtewsly to prosper. From London the xv day off Agust at yowr lordschyps to comand. †

ARTHUR DARCY.

---

* The words "your lover Henry Cumberland," of which a facsimile is given in Fig. 5, are in the handwriting of the Earl himself.

† This letter is printed literatim. The whole is in the hand-writing of Sir Arthur Darcy, and, as may be conceived from his autograph, (see Fig. 6,) it was no easy matter to decypher it.

AS will be seen, we have translated some of the documents printed in this Tract, literally, in other cases we have given a very free translation of the Latin, as we thought, (for reasons which we need not enter on here,) that, whilst one style was more suitable in some places, the other was best adapted for other portions, as it is no easy thing to translate old Legal documents in Latin, especially the "dog Latin" in which most of them are written, into modern English, at the same time retaining the general style of the originals.

T. B.

J. W. LAMBERT, PRINTER, SETTLE.

PARISH OF GIGGLESWICK.

POLL TAX, A.D. 1379.

FOLLOWERS OF LORD CLIFFORD,
A.D. 1510.

ASSOCIATION FOR THE PROSECUTION
OF FELONS, A.D. 1743.

LAND TAX, &c., A.D. 1800.

EDITED BY

THOS. BRAYSHAW.

* * * *

STACKHOUSE,

NEAR SETTLE,

DECEMBER 20TH, 1884.

This, the fourth of my series of "Local Tracts," consists in a great measure of lists of names of former inhabitants of the Parish of Giggleswick. To a stranger these lists will be exceedingly dull, but for those whose ancestors and connections have lived in this parish for generations, I venture to hope there will be a certain amount of interest in tracing the old names in the successive lists, which prove the tenacity with which the old Craven families cling to their native dales.

THOS. BRAYSHAW.

Twelve large and one hundred small paper copies printed for private circulation.

POLL TAX, A.D. 1379.

IN the second year of the reign of King Richard the Second (A.D. 1379,) the Parliament granted to the King a subsidy to enable him to carry on war against France, this subsidy being raised by a tax payable by all persons above the age of 16, (other than ecclesiastics and notorious mendicants,) according to their state and degree. The total amount raised in the West Riding was £604 19s. 4d., and of this sum the following townships in this neighbourhood contributed as follows:—

	£	s.	d.
Langclyff (Langcliffe)	0	8	4
Balghom (Malham)	0	16	2
Hamlych (Hanlith)	0	1	10
Scothorp (Scosthrop)	0	5	10
Preston (Long Preston)	0	15	6
Calton	0	15	0
Oterburn (Otterburn)	0	5	6
Rauchmell (Rathmell)	0	11	10
Setle (Settle)	0	17	10
Helyghfeld (Hellifield)	0	17	4
Halton West	0	10	10
Wyglesworth (Wigglesworth)	0	12	0
Kyrkby (Kirkby Malham)	0	5	0
Gygleswyk (Giggleswick)	1	1	8
Staynford (Stainforth)	1	12	0
Ayreton (Airton)	0	7	10
Clapham	1	3	6
Austwyk (Austwick)	1	6	6
Horton (Horton-in-Ribblesdale)	0	17	0

We thus see that the then parish of Giggleswick, consisting of the Townships of Giggleswick, Settle, Rathmell, Langcliffe, and Stainforth, contributed the respectable sum of £4 11s. 8d.

Comparing the above amounts with those of some other West Riding Townships, we may note that

	£	s.	d.
Sheffield paid	6	11	2
Huddersfield	0	19	4
Halifax	0	12	8
Bradford	1	3	0
and Leeds	3	0	4

From the returns we can approximately estimate the number of inhabitants of each village, and the relative importance at that day, not only of one township in the parish with another, but of each and all of them as compared with other places in the county.

The lists for this parish are as follows :—

LANGCLYFF (LANGCLIFFE.)

Willelmus filius* Thome & vx† iiij*d*.		Seruientes‡—Ricardus filius Laurencii . . . . iiij*d*.
Willelmus filius Ade & vx . iiij*d*.		Alicia vx Ade . . . iiij*d*.
Laurencius filius Ade & vx . iiij*d*.		Agnes filia§ Nicholai . . iiij*d*.
Laurencius filius Johannis & vx. . . . . . iiij*d*.		Matilda de Thorp . . iiij*d*.
Willelmus ffysch'r & vx . iiij*d*.		Matilda filia Willelmi . . iiij*d*.
Willelmus Prest & vx . . iiij*d*.		Emma ffyscher . . . iiij*d*.
Thomas Forester & vx . . iiij*d*.		Cecilia filia Willelmi . . iiij*d*.
Ricardus de Carr & vx . . iiij*d*.		Matheus ffyscher . . . iiij*d*.
Edmundus Suerdson & vx . iiij*d*.		Agnes Prest . . . . iiij*d*.
Thomas Ineson & vx . . xij*d*.		Alicia filia ejusdem . . iiij*d*.
Thomas Robertson & vx . iiij*d*.		Patricius Syke . . . iiij*d*.
Johannes de Armetstede & vx iiij*d*.		Summa‖—viij.*s*.iiij*d*.

RAUCHMELL (RATHMELL.)

Willelmus de Cote & vx . iiij*d*.		Johannes filius Alani & vx . iiij*d*.
Thomas filius Ade & vx . iiij*d*.		Willelmus Curtays & vx . iiij*d*.
Johannes Saylebank & vx . iiij*d*.		Johannes Webstre.†† *Textor*, & vx . . . . . vj*d*.
Ricardus de Carr & vx . iiij*d*.		Willelmus filius Agnetis & vx iiij*d*.
Hugo Schether & vx . . iiij*d*.		Willelmus Hendley & vx . iiij*d*.
Thomas Milner & vx . . iiij*d*.		Robertus filius Willelmi & vx iiij*d*.
Ricardus filius Johannis & vx iiij*d*.		Willelmus de Gisburn & vx . iiij*d*.
Adam Camle (?) & vx . . iiij*d*.		Robertus filius Alane & vx . iiij*d*.
Johannes Godson & vx . . iiij*d*.		*Seruient*—Magota Daudwyfe iiij*d*.
Willelmus filius Ade & vx . iiij*d*.		Matilda Daudoghter . . iiij*d*.
Willelmus Swane & vx . . iiij*d*.		Tillot' de Carr . . . iiij*d*.
Henricus Forster & vx . . iiij*d*.		Alicia de Akedeyn . . iiij*d*.
Johannes Lyndsey & vx . iiij*d*.		Anabilla Daugoghter' (*sic*) . iiij*d*.
Adam filius Ricardi & vx . iiij*d*.		Matilda soror‡‡ ejus . . iiij*d*.
Ricardus filius ejus & vx . iiij*d*.		Agnes de Broghton . . iiij*d*.
Willelmus Kokheued & vx . iiij*d*.		Willelmus Rydhowt . . iiij*d*.
Willelmus Walesman & vx. . iiij*d*.		Johannes Daudson . . iiij*d*.
Thomas filius Walteri & vx . iiij*d*.		

Summa xj.*s*.x.*d*.

*Son. †Wife. ‡Servants. §Daughter. ‖Total. ††Weaver. ‡‡Sister.

Setle (Settle.)

Johannes de Wadyngton & vx	iiijd.	Thomas Megson & vx	iiijd.
Simod Nicholson & vx .	iiijd.	Hanricus (sic) Helynson & vx	iiijd.
Laurencius Nellson & vx	iiijd.	Johannee Blyth', *Milner,* & vx	iiijd.
Johannes Walker & vx .	iiijd.	Johannes de Watre & vx	iiijd.
Robertus Betonson & vx	iiijd.	Johannes Baillie & vx .	iiijd.
Robertus Nellson & vx .	iiijd.	Thomas Manhyrd' & vx	iiijd.
Willelmus Sclater & vx	iiijd.	Johannes Stele & vx	iiijd.
Willelmus de Lyndesay & vx	vjd.	Willelmus Tyllson & vx	iiijd.
Johannes Smeth & vx .	vjd.	Thomas de Waddesworth & vx	iiijd.
Willelmus Broket & vx	iiijd.	Willelmus Hunter & vx	iiijd.
Robertus de Clare & vx	iiijd.	Elias Neleson & vx	iiijd.
Willelmus Wayt & vx .	iiijd.	Johannes Dyrton & vx	iiijd.
Adam filius Willelmi & vx	iiijd.	Magota de Yelbank	iiijd.
Willelmus de Clore & vx	iiijd.	Alicia de Gadby .	iiijd.
Adam de Ottlay & vx .	iiijd.	Agnes Jonwyfe	iiijd.
Rogerus Snell & vx	iiijd.	Tillot' Clynch	iiijd.
Johannes de Hege & vx	iiijd.	Hugo de Burn	iiijd.
Adam de Grene & vx	iiijd.	Willelmus filius Elie	iiijd.
Symon Kyd & vx	iiijd.	Seruie (sic)—Thomas Hunterman	iiijd.
Willelmus Brunson & vx	iiijd.		
Johannes de Langclyffe & vx	iiijd.	Willelmus Lawghman .	iiijd.
Thomas de Kyme & vx	iiijd.	Nell' de Hege	iiijd.
Thomas Schayl & vx .	iiijd.	Adam Broketman	iiijd.
Simon Belhyrd & vx	iiijd.	Alicia de Lytton	iiijd.
Willelmus Lauson & vx	iiijd.	Agnes Broket	iiijd.
Willelmus de Ouersetle & vx	iiijd.	Willelmus Toller .	iiijd.
Johannes Cleuache & vx	iiijd.	Summa—xvijs. xd.	

Gygleswyk (Giggleswick.)

Wilhelmus Monk & vx	iiijd.	Thomas Verty & vx	iiijd.
Johannes de Bland & vx	iiijd.	Ricardus de Heton & vx	iiijd.
Willelmus de Laukland & vx	iiijd.	Johannes Tailliour & vx	vjd.
Willelmus Jonson & vx	iiijd.	Johannes de Bland & vx	vjd.
Abraham filius Ade & vx	iiijd.	Willelmus de Langclyff & vx	iiijd.
Johannes de Bolton & vx	iiijd.	Willelmus de Vicars & vx	iiijd.
Johannes filius Ade & vx	iiijd.	Ricardus Ward & vx	iiijd.
Walterus Forstre & vx .	iiijd.	Johannes de Skar & vx.	iiijd.
Ricardus de Bank & vx.	xijd.	Willelmus Clerc & vx .	iiijd.
Willelmus be Bank & vx	iiijd.	Johannes de Telghfeld' & vx	iiijd.
Ricardus Prest & vx ,	iiijd.	Laurencius de Armetsted', ffrankleyn, & vx	xld.
Robertus de Bentham & vx .	iiijd.		
Willelmus Wylkynson & vx	iiijd.	Willelmus filius Thome &vx	iiijd.
Robertus Baillieman & xx	iiijd.	Adam filius Thome & vx	iiijd.
Thomas Cockeued & vx	iiijd.	Johannes Hunter' & vx	iiijd.
Willelmus de Bank junior & vx	iiijd.	Ricardus de Grenfell' & vx · .	iiijd.
Nicholaus Skynner & vx	iiijd.	Willelmus filius Ricardi' & vx	iiijd.
Johannes Jermowth & vx	iiijd.	Adam de Palay & vx	iiijd.
Johannes de Grenfell & vx	iiijd.	Johannes de Palay & vx	iiijd.
Willelmus Cockeued & vx	iiijd.	Walterus de Wod' & vx	iiijd.
Johannes Brone & vx .	iiijd.	Johannes Styegh' & vx	iiijd.

*Miller.

Gygleswyk (Giggleswick) continued.

Willelmus Kyd' & vx	iiijd.	Emma Harpour	iiijd.
Seruient'—Robertus Vessy	iiijd.	Willelmus de Grenfell'	iiijd.
Willelmus filius Thome	iiijd.	Isabella de Vicars	iiijd.
Agnes relicta Ricardi	iiijd.	Henricus Vicarman	iiijd.
Willelmus de Norham	iiijd.	Johannes Vicarman	iiijd.
Matilda Kemp	iiijd.	Summa—xxjs. viijd.	
Johannes seruiens Willelmi de Laukland'	iiijd.		

Staynford (Stainforth.)

Robertus de Staynford, dominus Ville	xxs.	Thomas Symson & vx	iiijd.
Willelmus de Austwyk & vx	iiijd.	Johannes filius Wilellmi & vx	iiijd.
Willelmus filius Roberti & vx	iiijd.	Henricus de Laukland & vx	iiijd.
Johannes Wayes & vx	iiijd.	Willelmus Schyrwod & vx	iiijd.
Johannes filius Ricardi Tyllson & vx	iiijd.	Ricardus Walays & vx	iiijd.
Gilbertus Milner & vx	iiijd.	Robertus Tailliour & vx	vjd.
Johannes Lemyng & vx	iiijd.	Johannes ffeton & vx	iiijd.
Stephanus Milner & vx	iiijd.	Adam filius Roberti & vx	iiijd.
Johannes Tomson & vx	iiijd.	Adam Benhowre & vx	iiijd.
Hugo Coyllyer & vx	iiijd.	Thomas Emanson & vx	iiijd.
Robertus Hyrd & vx	iiijd.	Willelmus Walays & vx	iiijd.
Johannes Turpyn & vx	iiijd.	Ricardus de Craueu & vx	iiijd.
Henricus Tomson & vx	iiijd.	Robertus Magson & vx	iiijd.
Johannes Preston & vx	iiijd.	Adam Derakes & vx	iiijd.
Thomas filius Ade & vx	iiijd.	Seruient—Agnes ffyscher	iiijd.
Willelmus Walker & vx	vjd.	Matilda filia Roberti	iiijd.
Henricus de Braychawe & vx	iiijd.	Robertus Gybson	iiijd.
		Johannes Robynson Hyrd	iiijd.
		Summa—xxxij.s.	

The different amounts paid by different individuals shewed their relative positions. An ordinary householder would pay 4d. Thomas Ineson of Langcliffe, and Richard de Bank of Giggleswick, were either merchants or innkeepers, and accordingly had to pay twelve pence each; those who paid six pence were either tradesmen or artificers.

The local swell however, was Robert de Stainford, Lord of the Manor of Stainford (Stainforth.) The family has now become extinct. A Chapel that belonged to them is in the north-east corner of Giggleswick Church.

The person of next importance to him seems to have been Lawrence de Armistead of Giggleswick, who, being a franklin, had to pay 3s. 4d.

FOLLOWERS OF LORD CLIFFORD, A.D. 1518.

THE Parish of Giggleswick was formerly part of the Percy Fee, (the Duke of Devonshire is still Lord of the Manor of Settle,) and in accordance with the custom of Feudal days many of the Tenants of the Lord were liable to be called on to serve under him in case of war. From the Household Book of Henry, Lord Clifford, made in the 2nd year of King Henry VIII, (A.D. 1510—1511,) we find that at that date the following men from this parish were liable to be called on to serve. The word "also" is used in the same sense that we now put "ditto."

GYGRESWYCK (GIGGLESWICK.)

Robt. Stakhouse, a bowe, able, and horse and harnes.
John Webster, a bowe also.
Thomas Paley, a bowe also.
James Carr, a bowe also.
Thomas Browne, a bille also.
Jack Stakhouse, a bowe also.
Rich. Brashay, a bowe.
Rich. Wilson, also.
Robt. Burton, a bille.
John Brashay, a bowe.

Thomas Taleyor, also.
Thomas Preston, also.
John Stakhouse, also.
Will-m Ryley, also.
Thomas Armested, also.
Henry Armested, also.
John Taleyor, also.
Henry Taleyor, also.
Thomas Newhouse, also.
Oliver Stakhouse, also.

SETTYLL (SETTLE.)

Rich. Browne, a bowe, able, and horse and harnes.
Will-m Talyr, a bowe also.
Oliver Foster, a bowe also.
Rich. Cokeson, a bowe also.
Will-m Knolle, a bille also.
Adam Browne, a bille also.
Rogr. Yveson, a bowe also.
Rawlyn Lawson, a bowe also.
Allen Procter, a bille also.
Henry Hoelson, a bowe also.
Rich. Carr, a bill also.
Rich. Tenant, bille.
Alan Proctor, also.
Edward Lawson, also.
Adam Browne, a bowe.
Oliver Taleyor, also.
Thomas Sume-skale, bille.

Will-m Symson, also.
Robert Taleyor, also.
John Watkynson, also.
Will-m Lawson, also.
Will-m Carr, a bowe.
Nicoll Carr, bille.
Robt. Medoppe, a bille.
Rich. Londe, a bowe.
Rich. Jackson, also.
Rogr. Carr, also.
Hug. Carr, also.
Will-m Taleyor, also.
Gyles Kokeson, also.
George Kokeson, also.
John Kokeson, also.
John Holson, also.
Rich. Lawson, also.

STONEFORD (STAINFORTH.)

James Foster, a bowe, able, horse and harnes.
Adam Palay, a bowe also.
Robt. Twisleton, a bowe also.
Rich. Franklyn, a bowe also.
Rich. Chew, a bowe also.
James Armisted, a bille also.
Adam Palay, a bille.
Rogr. Lawson, also.

Rogr. Swaynson, a bowe,
Rich. Palay, also.
James Armested, a bille.
John Kokeson, a bowe.
Olivr. Armested, also.
Henry Lawkland, also.
Will-m Foster, a bille.
John Yveson, also.
Rogr. Yveson, a bowe.

LANGCLYFF (LANGCLIFFE.)

Rich. Browne, a bowe, able, horse and harnes.
Roger Yveson, a bowe also.
Henry Pacock, a bille also.
Robt. Kydson, bille.

Rich. Kyng, also.
Robt. Kydd, also.
Will-m Yveson, also.
John Stakhouse, a bille.
Rog. Browne, a bowe.

Nicholson, the "Airedale Poet" takes this list as the muster-roll of those soldiers who fought under Lord Clifford at the battle of Flodden, two years later, viz., on the 9th Sept., 1513, and on this supposition introduces many of the names found in the list into his poem entitled "The Lyre of Ebor."

The two following passages in this poem relate to this parish.

> "Hundreds of names with care great Clifford kept
> Of those who centuries in the dust have slept,
> Who fought at Flodden, by their chieftain led,
> Nor sheathed their swords till every foe had fled.
> Marton sent forth bold Arnold in his mail,
> Four noble Tennants fought from Longstrodale;
> Hawkswick and Flasby, and old Hellifield,
> Sent Listers, who were never known to yield.
> Arncliffe and Sutton of the triumph shared,
> For these had sons who dangers never feared;
> Old Giggleswick, beneath her scraggy scar,
> Had fifty sons, who bravely fought in war.
> Stackhouse and Preston, with the bow and bill,
> Fought, with the Brayshaws, on old Flodden hill;
> The Summerscales, from Settle, cut their way
> Through files of Scots on that eventful day;
> And Keighley's warriors, led by Smith and Hall,
> Unparted fought, and made the Northerns fall."

"Old Castleberg, the torrent-wasted scar,
Uprears his head, where Romans met in war,
When on its topmost point the watch-tower stood,
And deep below, beheld the rolling flood.
Britons and Saxons have contended there,
And on the ramparts mixed spear with spear;
The warriors, tumbling headlong down the steep,
Pressed with their armour, plunged into the deep
But Time, who leaves behind all earthly things,
And overtakes fresh objects with his wings,
Has left so far behind swift-pinioned Fame,
She could not reach us with a warrior's name."

ASSOCIATION FOR THE PROSECUTION OF FELONS, A.D. 1743.

IN the middle of the last century, when the laws of the country were very severe on a criminal when *caught*, but the means for apprehending offenders and bringing them to justice were cumbersome and deficient, it was customary for the inhabitants of a parish to form an Association for the purpose of mutual assistance when any of the members had been wronged or robbed. This parish was not behindhand in forming such an Association, and the list of members comprised nearly all the principal inhabitants of the neighbourhood.

The Agreement mutually entered into, and the names of the subscribers, are as follows :—

"Whereas the expence that attends the prosecution of persons guilty of Felony, and other Crimes and Misdemeanors, is so great that they frequently go unpunished, to the great encouragement of Idleness and Villainy; To prevent which, as much as in us lye, It is agreed and concluded upon by, between, and amongst us who have hereunto subscribed our hands, being inhabitants of the Parish of Giggleswick, in the County of York, in manner as followeth.

First, It is agreed, and we who have subscribed our hands do mutually consent thereto, that all and every person and persons whatsoever, that shall at any time hereafter be found guilty, of any felony, murder, Robery, or other Crime, Misdemeanor, or unlawfull attempt whatsoever, against the persons, houses, goods, or chattells of us or any of us, That then and in such case such person or persons so guilty, or suspected so to be, shall be pursued, apprehended, committed, and prosecuted, at the Joint and Equal Expence of every of us who have consented unto and subscribed this Agreement, so as such prosecution be carried on by and with the consent of five or more of us.

And it is further agreed that when, and as often as it shall hereafter happen that, such Crimes and Misdemeanors as aforesaid, shall be done or committed, and the person or persons guilty thereof cannot easily be apprehended, that then and in such case it shall and may be lawfull, to and for any of us to publish and propose such a reward as shall be deemed reasonable by five or more of us, and the same to be paid at the joint and equal expence of us who have hereunto set our hands.

And we do hereby further agree that when, and as often as shall hereafter happen that, and of us subscribers hereto shall be obliged to prosecute any person or persons for such crimes or misdemeanors as aforesaid, and cannot conveniently spare so much money as must be necessarily expended in such prosecutions, That then and in such case such prosecutors shall, by publick notice published at the door of the Parish Church of Giggleswick aforesaid, Desire all persons that have subscribed this Agreement to meet at a time and place therein mentioned, and the majority of us that shall meet pursuant to the said notice, shall determine what sum ought to be raised for carrying on such prosecution. And we hereby Agree that the same shall be raised and paid by us all share and share alike.

And lastly we who have hereunto subscribed our hands Do hereby severally promise to pay to such prosecutor or prosecutors, (as shall at any time hereafter carry on any prosecution by virtue of this Agreement,) our and each of our several shares and proportionable parts of the expence of such prosecutions on demand, the same being equally and fairly divided amongst us.

AS WITNESS our hands this ninth day of November in the year of our Lord 1743.

The names of all those persons that signed the Agreement for prosecuting Rogues, dated 9th November, 1743.

Wm. Dawson	Allan Carr
Charles Nowell	Jno. Foster
Sus. Harris	Wm. Carr
Susan Whalley	Robt. Brown
Anth. Lister	Wm. Bradley
Bryan Waller	John Hirdsworth
John Kendall	Jos. Morley
Richd. Brayshaw	Anth. Lister (Vicar)
Wm. Brown	Jno. Richardson

Thos. Brayshaw
Thos. Clapham
Edwd. Cooke
Wm. Hall
Jno. Lister
Edmund Wilson
John Hargraves
Henry Town
Jane Hargraves
J. Bell
Sarah Carr
Jos. Hall
Margt. Hargraves
Robt. Roberts
John Windsor
Wm. Bousfield
John Tatham
Robt. Hardcastle
Wm. Peart
R. Barnard
James Johnson
Richd. Moore
John Paley
John Armitstead
Chris. Picard
Rich. Dobson
John Armitstead
Isaac Armitstead
Thos. Preston
George Carr
Thomas Settle

Christp. Clapham
Wm. Birkbeck
Wm. Birkbeck, jun.
Thos. Williams
Richard Horner
Jer. Bowskill
Thos. Taylor
Samuel Lucas
Sarah Maud
Anthony Clark
Thomas Tomlinson
Thomas Lawson
Wm. Tyson
William Pailey
John Shackleton
Wm. Carr
Edward Slater
Jos Bell
Hugh Hall
John Shackleton
Charles Abbotson
Wm. Hargraves
Wm. Birkett
William Husband
Thomas Carr
William Carr
Robert Mason
Roger Armitstead
Robert Armitstead
Lawrence Knowles
William Silverwood

TAXES FOR THE TOWNSHIP OF GIGGLESWICK, A.D. 1800.

IT is of course the privilege of every Englishman to grumble, and there is nothing John Bull likes to growl at so much as the taxes, and it must in justice be admitted that he frequently has good cause for thus giving vent to his feelings.

Some time since the Tax collectors' accounts for the year 1800, so far as they relate to this parish, fell into my hands, and I think they are interesting as shewing what taxes our ancesters had to submit to, for, although they had not those "sweet boons" the Sewerage and other like rates that we are now blessed with, they had to pay heavy taxes on windows; £1 10s. 0d. for each male servant; £1 4s. 0d. if they kept one saddle or carriage horse, and £3 12s. 0d. if they kept two; 6s. 0d. for each cart horse; 4s. 0d. for a dog, and £9 12s. 0d. for a four-wheel carriage, of which there only seems to have been one in the parish.

The accounts are as follows:—

GIGGLESWICK LAND TAX FOR 1800. EXONERATED.

	£	s.	d.
Atkinsons Isabel and Alice	3	3	3
Brayshaw Thomas	2	17	9½
Bolland Agnes	0	16	5¾
Birkbeck John	0	5	8
Barker John	1	11	1
Brown Robert	1	9	1
Clapham Thomas	9	13	0
Clapham John, Revd.	0	10	2
Do. for Mr. J. Hargraves	0	3	6
Carr William	2	19	2
Claytons & Walshman	0	7	6

	£	s.	d.
Cork Richard ...	0	0	4
Clapham Thos., for Tythes ..	1	6	2
Dawson Richd., Revd.	0	6	8
Foster John ...	2	2	11¾
Frankland Richard ...	3	16	2
Frankland John	2	16	3
Green Richd. Robt. Germain	0	0	1
Hesleden William	1	15	11½
Hardacre Richard	1	19	1
Hargraves Agnes	0	6	6
Jackson James	0	3	9
Kirkley Thomas	0	15	8
Lister Anthony	9	5	2
Lund John ...	1	4	2
Lawson William	0	11	5
Maudsley Henry	2	12	2
Maudsley Thomas	1	14	0
Moreley Wilson	2	11.	7
Occupier of Bull Ing, Henry Wood	0	1	8
Occupier of New Hall, Wm. Kendal, for Morley	0	1	1
Paley Wm., Revd. ..	1	18	11¾
Paley Thomas	0	1	3
Stackhouse Anthony ...	0	3	10¾
Stackhouse John	0	7	11
Slinger Francis	0	3	0
Silverwood Robert	0	0	8
Shackleton Ann, Trustees	0	0	3
Wood Henry ...	2	13	1½
Wildman William	1	18	11

Total Exonerated £64 15 6½

Land Tax Not Exonerated.

	Yearly.			Quarterly.		
	£	s.	d.	£	s.	d.
Armitstead John, Oxscarr Gates	0	8	0¾	0	2	0¼
Backhouse Mrs. Jane	1	18	3½	0	9	7
Bradley Elizabeth	0	2	7	0	0	7¾
Bradley Mary, Adam Lawson	0	6	0	0	1	6
Barrow Elizabeth	0	1	0	0	0	3
Bank William	0	7	5	0	1	10¼
Brennand James, H. Wood	0	1	3	0	0	3¾
Brown Edward	0	2	2	0	0	6½
Coar Thomas	0	0	8	0	0	2
Clapham John, Vicarage	0	2	11½	0	0	9
Dawson Stephen	0	1	4	0	0	4
Foster William	0	1	4	0	0	4
Green Rebecca	0	2	2	0	0	6½
Green Richd. Robt. Germain	0	0	3	0	0	0¾
Greenwood John, for Sugden	0	0	11¾	0	0	3
Hodgson Pheby	0	2	8	0	0	8
Hutton William	0	0	4	0	0	1
Johnson Jane, Stephen Dawson	1	16	6	0	9	1½
Kirkley Thos., for Poor Close	0	2	6	0	0	7½
Kidd John	0	0	3	0	0	0¾
Moore Margaret	0	5	4	0	1	4
Occupiers of Mill, Jno. Birkbeck & Co.	1	12	2	0	8	0½
Overseers	0	0	6	0	0	1½
Preston Wm., Paley Green	8	19	4	2	4	10
Do. for Trustees of Shutfield	0	4	0	0	1	0
Pollard Elias	0	0	3	0	0	0¾
Preston Mary	0	0	2	0	0	0½
Ralph John	0	1	4	0	0	4
Towler John, John Johnson	0	7	10	0	1	11½
Taylor Robert and Agnes	0	3	0	0	0	9
Tennant Elizabeth	0	2	8	0	0	8
Tennant Christopher	0	0	10	0	0	2½
Tomlinson John	0	1	1	0	0	3¼
Wilman John, per Place	1	9	11	0	7	5¾
Waller John, per Tyson	0	2	10	0	0	8½
Not exonerated	£19	9	11½	4	17	6¼

WINDOW TAX &c., FOR 1800.

			Yearly.	Quarterly.
	£ s. d.		£ s. d.	£ s. d.
Backhouse Jane,				
26 Windows	11 2 0			
House Duty	0 3 4			
1 Male Servant	1 10 0			
1 four-wheel Carriage	9 12 0			
2 Horses (saddle)	3 12 0			
1 Horse (cart)	0 6 0			
1 Dog	0 4 0			
			26 9 4 ... 6 12 4	
Brayshaw Thos.,				
12 Windows	2 16 0			
House Duty	0 3 4			
1 Horse	1 4 0			
1 Horse	0 6 0			
			4 9 4 ... 1 2 4	
Brennand Robert,				
6 Windows	..	...	0 4 6 ... 0 1 1½	
Bolland Agnes				
1 Male Servant	1 10 0			
1 Saddle Horse	1 4 0			
1 Cart Horse	0 6 0			
			3 0 0 ... 0 15 0	
Bentley Anthony,				
6 Windows	0 4 6			
2 Cart Horses	0 12 0			
1 Dog	0 4 0			
			1 0 6 ... 0 5 1½	
Bank Wm.,				
6 Windows	0 4 6			
1 Cart Horse	0 6 0			
			0 10 6 ... 0 2 7½	
Bolland Fawcett,				
9 Windows	1 7 0			
1 Saddle Horse	1 4 0			
1 Cart Horse	0 6 0			
			2 17 0 ... 0 14 3	
Barrows Elizabeth,				
6 Windows	...	...	0 4 6 ... 0 1 1½	

	£ s. d.	Yearly. £ s. d.	Quarterly. £ s. d.
Clapham Thos.,			
15 Windows	4 12 0		
1 Male Servant	1 10 0		
1 Cart Horse	0 6 0	6 8 0 ... 1 12 0	
Clapham Wm.,			
20 Windows	7 12 0		
1 Male Servant	1 10 0		
2 Saddle Horses	3 12 0		
4 Cart Horses	1 4 0	13 18 0 ... 3 9 6	
Clapham John,			
14 Windows	4 0 0		
House Duty	0 3 4		
1 Male Servant	1 10 0		
1 Saddle Horse	1 4 0		
1 Cart Horse	0 6 0		
1 Dog	0 6 0	7 9 4 ... 1 17 4	
Carr Wm.,			
15 Windows	4 12 0		
House Duty	0 3 4		
1 Saddle Horse	1 4 0		
2 Dogs	0 12 0	6 11 4 ... 1 12 10	
Carr John,			
8 Windows	1 1 0		
1 Saddle Horse	1 4 0		
2 Cart Horses	0 12 0	2 17 0 ... 0 14 3	
Carr Thomas,			
8 Windows	...	... 1 1 0 ... 0 5 3	
Dawson Stephen,			
6 Windows	0 4 6		
1 Saddle Horse	1 4 0		
1 Cart Horse	0 6 0		
1 Dog	0 4 0	1 18 6 .. 0 9 7½	
Ducket John,			
6 Windows	0 4 6		
1 Cart Horse	0 6 0	0 10 6 ... 0 2 7½	

		£ s. d.	Yearly. £ s. d.	Quarterly. £ s. d.
Frankland Richd.,				
10 Windows	...	1 14 0		
2 Cart Horses	...	0 12 0		
1 Dog	...	0 4 0		
			2 10 0 ... 0 12 6	
Frankland Jno.,				
1 Saddle Horse	...		1 4 0 ... 0 6 0	
Foster John,				
18 Windows	...	6 8 0		
House Duty	...	0 3 4		
1 Male Servant	...	1 10 0		
2 Saddle Horses	...	3 12 0		
3 Cart Horses	...	0 18 0		
12 Dogs	...	3 12 0		
			16 3 4 .. 4 0 10	
Fearnside Lawce,				
6 Windows	...	0 4 6		
1 Saddle Horse	...	1 4 0		
1 Cart Horse	...	0 6 0		
1 Dog	...	0 4 0		
			1 18 6 ... 0 9 7½	
Green Rebecca,				
6 Windows	...	...	0 4 6 ... 0 1 1½	
Hargreaves Agnes,				
15 Windows	...	4 12 0		
House Duty	...	0 3 4		
			4 15 4 ... 1 3 10	
Harrison Ann,				
7 Windows	...	...	0 14 6 ... 0 3 7½	
Hargraves John,				
6 Windows	...	0 4 6		
3 Cart Horses	...	0 18 0		
1 Dog	...	0 4 0		
			1 6 6 ... 0 6 7½	
Hodgson Phebe,				
6 Windows	...	...	0 4 6 ... 0 1 1½	
Hargraves Jno.,				
6 Windows ...	...	...	0 4 6 ... 0 1 1½	
Appealed off.				

		Yearly.	Quarterly.
		£ s. d.	£ s. d.
Holden Rebecca,			
9 Windows	... ...	... 1 7 0	... 0 6 9
Hutton Wm.,			
6 Windows	... ...	... 0 4 6	... 0 1 1½
Johnson Gilbert			
6 Windows	... ...	... 0 4 6	... 0 1 1½
Johnson Jno.,			
6 Windows	... ...	... 0 4 6	... 0 1 1½
Kirkley Thos.,			
13 Windows	... ... 3 8 0		
House Duty	... ... 0 3 4		
1 Cart Horse	... ... 0 6 0		
		3 17 4	... 0 19 4
Kendall Jno.,			
6 Windows	... ... 0 4 6		
1 Cart Horse	... ... 0 6 0		
		0 10 6	... 0 2 7½
Knight Jno.,			
6 Windows	... ... 0 4 6		
2 Cart Horses	... ... 0 12 0		
1 Dog	... ... 0 4 0		
		1 0 6	... 0 5 1½
Knight Lawrence,			
6 Windows	... ...	... 0 4 6	... 0 1 1½
Kidd John,			
6 Windows	... ...	... 0 4 6	... 0 1 1½
Kayley Lettice,			
6 Windows	... ...	... 0 4 6	... 0 1 1½
Lister Anthony,			
15 Windows	... ... 4 12 0		
House Duty	... ... 0 3 4		
1 Male Servant	... ... 1 10 0		
1 Saddle Horse	... ... 1 4 0		
1 Cart Horse	... ... 0 6 0		
6 Dogs	... ... 1 16 0		
		9 11 4	... 2 7 10
Lund Jno.,			
12 Windows	... ... 2 16 0		
1 Saddle Horse	... ... 1 4 0		
1 Male Servant	... ... 1 10 0		
1 Cart Horse	... ... 0 6 0		
1 Dog	... ... 0 4 0		
Lund Mary, 1 Horse	... ... 1 4 0		
		7 4 0	... 1 16 0

	£ s. d.	Yearly. £ s. d.	Quarterly. £ s. d.
Lawson Wm.,			
12 Windows	2 16 0		
House Duty	0 3 4		
		2 19 4 ... 0 14 10	
Maudsley Thos.,			
10 Windows	1 14 0		
1 Saddle Horse	1 4 0		
2 Horses	0 12 0		
1 Dog	0 4 0		
		3 14 0 ... 0 18 6	
Maudsley Henry,			
6 Windows	...	0 4 6 ... 0 1 1½	
Maudsley Joseph,			
6 Windows	0 4 6		
2 Cart Horses	0 12 0		
		0 16 6 ... 0 4 1½	
Mellisent F.,			
Taxed Cart	1 4 0		
1 Horse	0 6 0		
		1 10 0 ... 0 7 6	
Moore Margaret,			
9 Windows	...	1 7 0 ... 0 6 9	
Monkhouse Thos.,			
6 Windows	...	0 4 6 ... 0 1 1½	
Preston Wm.,			
15 Windows	4 12 0		
House Duty	0 3 4		
1 Saddle Horse	1 4 0		
2 Cart Horses	0 12 0		
		6 11 4 ... 1 12 10	
Newsolme Henry,			
6 Windows	0 4 6		
1 Cart Horse	0 6 0		
		0 10 6 ... 0 2 7½	
Paley Mary,			
15 Windows	4 12 0		
House Duty	0 3 4		
		4 15 4 ... 1 3 10	
Preston Jno.,			
6 Windows	0 4 6		
3 Cart Horses	0 18 0		
		1 2 6 ... 0 5 7½	

23

	Yearly			Quarterly		
	£	s.	d.	£	s.	d.
Settle Margaret						
6 Windows	0	4	6	0	1	1½
Smith Hannah,						
6 Windows	0	4	6	0	1	1½
Silverwood Robert,						
6 Windows	0	4	6	0	1	1½
Seedle Thos.						
6 Windows	0	4	6	0	1	1½
Taylor Robert,						
6 Windows	0	4	6	0	1	1½
Tennant Elizabeth,						
6 Windows	0	4	6	0	1	1½
Tomlinson John,						
6 Windows	0	4	6	0	1	1½
Towler George,						
6 Windows	0	4	6	0	1	1½
Wood Henry,						
8 Windows 1 1 0						
1 Saddle Horse ... 1 4 0						
1 Cart Horse 0 6 0						
1 Dog 0 4 0						
	2	15	0	0	13	9
Waller John,						
9 Windows	1	7	0	0	6	9
Wildman William,						
6 Windows	0	4	6	0	1	1½
Waller Thomas						
1 Cart Horse	0	6	0	0	1	6
Preston Wm.,						
6 Windows 0 4 6						
2 Cart Horses 0 12 0						
(Instead of his Brother's Horses)	0	16	6	0	4	1½

June 21st, 1800. LAND, SESSES, WINDOWS, &c.

Bradley Elizabeth, Land ...	...	0	0	7¾			
9 Sesses	...	0	4	10¼			
One Quarter's Windows, &c. ...	...	0	6	9			
					0	12	3¼
Bradley Mary, Land	...	0	1	6			
9 Sesses	...	0	7	6			
Adam Lawson					0	9	0

		£	s.	d.	£	s.	d.
Barrows Elizabeth, Land	...	0	0	3			
9 Sesses	...	0	1	1½			
One Quarter's Windows	...	0	1	1½			
					0	2	6
Brennand James, Land ...	...	0	0	3¾			
9 Sesses	...	0	1	10½			
H. Wood					0	2	2¼
Backhouse Jane, Land ...	...	0	9	7			
9 Poor Rates	...	2	0	6			
One Quarter's Windows, &c....	...	6	12	4			
					9	2	5
Armitstead John, Land ...	...	0	2	0¼			
9 Sesses	...	0	8	5¼			
					0	10	5½
Brayshaw Thos., 9 Sesses	...	3	6	9			
One Quarter's Windows, &c....	...	1	2	4			
					4	9	1
Brown Edward, Land ...	...	0	0	6½			
9 Sesses	...	0	2	3			
					0	2	9½
Bank William, Land ...	...	0	1	10¼			
9 Sesses	...	0	7	3¾			
One Quarter's Windows, &c....	...	0	2	7½			
					0	11	9½
Barker Jno., 9 Sesses ...	...	1	13	4¼			
Jos. Maudsley, One Quarter	...	0	4	1½			
					1	17	6
Clapham John, Land ...	...	0	0	9			
9 Sesses	...	0	11	0¾			
One Quarter's Windows, &c.	...	1	17	4			
					2	9	1¾
Clapham Wm.							
One Quarter's Windows, &c....	...	...	...	...	3	9	6
Bolland Agnes, 9 Sesses ...	...	0	18	4½			
One Quarter's Servant & Horses	...	0	15	0			
					1	13	4½
Bolland Fawcett, 9 Sesses ...	...	0	15	9			
One Quarter's Horses and Windows		0	14	3			
					1	10	0
Clapham Thos., 9 Sesses ...	...	0	7	1½			
One Quarter's Windows, &c ...	..	1	12	0			
					1	19	1½

	£	s.	d.	£	s.	d.
Coar Thos., Land	0	0	2			
9 Sesses	0	0	9			
One Quarter's Windows, &c.	0	5	3			
				0	6	2
Carr Wm.,						
One Quarter's Windows, &c.	1	12	10			
Carr John, 9 Sesses	3	11	3			
One Quarter's Windows, &c.	0	14	3			
				5	18	4
Frankland Richard,						
One Quarter's Windows, &c.		..		0	12	6
Frankland John, 9 Sesses	2	19	7½			
One Saddle Horse, one quarter	0	6	0			
				3	5	7½
Fearenside Lawrence, 9 Sesses	2	1	3			
One Quarter's Windows, &c.	0	9	7½			
				2	10	10½
Dawson Stephen, Land	0	0	4			
9 Sesses	0	2	3			
One Quarter's Windows, &c.	0	9	7½			
	0	12	2½			
Per Johnson	2	11	10½			
				3	4	1
Foster John, 9 Sesses	2	12	1½			
One Quarter's Windows, &c,	4	0	10			
				6	12	11½
Foster Wm., Land	0	0	4			
9 Sesses	0	1	6			
				0	1	10
Green Rebecca, Land	0	0	6½			
9 Sesses	0	3	0			
One Quarter's Windows	0	1	1½			
				0	4	8
Hargraves Agnes, 9 Sesses	0	4	6			
One Quarter's Windows, &c.	1	3	10			
				1	8	4
Hodgson Phebe, Land	0	0	8			
9 Sesses	0	1	6			
One Quarter's Windows	0	1	1½			
				0	3	3½
Johnson John, Land	0	9	1½			
9 Sesses ..	2	2	9			
				2	11	10½

	£ s. d.	£ s. d.
Green Richard, Land	... 0 0 0¾	
9 Sesses	... 0 3 9	
Robert Germain, 3/9 received		0 3 9¾
Greenwood Jno., Land	... 0 0 3	
9 Sesses	... 0 1 6	
		0 1 9
Hutton Wm., Land	... 0 0 1	
9 Sesses	... 0 1 10½	
One Quarter's Windows ...	... 0 1 1½	
		0 3 1
Kidd John, Land...	... 0 0 0¾	
9 Sesses	... 0 2 0¾	
One Quarter's Windows ...	... 0 1 1½	
		0 3 3
Kirkley Thos., Land	... 0 0 7½	
9 Sesses	... 0 19 8¼	
One Quarter's Windows, &c.	... 0 19 4	
		1 19 7¾
Maudsley Thos. 9 Sesses ...	... 4 11 10½	
One Quarter's Windows, &c.	... 0 18 6	
One Quarter, Henry's Windows	... 0 1 1½	
		5 11 6
Occupiers of Mill Land	... 0 8 0½	
9 Sesses	... 1 17 6	
John Birkbeck	... 2 5 6½	
Do.	... 0 6 4½	
		2 11 11
Lister Anthony,		
One Quarter's Windows &c. ...	... ...	2 7 10
Lund Jno., 9 Sesses	... 1 7 0	
One Quarter's Windows, &c....	... 1 16 0	
		3 3 0
Lawson Wm., 9 Sesses	... 0 9 4½	
One Quarter's Windows, &c....	... 0 14 10	
		1 4 2½
Moore Margaret, Land	... 0 1 4	
9 Sesses	... 0 5 7½	
One Quarter's Windows, &c....	... 0 6 9	
		0 13 8½
Overseers, Land	... 0 0 1½	
9 Sesses	... 0 3 4½	
		0 3 6

	£	s.	d.	£	s.	d.
Paley Mary, 9 Sesses	... 2	2	4½			
One Quarter's Windows, &c....	... 1	3	10			
				3	6	2½
Preston Mary, Land	... 0	0	0½			
9 Sesses	... 0	1	6			
				0	1	6½
Smith Hannah, 9 Sesses ...	... 0	1	3¾			
One Quarter's Windows, &c....	... 0	1	1½			
				0	2	5¼
Preston Wm., Land	... 2	5	10			
One Quarter's Windows, &c....	... 1	12	10			
9 Sesses	... 9	14	7½			
				13	13	3½
Pollard Elias, Land	... 0	0	0¾			
9 Sesses	... 0	1	6			
				0	1	6¾
Ralph Jno., Land...	... 0	0	4			
9 Sesses	... 0	1	6			
One Quarter, per Dawson ...	... 0	7	3¾			
				0	9	1¾
Towler Jno., Land	... 0	1	11½			
9 Sesses	... 0	7	6			
				0	9	5½
Taylor Robert, Land	... 0	0	9			
9 Sesses	... 0	6	0			
One Quarter's Windows ...	... 0	1	1½			
				0	7	10½
Wood Henry, 9 Sesses	... 3	0	9			
One Quarter's Windows, &c....	... 0	13	9			
Brennand's	... 0	2	2¼			
Bull Ing...	... 0	1	10½			
				3	18	6¾
Silverwood Robert, Windows ...	... 0	1	1½			
9 Sesses	... 0	1	6			
Ann Shackleton	... 0	1	6			
				0	4	1½
Tennant Elizabeth, Land ...	... 0	0	8			
9 Sesses	... 0	1	6			
One Quarter's Windows ...	... 0	1	1½			
				0	3	3½
Tennant Christopher, Land ...	.. 0	0	2½			
9 Sesses	... 0	1	1½			
				0	1	4

	£	s.	d.	£	s.	d.
Tomlinson Jno., Land	0	0	3¼			
9 Sesses	0	1	6			
One Quarter's Windows	0	1	1½			
				0	2	10¾
Wilman Jno., Land	0	7	5¾			
9 Sesses	1	11	10½			
				1	19	4¼
Waller Jno., Land	0	0	8½			
9 Sesses	0	3	4½			
One Quarter's Windows	0	6	9			
				0	10	10
Wildman Wm., Windows	0	1	1½			
9 Sesses	0	9	0			
Hardacre, 9 Sesses	0	2	7½			
				0	12	9

September 20th, 1800.

	£	s.	d.	£	s.	d.
Armitstead John, Land	0	2	0¼			
11 Sesses...	0	10	3¾			
				0	12	4
Brayshaw Thos.,						
11 Sesses	4	1	7			
One Quarter's Windows, &c.... ...	1	2	4			
				5	3	11
Backhouse Jane, Land	0	9	7			
11 Sesses	2	9	6			
One Quarter's Windows, &c.... ...	6	12	4			
				9	11	5
Bradley Elizabeth, Land	0	0	7¾			
11 Sesses	0	5	11½			
One Quarter's Windows	0	6	9			
				0	13	4¼
Bradley Mary, Land	0	1	6			
11 Sesses	0	9	2			
A. Lawson				0	10	8
Bank Wm., Land	0	1	10¼			
11 Sesses	0	8	11¼			
One Quarter's Windows, &c.... ...	0	2	7½			
				0	13	5
Brenand Jas., Land	0	0	3¾			
11 Sesses	0	2	3½			
				0	2	7¼

	£	s.	d.	£	s.	d.
Barker John, 11 Sesses	2	0	9½			
J. Maudsley, One Quarter	0	4	1½			
				2	4	11
Barrows Elizabeth, Land	0	0	3			
11 Sesses	0	1	4½			
One Quarter's Windows	0	1	1¼			
				0	2	9
Brown Edward, Land	0	0	6½			
11 Sesses	0	2	9			
				0	3	3½
Bolland Agnes						
11 Sesses	1	2	5½			
One Quarter's Servant and Horses	0	15	0			
				1	17	5½
Bolland Fawcett,						
11 Sesses	0	19	3			
One Quarter's Windows and Horses	0	14	3			
				1	13	6
Clapham Thos.,						
11 Sesses	0	8	8½			
One Quarter's Windows, &c.	1	12	0			
				2	0	8½
Clapham Jno., Land	0	0	9			
11 Sesses	0	13	6¼			
One Quarter's Windows, &c.	1	17	4			
				2	11	7¼
Dawson Stephen, Land	0	0	4			
11 Sesses	0	2	9			
One Quarter's Windows, &c.	0	9	7½			
Per Johnson	3	1	4½			
				3	14	1
Clapham Wm.,						
11 Sesses	13	1	3			
One Quarter's Windows, &c.	3	9	6			
				16	10	9
Carr Wm., One Quarter's Windows	1	12	10			
Carr John, 11 Sesses	4	7	1			
One Quarter's Windows	0	14	3			
				6	14	2

		£	s.	d.	£	s.	d.
Coar Thos., Land	...	0	0	2			
11 Sesses	...	0	0	11			
One Quarter's Windows	...	0	5	3			
June 21st. For Hunter	...	0	2	3			
Sep. 20th. Do.	...	0	2	9			
					0	11	4
Frankland Richard							
11 Sesses	...	4	18	9¼			
One Quarter's Windows, &c.	...	0	12	6			
					5	11	3¼
Frankland Jno.,							
11 Sesses	...	3	12	10½			
1 Saddle Horse, one Quarter	...	0	6	0			
					3	18	10½
Fearenside Lawrence,							
11 Sesses	...	2	10	5			
One Quarter's Windows, &c.	...	0	9	7½			
					3	0	0½
Greenwood Jno., Land	...	0	0	3			
11 Sesses	...	0	1	10			
					0	2	1
Foster Jno., 11 Sesses	...	3	3	8½			
One Quarter's Windows, &c.	...	4	0	10			
					7	4	6½
Foster Wm., Land	...	0	0	4			
11 Sesses	...	0	1	10			
					0	2	2
Green Richard, half-year, Land	...	0	0	1½			
11 Sesses	...	0	4	7			
					0	4	8½
Green Rebecca, Land	...	0	0	6½			
11 Sesses	...	0	3	8			
One Quarter's Windows	...	0	1	1½			
					0	5	4
Hutton Wm., Land	...	0	0	1			
11 Sesses	...	0	2	3½			
One Quarter's Windows	...	0	1	1½			
					0	3	6
Johnson Jno., Land	...	0	9	1½			
11 Sesses	...	2	12	3			
					3	1	4½

	£	s.	d.	£	s.	d.
Kidd Jno., Land	0	0	0¾			
11 Sesses	0	2	6¼			
One Quarter's Windows	0	1	1½			
				0	3	8½
Lund John,						
11 Sesses	1	13	0			
One Quarter's Windows, &c.	1	16	0			
				3	9	0
Hargraves Agnes, 11 Sesses	0	5	6			
One Quarter's Windows, &c.	1	3	10			
				1	9	4
Hodgson Phebe, Land	0	0	8			
11 Sesses	0	1	10			
One Quarter's Windows	0	1	1½			
				0	3	7½
Kirkley Thos., Land	0	0	7½			
11 Sesses	1	4	0¾			
One Quarter's Windows, &c.	0	19	4			
				2	4	0¼
Lister Anthony, 11 Sesses	12	2	11			
One Quarter's Windows, &c.	2	7	10			
				14	10	9
Maudsley Thos., 11 Sesses	5	12	3½			
One Quarter's Windows, &c.	0	18	6			
Henry, One Quarter	0	1	1½			
				6	11	11
Occupiers of Mill Land	0	8	0½			
11 Sesses	2	5	10			
John Birkbeck	2	13	10½			
Do.	0	7	9½			
				3	1	8
Preston Wm., Land	2	5	10			
11 Sesses	11	17	10½			
One Quarter's Windows, &c.	1	12	10			
				15	16	6½
Preston Mary, Land	0	0	0½			
11 Sesses	0	1	10			
				0	1	10½
Lawson Wm., 11 Sesses	0	11	5½			
One Quarter's Windows, &c.	0	14	10			
				1	6	3½

				£	s.	d.	£	s.	d.
Moore Margt., Land	...	...	...	0	1	4			
11 Sesses	...	...	...	0	6	10½			
One Quarter's Windows		...	...	0	6	9			
							0	14	11½
Overseer, Land	...	...	...	0	0	1½			
11 Sesses	...	...	...	0	4	1½			
							0	4	3
Paley Rev., 11 Sesses	...	...	...	2	11	9½			
Paley Miss, Windows	...	...	...	1	3	10			
							3	15	7½
Pollard Elias, Land	...	...	...	0	0	0¾			
11 Sesses	...	...	...	0	1	10			
							0	1	10¾
Ralph Jno., Land	...	...	...	0	0	4			
11 Sesses	...	...	...	0	1	10			
Per Dawson	...	...	...	0	8	11¼			
							0	11	1¼
Towler Jno., Land	...	...		0	1	11½			
11 Sesses	...	...	...	0	9	2			
							0	11	1½
Taylor Robert, Land	...	...	...	0	0	9			
11 Sesses	...	...	...	0	7	4			
One Quarter's Windows		...	...	0	1	1½			
							0	9	2½
Tomlinson Jno., Land	...	...	...	0	0	3¼			
11 Sesses	...	...	...	0	1	10			
One Quarter's Windows		...	...	0	1	1½			
Last Quarter	...	...	...	0	2	10¾			
							0	6	1½
Silverwood Robert, Windows		...	...	0	1	1½			
11 Sesses	...	...	...	0	1	10			
Ann Shackleton, do.		...	...	0	1	10			
							0	4	9½
Smith Hannah, Windows		...	...	0	1	1½			
11 Sesses	...	...	...	0	1	7¼			
Last quarter	...	...	...	0	2	5¼			
							0	5	2
Tennant Elizabeth, Land		...	...	0	0	8			
11 Sesses	...	...	...	0	1	10			
One Quarter's Windows		...	...	0	1	1½			
							0	3	7½

			£	s.	d.	£	s.	d.
Tennant Christr., Land	...	...	0	0	2½			
11 Sesses	...	...	0	1	4½			
						0	1	7
Wilman Jno., Land	...	...	0	7	5¾			
11 Sesses	...	...	1	18	11½			
						2	6	5¼
Waller Jno., Land	...	...	0	0	8½			
11 Sesses	...	...	0	4	1½			
Windows	...	...	0	6	9			
						0	11	7
Wood Henry, 11 Sesses	...	...	3	14	3			
One Quarter's Windows, &c.	...		0	13	9			
Brennands	...	...	0	2	7¼			
Bull Ing...	...	...	0	2	3½			
						4	12	10¾
Wildman Wm., Windows	...		0	1	1½			
11 Sesses	...	...	0	11	0			
For Hardacre	...	...	0	3	2½			
						0	15	4

Oct. 18th, 1800

Received of Jno. Carr	...	...	7	5	0
His Assessments	...	...	6	14	2
This towards Income	...	...	0	10	10
Received Jno. Carr	...	...	5	5	0

"COLLECTANEA GIGGLESWICKIANA."

PART I.

WITH ILLUSTRATIONS.

COMPILED BY THOS. BRAYSHAW.

* * * * * * *

STACKHOUSE,

NEAR SETTLE,

October, 1886.

In this number of my "Local Tracts" I have thrown together a few miscellaneous items relating to our parish. I trust the illustrations I have given with them will add to their interest.

THOS. BRAYSHAW.

Twelve large and one hundred small paper copies printed for private circulation.

"COLLECTANEA GIGGLESWICKIANA."

I have only come across a single copy of an old Settle-printed "Broadside," and as this is also, so far as I know, the earliest specimen of typography now in existence, from the press of that town, it possesses double interest for us.

The broadside consists of the two following poems, but unfortunately the *poet's* name is not given, and I fear is now irrevokably lost,—a sad commentary on the wish he expresses that "Our names shall be recorded amongst those who are great," as I consider the second of his effusions to be "a thing of beauty and a joy for ever."

FAREWEL TO OLD ENGLAND.

Farewel to Old England since we must leave the shore,
And perhaps never see our dear island no more,
Leaving father and mother and sister to moan,
And all for the sake of onr dear darling swain.
Here is something to relate which grieves my heart sore,
That's to go and leave my charmer whom I adore.

In fair London city I took great delight,
Both in pleasure and pastime by day and by night
For the music in Hyde Park so sweetly did play,
Ten thousand strange faces we SEE every DAY
But now it's all over we must play there no more
We must go to hear the music where the cannons do roar.

Come, come my brave lads LET us never repine,
With honor and glory our army WE'LL join,
With our 36 pounders we'll face our proud FOE,
We'll make them surrender wherever WE go,
If it BE our lot to fall in THE FIELD
My lads BE not daunted we NEVER will yield.

And if to Old England WE return back again,
FREE from all sorrow vexation and pain,
Our fathers shall sing and our mothers REJOICE
And it's all for the sake of their own darling boys
Our names shall be recorded amongst those who are great,
And for ages to come shall read of our fate.

THE FALSE-HEARTED LOVER.

It was early in the spring,
I went on board to serve the King,
Leaving MY dearest dear behind,
She oft told me her heart was mine,
When I had her all in my arms.
With solemn vows and kisses sweet
Love, we will be married next time we meet
O then I sail'd on the raging seas.
O then I spy'd my opportunity.
In writing letters to my dearest dear
But not a word could from her hear
O then I came to her fathers hall,
And for my fair one aloud did call
Her father made this reply,
Above all Men she does you deny.
O then I ask'd him what he meant
He told me married she had been.
My daughter is married for a term of life
So pray young Man seek another wife
I curse your gold and riches bright,
For I have lost my heart's delight
And all false lovers that such vows doth make
That may break their vows for riches sake
If you sent letters into this town,
I do declare I have had none but one,
The faults my fathers it is none of mine,
So do not blame young women kind.
I do declare I must leave this town
Since hard fortune has on me frown,
I'll plow the ocean till I die,
And I'll shun all womens company
O stay O stay young man said she,
There is far handsomer girls than me
There is far handsomer girls than I
So go no more where the bullets fly.
Then as he walk'd up London streets
He kicked a letter before his feet,
And on the bottom these lines was wrote
Love seldom seen and soon forgot.

[HAYES, PRINTER, SETTLE.

PROPOSED CANALS TO SETTLE.

Every now and then we find in the history of the commercial world, that some mania seizes on the minds of promoters and speculators. A few years since, the electric light; forty years since, railways; and last century canals, were a craze of the investing public, and this craze found partial vent in the proposal to connect this town with the southern parts of Yorkshire and Lancashire, by means of a canal. In 1774, the canal between Leeds and Liverpool was nearly completed, and some inventive genius thought it a pity that an important place like Settle should be left out in the cold, so a route for the proposed canal, which was to join the Leeds and Liverpool one at Foulridge, near Colne, was actually surveyed and prospectuses printed.

Another projected canal was to run from Settle to Lancaster, by way of Ingleton. One of the main features of this latter scheme was a great tunnel under Huntworth.

The terminus of the first-named canal seems, from the plan, to have been at a spot called "Paley Puddle," and I should fancy it was situate in what is now "Duke Street," in Settle.

Query? Was not *Duke* Street originally *Duck* Street.

The "Case" in support of the formation of the canal was as follows:

"CASE IN FAVOUR OF THE SETTLE CANAL."

"The advantages derived from Canal Navigations to a commercial and manufacturing country, are so numerous and so generally understood, that it is unnecessary to enumerate them.

"At the time when the grand communication between the Eastern and Western Oceans, by means of a canal from Leeds to Liverpool, was under contemplation, various branches were proposed to be made to the trading towns and places lying near the line of it; and particularly a branch was proposed, and actually surveyed, from Settle, in the County of York, to join the same, between Gargrave and Foulridge near Colne, in Lancashire; but the grand canal being an undertaking of so great a magnitude, it was thought proper to defer applying to Parliament for powers to make the canal from Settle, until the grand canal should be cut near to the place of junction.

"That the grand canal is now cut within a few miles of the proposed junction, and the inhabitants and tradesmen of Settle and other places in Craven, in Yorkshire, being anxious to partake the benefit of a Canal Navigation, have thought proper to apply to Parliament for powers to make the proposed branch to Settle.

"It is presumed very few countries stand so much in need, or would be so much benefitted by a canal, as that through which the proposed canal runs, and in order to form a judgment of its importance, it may not be improper to observe:

"That there are no coal mines within many miles of its course; that coals are now brought by land carriage at a very great expense, whereby the poor are distressed, the increase of manufactures greatly hindered, and the improvement of lands discouraged, although the country abounds with limestone, which, when burnt, is a manure peculiarly adapted to that country.

"That the land-owners through the extent of country, in the line of the proposed canal, generally prohibit the use of the plough in the best soil, well knowing that coarse and barren lands, when manured with lime, will produce good crops of oats, though otherwise of little value; yet thousands of acres of this improveable ground lye almost useless, occasioned by the present great expense and difficulty of procuring coals for burning that abundant stock of limestone which nature has hitherto in vain distributed; hence this country in its present situation, is not able to produce grain sufficient for its own consumption, so that the inhabitants are under a necessity of bringing malt, wheat, flour, &c., from very considerable distances by expensive land carriage, which the execution of this branch will prevent.

"That vast quantities of grit-stone suitable for building and other purposes are placed upon and towards the extremity of this branch; but the south part of the line and for several miles upon the grand canal, on each side of the junction, is destitute of this useful article; besides this, there are many inexhaustible quarries of blue-flags, grit-flags, excellent blue slate, and grit-slate in the neighbourhood of Settle, which will undoubtedly pass along this branch, and the grand canal, to a considerable distance.

"That great quantities of goods and merchandise now pass by land carriage, at a very great expense, from London, Hull, Sheffield, Leeds, Halifax, &c., through Settle to Kendall, and the north-west parts of this Kingdom, and of heavy manufactured goods from Kendal to the London market and other places, the expense of which will be greatly reduced by means of this canal.

"That if the proposed canal was completed, there is not the least doubt but it would be the means of increasing the trade and manufactures now carried on at Settle, and in the neighbourhood, to the unspeakable advantage of the country."

OLD SEARCH WARRANT.

Divisions of *Staincliffe* and *Ewcross*, in the West-Riding of the County of York.

To the Constable of Giggleswick in the said Division.

THESE are in his Majesty's Name to charge and command you that, taking to your Assistance sufficient Men within your Constablewick, (who are hereby required to assist you accordingly) you to make a General Privy Search in the Night of the 24th Day of April Inst., throughout your said Constablewick, and also at all other Times, so often as you find Occasion, for the finding out and apprehending all Rogues and Vagabonds, and wandering idle Persons: And all such as shall be found dangerous or incorrigible, that then you cause such to be brought before some of his Majesty's Justices of the Peace for the said Riding, to be farther dealt withall according to Law. And herein fail not. This our Warrant to continue in Force Three Months.

GIVEN under our Hands and Seals, being two of his Majesty's Justices of the Peace for the said Riding, the 8th Day of April in the Year of our Lord 1784.

	L.S.
HEN. WICKHAM,	O
	L.S.
J. A. BUSHFEILD.	O

THE EBBING AND FLOWING WELL AT GIGGLESWICK.

This remarkable Well is situated about a mile to the north of Giggleswick. It is very unpretentious affair, to the casual observer being nothing more than one of the ordinary roadside wells, so frequently to be found in this neighbourhood, that have been erected for the use of the wayfarer and passing horses and cattle. And even should the tourist who visits the well take the trouble to stay some time, it by no means follows that he will be rewarded for his pains, because in very wet or very dry weather, the ebbing and flowing of the well almost entirely ceases, but when there is a medium supply of water it is commonly in full activity, rising and falling rapidly, sometimes without intermission, and at other times with irregular intervals.

The distance between its flux and reflux varies from a few inches to half a yard. Different explanations of this phenomenen have been given, but none that satisfactorily accounted both for the reciprocation and its irregularity, as well as for the influence of wet and dry seasons, until a solution on the principal of the double syphon was given by the late Thomas Hargreaves, of Settle, who constructrd a model, which exactly imitated the eccentric habits of the Well, and this model was for some time disposited in the library of the Settle Mechanics' Institute. It is impossible to explain the solution without the aid of a diagram.

As to the origin of this Well, the local legend is that "once upon a time" a nymph, who dwelt in this locality, was seen by a satyr, who at once fell in love with her. Finding his attentions becoming inconviently pressing, the nymph fled away from him, with her tormentor in hot pursuit. To her consternation she found that he was rapidly gaining on her, and so she prayed to the gods to change her into a spring, so that she might escape him. The gods acceeded to her request, and the Well, as it ebbs and flows, is supposed to be the nymph panting.

Drayton, in his "Polyolbion" (published in 1612), has put this legend into verse, as follows:—

> In all my spacious tract, let them (so wise) survey
> My Ribble's rising banks, their worst, and let them say;
> At Giggleswick, where I a fountain can you show,
> That eight times in a day is said to ebb and flow!
> Who sometime was a nymph, and in the mountains high
> Of Craven, whose blue heads, for caps, put on the sky,
> Amongst the oreads there, and sylvans, made abode
> (It was ere human foot upon those hills had trod),
> Of all the mountain-kind and since she was most fair;
> It was a satyr's chance to see her silver hair
> Flow loosely at her back, as up a cliff she clame,
> Her beauties nothing well, her features, and her frame,
> And after her he goes; which when she did espy,
> Before him, like the wind, the nimble nymph did fly.
> They hurry down the rocks, o'er hill and dale they drive,
> To take her he doth strain, t'outstrip him she doth strive,
> Like one his kind that knew, and greatly fear'd his rape,
> And to the Topic gods by praying to escape,
> They turn'd her to a spring, which, as she then did pant,
> When, wearied with her course, her breath grew wondrous scant,
> Even as the fearful nymph then thick and short did blow,
> Now made by them a spring, so doth she ebb and flow.

Some twenty or thirty years after Drayton published his "Polyolbion," Richard Braithwaite, better known as "Drunken Barnaby," passed through Giggleswick on one of his tours, and he has made mention of the well in the following Latin verse :—

> Veni Giggleswick; parum frugis
> Profert tellus clausa jugis;
> Ibi vena prope viae
> Fluit, refluit, nocte, die,
> Neque norunt unde vena
> An a sale vel arena.

This is freely translated as follows:—

> Thence to Giggleswick most sterile,
> Hemm'd with rocks and shelves of peril,
> Near to th' way as traveller goeth,
> A fresh spring both ebbs and floweth;
> Neither known the learned that travel
> What procures it, salt or gravel.

I suppose the last line refers to the belief that was formerly entertained, that the ebbing and flowing of the well had some mysterious connection with the tides.

Many travellers and tourists have taken notice of the well in their published works. A writer in the " Gentleman's Magazine" for 1760 says the well "is enclosed in a quadrangle of stone flags of about two foot square, and had formerly proper outlets for the current to enable the spectator to distinguish the degrees of its rise and fall with more exactness. But it is now much neglected and out of order, which is a little surprising, as it is the capital curiosity of the country."

The illustration I give is a facsimile of a curious old picture engraved by Buck and Feary in 1778. From this it seems that the well was at that day situated a short distance above the road, (the new highway runs higher up and close to the well), and from it two copious streams flowed into Giggleswick Tarn, which then lay at the foot of the scar; the road crossing the head of the tarn by a ford. The inscription at the foot of the engraving is as follows " The amazing Flowing and Ebbing Well in Giggleswick Scarr, in the Road to Kendal."

Montagu, in his " Gleanings in Craven," Burlin in " The Northern Star" for 1817, and a host of others, testify to their astonishment at the ebbing and flowing of the well; but it has been reserved for a recent writer to doubt its peculiarities. Mr. Burkill, however, in his foolish " Reminiscences," puts it down as a " sell," and compares it to spirit-rapping and suchlike nonsense. Mr. Burkill courteously states that "the aborigines at Settle thoroughly believe in in it, however, and are not at all pleased to hear anyone express disappointment or disbelief." That a casual visitor should express "disappointment" if he does not see the well ebb and flow may be natural, but Mr. Burkill's "disbelief" has not much weight against the belief of "the aborigines at Settle" simply because he did not observe anything peculiar in the well when he paid it a chance visit one Christmas morning.

In connection with this well I may mention an old custom that is still kept up in the neighbourhood. On the afternoon of every Easter Sunday, hundreds of children and young people take a piece of " black Spanish " and a bottle to the well, and by dissolving the lump of " Spanish " in a bottleful of the water of the spring they concoct a sweet drink.

When the water in the well is at the lowest point there may occasionally be seen what is known as the "silver thread." This is nothing more than a tiny current of air running from end to end of the well, but on account of its rare appearance the superstitious consider it as a token of good luck to the person who is fortunate enough to see it.

It was "the spirit of the well," that according to the local legend, gave the magic bridle to Nevison, the highwayman, when he was pursued, by the aid of which he was enabled to ride up Giggleswick Scars, at the point still known as "Nevison's Nick," and also to leap over the chasm at the head of Gordale, and so escape.

The Rev. Thomas Cox, in his history of Yorkshire, published in the last century, has the following account of the well :—

Giggleswick, a Village situate upon the River *Ribble*, where at the foot of a very high Mountain, is the most noted spring in *England* for Ebbing and flowing ; sometimes thrice in an hour, and the water subsides three quarters of a yard at the reflux, though thirty miles from the Sea.

GRANT TO HOLD FAIR.

Settle has had several charters granted to it at various times for the holding of fairs and markets. The following grant of one to the Earl of Burlington is now in the British Museum :

A CONFIRMATION to Richard, Earl of Burlington and his heirs of an antient Weekly Market on Tuesday, and a Fair yearly held for three days on the Vigil, upon the day, and on the morrow of St. Lawrence within the manor of Setel in the County of York. AND ALSO a grant to him and his heires of severall other new ffaires to be held yearly within the towne of Setel in the said County on the days following, vizt.— One ffair on the Tuesday next before Palm Sunday for the buying and selling all sorts of Cattle, goods, wares, and merchandizes. Another on the 15th of April for sheep, another on Tuesday next after Whit-sunday, for all sorts of cattle, goods, wares and merchandizes, another on the 23rd June for lambs, another on the 12th of October for sheep, another on the Tuesday next after the 16th day of October for all sorts of cattle, goods, wares and merchandizes, and another on Fryday in every other weeke during three months successively, yearly, to begin on ffryday before Easter, for buying and selling all sorts of cattle.

According to Her Majestie's pleasure signified by Warrant, under Her Royal Signe Manual, countersigned by Mr. Secretary Boyle, subscribed by Mr. Solicitor Generall.

John Tench, Deputy to Thomas Gosling, Esq.

[Inscribed on the back.]

" DACQUET for the Most Noble John, Duke of Newcastle, Lord Privy Seale. Sealed the 24th day of May, 1708.

SHORT EXTRACTS FROM SUBSIDY ROLLS.

In a Subsidy Roll temp. Edward I., I find that Henry de Percy* paid a Knight's fee of 7s. 2¾d. for 2½ carncates of land in "Gikeleswike" (Subsidy Roll No. $\frac{206}{9}$).

In a roll of the Assessment of the "*Vicesima*" in the 1st year of Edward III. in the various Wapentakes in the West Riding of Yorkshire, I find under the heading of Staincliffe:

GIGLESWYK.

D. Willo. le Chapman	iij s	vi d
D. Rad. de Bank	iij s	iij d
D. Rico de Saylbank	ii s	iij d
D. Ad. de Lawkallides (?) ...	ii s	ix d
D. Laur. fil Rogi	ii s	iij d
D. Johne de Gr . . . st	iii s	
D. Johne de Cochend	ii s	
D. Rico fil Laur	xii d	

(Subsidy Roll No. $\frac{206}{14}$)

A later Roll of the Assessment of Tenths and Fifteenths (also temp. Edward III.) contains the following.

WESTRICHING.   STAYNCLIF.

GYCLESWYKE.
{ De. Ad de Grenefell
De Willo. Chapman
De Johe fil Serlou
De Rico. Husband
De Johe le lang
De Rico fil Laurenc
De Thom. del Sterr (?) }

(Subsidy Roll $\frac{206}{47}$ M. i. Coll. ii.)

---

* In the year 1316 the Abbot of Furness and the heirs of Henry de Percy were returned as Lords of the Townships of Giggleswick and Settle.

SETTLE TOKENS.

During the 17th Century there was a great scarcity of of copper coinage in England, the result of which was that many tradesmen coined their own pence and half-pence, these coins being known as tokens. Amongst others, Settle tradesmen issued three separate tokens, viz : two pennies and one half-penny, and of these tokens I give engravings.

The first is as follows. Observe, round the edge :

WILLIAM · TAYLOR · IN · SETLE

In the field : the arms of the Drapers' Company.

Reverse, round the edge :

I · WILL · EXCHAING · MY ·

In the field :

PENNY · 1668.

From the arms on the obverse, we conclude that William Taylor was a draper.

The second token has on the obverse, round the edge :

IOHN · & · STEVEN · SIDGSWICK ·

In the field : an arm grasping a circle with a bar across it.

Reverse, round the edge :

OF · SETTLE · WILL · EXCHEINGE ·

In the field :

THEIR · PENEY · 1672.

We do not know what trade the Sidgswicks carried on, probably the circle with the bar across it has some reference to it, but what it is, we cannot say.

The Third token is a half-penny one, and is the most noteworthy of the set. On the obverse : round the edge :

FOR · THE · COMPANY · OF ·

In the field :

AGREED · IN · ONE ·

With two hands clasping each other.

Reverse, round the edge :

GROCERS · IN · SETTLE ·

In the field :

THEIR · HALFE PENNY.

This token is particularly valuable from the fact of its being what is called a "town piece," that is, issued by a corporation, company, or public body. Out of the four hundred tokens issued in Yorkshire at this period, there are only two such "town pieces" viz: the one we are now discussing and one issued by the overseers of the poor at Bridlington, and what makes it more remarkable is the fact that, so far as I can discover, it is the only one of the 10,000 tokens issued in England during the latter half of the 17th century, that was issued by a company of traders. It shews us that even two hundred years ago the benefits of united action were known and appreciated by the shrewd tradesmen of Settle. In an old number of the Settle Chronicle there is a query by some writer who had come across one of these Settle Tokens—" Was the business of the tradesman so large as to render it necessary for him to have a special mint of his own ?"

THE OLD SUN-DIAL ON CASTLEBERG.

On the opposite page I give a facsimile reproduction, though of course much reduced in size from the original, of the very scarce and curious old engraving of the Sun-dial at Settle.

This Engraving bears the inscription "The very extraordinary Sun-dial facing the Market place at Settle in the West Riding of Yorkshire. Drawn engraved and publish'd by S. Buck and J. Feary according to Act of Parliament, May 18th, 1778."

Mr. H. Ecroyd Smith, in his " Illustrations of Old Yorkshire" gives a photograph of this engraving, and has the following remarks on the subject:—" Yet upon strict enquiry we find the very *tradition* of this unique structure to have become lost to the memory of the oldest inhabitants. The Rev. Dean Howson, who was educated at the neighbouring Giggleswick Grammar School, informs us, however, that he remembers old people who had heard of, if they had not seen it. Apparently large slabs of limestone, engraved with letters to indicate the hours from 8 to 12, have been inserted in the turfy slope of the hill, and the pinnacled Scar on its summit formed the *gnomon* of this singular dial, which seems to have been altogether unknown to the late Mrs. Alfred Gatty when inditing her recent work " A History of Sun-Dials."

The Rev. John Hutton, passing through Settle on a tour, in the year 1779 (the year following the one in which the picture was engraved), has the following remarks on Castleberg, and as he makes no reference to the Dial we may safely conclude that it was not in existence at the date of the engraving.

" As we approached towards Settle in our return, a white rock like a tower, called *Castleber*, immediately above the town, and about 20 or 30 yards in perpendicular height, engaged our attention. We were told a curious anecdote of this rocky mount. As limestone was daily got there to supply a kiln at the bottom, the inhabitants had the lime-burner presented at the court of the Lord of the Manour, fearing that if any more was dug out, the rock might fall and bury the whole town in ruins, a stone having once tumbled down and broken through a garden wall beneath, in its impetuous course torards the

houses. Twelve wise and just men were impanelled as jurors, and sent to view this impending nuisance; the verdict they returned was that if ever it fell *it would tumble not towards the town, but the direct contrary way.* On the other side it rests against the base of an high mountain. The hills and mountains all round were limestone to a prodigious depth; yet, strange to tell, we were informed there was a monopoly of this commodity, one lime-burner, or one company of lime-burners having engrossed the whole of it."

Having arrived at the conclusion that the Sun-dial did not exist at the time the engraving was made, leads us on to consider the point " *Did it ever exist ?.*" Having regard to the fact that we have no mention whatever of it *previous to* 1778; that it was not there *in* that year, and that there has certainly been no such thing *since*, I am forced to arrive at the conclusion that the only answer we can give to the query, is "*No.*" The tradition is a pleasing one, and I wish I could place credence in it, but when we come to examine the point carefully, it seems to be clear that there never existed such a Sundial as is represented in our illustration. Of course it is quite possible that by natural marks on the hill, or something of that sort (in lieu of the large slabs as postrayed), the villagers may have been able to make a rough guess at the time, but even this I doubt.

It is true that Dr. Whitaker, in his " History of Craven," accepts the tradition of the Sun-Dial, as he remarks:—

" The Summit of Castleberg once formed the gnomon of a rude but magnificent Sun-dial, the shadow of which, passing over some gray self-stones upon its side, marked the progress of time to the inhabitants of the town beneath; an instrument more antient than the dial of Ahaz. But the hour-marks have long been removed, and few remember the history of their old benefactor, whose shadow now takes its daily tour unobserved."

It is evident from the words "few remember," that the learned Docter had no very strong evidence to support his belief.

My readers may have noticed that an outline sketch of the engraving forms the background of my book-plate, of which a copy appears on the cover of these " Local Tracts."

AGRICULTURE IN 1793.

In 1793, Commissioners were appointed by the Government to inspect and report on the state of Agriculture in the kingdom. The following items are extracted from the report issued by the Commissioners :—" At Settle and Skipton, we found that land let so high as 40s. and 50s. per acre, while, from the best accounts we could receive in the country, 20s. and 30s. was then considered as a high rent, and in many places it was much lower."

" As for the old rich pastures about Skipton, Settle and other places, it is not easy to say what they have originally been sown with.

Leaving Grassington we passed through a wide range of uncultivated moors, and arrived at Settle. At this place we saw the finest grass we ever viewed. Indeed the richness of the soil is hardly credible to those who have not seen it, and the possessors were unanimously of opinion that it is of greater value to them when kept in grass, than when cultivated by the plough.

The nature of the soil in the neighbourhood of Settle is what is called a hazel mould, incumbent upon a dry bottom. The farms are generally small, and the occupiers seldom have leases. Great part of the higher grounds are still common, and consequently unimproved; they are pastured with sheep and Scots cattle, which are afterwards fed off upon the lower grounds. The sheep bred here are called the Malham breed, and we received favourable accounts of them. Considering the great quantity of waste ground, it is surprising the proprietors have not turned their attention more to planting, as we received great complaints of the scarcity of wood. Coals are likewise scarce which it was thought might be remedied, if proprietors were disposed to hold out rewards or favourable leases to those who discovered them.

At Settle we had an opportunity of seeing a great show of fat cattle of the country breed. They were all long horned, and seemed in shape, skin, and other circumstances, to be nearly the same as the Irish breed. We learned that of late there had not been the same attention paid as formerly to keep the breed pure, by selecting proper bulls.

Be that as it may, the long horned breed of cattle which prevails over the western part of this island, from the thickness of their skin, and the hardness of their constitutions, are much better calculated to undergo the vicissitudes of this climate, than the short horned breed of the eastern coasts.

Price of labour. A man servant about ten guineas per year, with board and washing in his master's house; a woman about five guineas, with the same; day labourers in husbandry about 2s. or 2s. 6d. per day, finding their own victuals: about ten years ago 1s. or 1s. 2d. was the common price; the advance owing to the introduction of the cotton manufactory into a country so little populous. They work from six to six in the summer, and from eight to dark in winter.

Price of provisions for the last year; beef, mutton, veal and pork, about $4\frac{1}{2}$d. per pound of sixteen ounces; butter about 1s. or 1s. 1d. per pound of 22 ounces; wheat about 8s. per Winchester bushel: oats 28 or 30s. per quarter.

Parish of Giggleswick:

    2,200 Inhabitants
    16,500 Acres by estimation
    14,685 Acress grass
       315 Acres arable
       150 Acres waste
       300 Acres, in oats
        15 Acres barley

500 acres are occasionally plowed in small quantities."

COL. THORNTON'S TOUR.

In 1802 or 1803 Colonel Thornton of Thornville Royal, Yorkshire, undertook a tour in Scotland and the North of England. His remarks on Settle are as follows :—

Trotting on briskly (from Kirkby Lonsdale), I perceived, to the left, that stupendous and well known mountain Ingleborough and came in view of a town which I took for Settle; passed under the high and romantic rocks called Giggleswick Scar, and saw a well by the road side, which struck me to be the one I had heard so much of that ebbs and flows; but I did not perceive that singularity while I remained, which indeed I could not do so long as I wished, fearing I should arrive too late at Marshfield.

Proceeded and entering the town, I was informed that what I had conceived to be Settle was Giggleswick, but that I had not deviated above a quarter of a mile from the road. Soon arrived at Marshfield, the seat of Mr. Parker, near Settle; and on the groom's taking my mare, enquired when dinner would be ready, but can scarcely say whether I was most vexed or satisfied on hearing that it would not be ready for an hour and a half; I had understood from my friend Sir Michael Le Fleming, who is related to Mr. Parker, that his dinner hour was three o'clock, and had made what expedition I could, but the trot at which I had come, surpassed all my former journeys, for though I had gone a little out of the road, forming a ride of thirty three miles and a half, I found, by my watch, I had performed this journey in two hours and forty-two minutes; and when the road, which is rather hilly, is considered, and the low state to which bad Highland hay and worse corn had reduced my horses, with the time taken up in feeding the mare at Kirkby Lonsdale, I think about fourteen minutes, it was performed in a surprising short time.

The mare I rode was certainly a very astonishing creature, not fourteen hands high, and mistress of sixteen stone, she won several trotting matches of sixteen miles within the hour, but her bottom was her great fort, for it appeared to me, as the ride will testify, that she varied very little in the two hours and twenty-eight minutes she was on the road.

My friend not being returned from his morning ride, I soon got dressed, and amused myself before dinner with admiring the infinite neatness that reigned both within and without in every department of this very enviable little pavilion.*

It gave me great pleasure on our meeting to find my old acquaintance, and his lady, in that perfect health which is commonly enjoyed by those who inhabit the salubrious air of Craven.

We passed the remainder of the day in the most social manner, and in the course of the evening, the conversation, turning amongst other things, upon the subject of expeditious journeys, occasioned by my ride in the morning.

Morning charming; the air rather sharp. Mr. Parker being politely desirous of showing me the objects around him most worthy of attention, we mounted or horses, and after passing through some noble pastures, clothed with the finest grass, and chequered with herds of long-horned, or as they are generally called Craven Cattle, and sheep, came on the edge of the moors, where indeed the road was but indifferent.

With some difficulty we got to Malmstarn, [Malham Tarn] a sporting seat of Mr. Lister, brother-in-law to Mr. Parker.

We found that gentleman at home, and after showing me the inside of his lodge, which is commodious enough, he gave me some idea of his future plans of improvement; no place in England can be better situated for the amusements of the field. In the "tarn" or little lake, which lies directly in the front of his house is very good trout and perch fishing, and both fish are esteemed the best of the kind. I saw some very fine ones of both sorts. Trout are taken of six or seven pounds, and perch of not much inferior weight. There is also the best moor-game shooting in the county, and no better coursing even at Newmarket.

* Since the above was written, this charming box has been destroyed by fire; but, to a man of Mr. P's forture, as most of the valuable furniture was saved, it was of less consequence and gave scope to his elegant taste in rebuilding a larger, though not more desirable, residence.

Having some spare time before dinner, Mr. Parker was pleased to show me, as we returned from Malham, at the back of Marshfield, and directly above the town of Settle, a white rock, not unlike a tower, called Castle-Bar, about nineteen or twenty yards in perpendicular height. I confess I wa much pleased with it. This natural precipice has been much assisted by art, and will be daily more so, and rendered additionally awful by quantity of limestone dug from the cavity at its base, to supply an adjacent kiln.

Mr. Parker, being a member of the Falconer's Club, and one of the finest promoters of conviviality at home and abroad, had contrived to invite several of those jolly mortals to meet me at dinner, when we passed the remainder of the day together most happily, and recounted the different long flights we had had after kites, herns, hares, &c.

Rose early, wishing to get to Thornville as soon as possible. Passed through Settle, a small town, but possessed of some trade, and a market-place so spacious that it is out of all proportion to its size. The houses here, in general, are old and low, and there are but very few good ones, which may be owing to two causes: the situation of the town, which is directly under rocky hills, and its Parish Church being at Giggleswick, near to which the gentry have erected very neat boxes, and formed a kind of separation from the tradesmen.

Having sent on my servants the night before, I rode one of Mr. Parker's hacks, at a trot, I believe, it had not been accustomed to, in order to get to Skipton to breakfast.

SETTLE IN 1822.

On the opposite page I give a facsimile of a view by George Nicholson, the artist, of " Settle on a Market Day." The Sketch was made in 1822 and gives a good idea of the place at that date. The view is taken from the front of what is now Mr. Leeming's shop. In the back ground is Castleberg, before it was planted and laid out as gardens. In the centre is the old Tolbooth, which stood on the site of the present Town Hall. To the right is the building now occupied by Mr. Thomas Clark, and to the left the picturesque but unsavoury " shambles."

What I am most puzzled about is the object in the right foreground. It looks very much like a draw-well, but I hardly think it can be intended for one.

Judging from the attitude of the figures in the picture, trade does not seem to have been particularly brisk.

The following description of the town at the early part of this century, is from Daye's " Picturesque Tour", and is a fitting accompaniment to the engraving.

"From Skipton it is sixteen miles to Settle. This town is situated in the midst of barren hills, which present their rocky fronts to the eye from all points. Romantic as the situation may be, the town itself is equally so, the houses being the most whimsical, picturesque, and odd anywhere to be met with. The market place in particular, had to me, the strangest effect imaginable; it not appearing like English nature. The evening being fine and clear, the lengthened shadows of the houses were swept over the foreground, reducing the whole to one expansive dark; except where, here and there on its verge, a small group of figures glittered, from an elegant touch of the departing rays of the sun. Full in the light appeared the market house, raised on an arcade, above which, in a gallery that leads to different dwellings, were seen various people, busily employed in humble occupations. Add to the whole, by way of back--ground a tremendous cliff, 300 feet high, which impends fearfully over the back of the town, in the most terrific manner, and some idea of the scene may be formed.

In Settle, many of the houses about the market place, have their ascent to the upper storey on the outside; and where the cliff, or scar, which hangs frowning over the town, can be brought into the view, a subject highly picturesque will be obtained. On the whole, had I come all this way without meeting one object worthy of my attentton, I should have been satisfied for my trouble with what I found here."

ROMAN CATHOLICS IN 1604.

In 1604 a Return of all Roman Catholics was ordered to be made by King James I., and from this Return we find that only one, viz. a widow called Margaret Frankland, was living in the Parish at that time.

ANCIENT POWER OF ATTORNEY.

The following old deed of the year 1248 is interesting :

Noverint universi per presentis me Alicium filiam Petri Tempest militis attornasse et loco meo posnisse delectum michi in Christo Rogerum Tempest fidelum attornatum meum ad recipiendum seisinam de et in Cunctis terris et tementis in Villis et territorus de Gygleswyk Setyll Rawthmell Garegrave Newton et Conyston secundum vim forman et effectum cujusdam Carte Ricardi Pudsey Thome Dank de Gygleswyk Thome Quarf et Ade de Walsthawe inde mihi confectum ratum et gratum habituro quicquid predictus attornatus mens fecit nomine meo in premissis. In cujus rei testimonium presentibus sigillum meum apposin Datum xx die Semptembris Anno regni regis Henrici Sextio post conquestum Anglie Sexto.

(Translation.) Know all by these presents, that I, Alice, daughter of Peter Tempest, Knight, have attorned and put in my place, my beloved in Christ, Roger Tempest, my faithful attorney, to receive in my name full and peaceable possession of and in all lands and tenements in the vills and territories of Gygleswyk, Setyll, Rawthmell, Garegrave, Newton, and Coniston, according to the force, form, and effect of a certain charter of Richard Pudsey, Thomas Dank, of Gygleswick, and Adam de Walsthawe, I thenceforth holding as done, ratified, and satisfied whatever my said attorney has done in my name in the premises. In testimony whereof to these presents I have affixed my seal. Dated 20th September in the 6th year of the reign of Henry the 6th after the conquest.

LOCAL NOTES.

(Reprinted, as revised, from the Settle Household Almanac for 1896.)

Compiled by Thos. Brayshaw.

SETTLE:
CRAVEN PRINTING & STATIONERY COMPANY, LIMITED.

LOCAL NOTES.

Joseph Broader, of Settle, invented a "System of Artificial Memory," 1827.

Sir Joseph Banks was descended from the Giggleswick family of that name.

There was a "Soke Mill" at Anley in A.D. 1080.

Weekly Offertories commenced in Settle Church in 1864.

The interior walls of Giggleswick Church were formerly covered with Texts and Scroll-work.

Settle Mechanics' Institute was founded in 1831.

20,000 Sheep were shown at Settle "October" Fair in 1859.

There was a great Hurricane at Settle, January 7th, 1839.

Dr. Pococke saw the Sundial on Castleberg in 1750.

There are 1461 Pipes in Giggleswick Church Organ.

The boys of Giggleswick School used to "beat the boundaries" once every year.

Dr. George Birkbeck was born at Settle, January 10th, 1776.

C. Walker, P.D., of Settle, invented a System of Shorthand.

Settle Mechanics' Hall was formally opened by the Earl of Carlisle in 1855.

The Settle Mining Company had a capital of £1000.

The Countess Gyllenborg died at Settle in 1766.

The last Bull-baiting at Settle was at "Halsteads."

Settle was first lighted with Gas in January, 1853.

Barker's Beck, Settle, was supposed to be haunted by a headless man.

Mr. John Hare first acted in public at the Mechanics' Hall, Settle, in 1863.

Hat-making was formerly carried on in Settle.

The "Settle Chronicle" appeared from 1854 to 1866.

A fatal fire occurred at King's Mill in 1829.

The Settle Temperance Society was founded in 1834.

The making of Base Coins was formerly extensively carried on at Settle.

There was a fatal accident at Giggleswick Station in Feb. 1857.

Two Gallows stood at Settle in A.D. 1278.

There was a fire at King's Mill in February, 1854.

The Settle Market Charter used to be read once a year, at the Cross.

Tom Sayers visited Settle in 1862.

A Maypole formerly stood in Upper Settle.

The "Amicable" Society was founded at Giggleswick in 1789.

Much Ingleton Coal used to be sold at Settle.

Pope Gregory issued a "Bull" respecting Giggleswick Church in A.D. 1232.

The old Halberds, Standard Measures, &c., of Settle are now in the possession of the Duke of Devonshire.

Giggleswick Fair was re-established in 1842.

Settle used to be a great centre for the Leather Trade.

The Highlanders passed through Settle in 1729.

The Lancaster and Settle Mail Coach was started in 1839.

Ten Gallons of Wine were used at Communion Service in Giggleswick Church on Good Friday, 1739.

There was an outbreak of Cattle Plague at Settle in 1749.

The Benevolent Society (Wesleyan) was established at Settle in 1806.

Only 8 prisoners were brought before the Settle Magistrates in 1854.

A Ballot for the Militia was held at Settle in 1766.

The Settle Cricket Club was founded in 1854.

A Proclamation against Rogues and Vagabonds was made at Settle in 1598.

The Market Place, Settle, is 507 feet above sea level.

Settle is situate Lat. 54·4' North; Long. 2·16'·34" West.

The Order of Foresters established a Lodge at Giggleswick in 1853.

Dean Howson was born at Giggleswick in 1816.

£760 was raised for the local " Patriotic Fund " in 1855.

Astley's Circus visited Settle in 1822.

Settle Market Charter was confirmed in 1708.

The Giggleswick Tithe dispute was settled in 1845.

Giggleswick School obtained a Royal Charter in 1553.

Schemes for three Railways through Settle were made in 1845.

The " Craven Magazine " was published at Settle in 1836.

The Settle Wesleyan Sunday School was opened in 1809.

John Wesley preached at Settle in 1777.

The Primitive Methodists were first established at Settle in 1836.

The Settle Independent Chapel was opened in 1817.

Tradition says that four Knights formerly lived at Little Stainforth.

A Local Volunteer Force was raised in 1794.

Victoria Cave was first known as " The Clay-Pits."

A Flag-Pole was erected on Castleberg to commemorate the Queen's Coronation.

The present Rifle Corps was established at Settle in 1859.

Richard Frankland was excommunicated and absolved in Giggleswick Church.

There was a great " Bachelors' Ball " in a field near Stackhouse in 1839.

In Bulkeley's poems is a Sonnet " By Settle Railway Bridge."

Queen Adelaide passed through Settle in 1840.

The Railway from Skipton to Ingleton was opened in 1849.

Paley sent a Fly-Orchis from Settle, as a " prodigious rarity."

The present fountain in Settle Market Place was erected in 1863.

The Rev. Oliver Heywood visited Settle in 1679.

Giggleswick Select Vestry for poor-relief was established in 1824.

About £1000 was spent in exploring Victoria Cave.

The 9th of August was locally celebrated as "Kennel" night.

"The old wives of Bruncton" was a standing toast at Giggleswick School Dinner.

General Lambert was at Settle in 1641.

Giggleswick Church will seat 350 fewer people than before Restoration.

Giggleswick Township Cottages were sold in 1834.

Roger Dodsworth, the Antiquary, was at Giggleswick in 1620.

The old Parish Constables of Settle were paid £15 and £2 per annum.

Denny, the Classical itinerant, was buried at Giggleswick in 1748,

Part of King's Mill was formerly a snuff manufactory.

Many Settle men fought at Flodden Field in 1513.

The Vagrant Ward at Giggleswick had 373 occupants the first year it was opened.

A madman caused a panic at Giggleswick Church in 1833.

The Settle Sunday School Sick Club was founded in 1848.

Stainforth and Rathmell Churches were consecrated in 1842.

Wm. Dewsbury introduced Quakerism into Settle, about 1652.

The Victoria Hall (then "Music Hall") was opened in 1853.

Gray, the poet, visited Settle in 1769.

William Birkbeck, of Settle, was the first Quaker Magistrate in England.

The Cattle Plague broke out at Settle in Oct., 1865.

Four Settle Tradesmen issued Tokens in the 17th century.

The Settle Union Farmers Association was founded in 1854.

700 copies of No. 1 of "The Settle Chronicle" (February 1854) were sold.

There was a great flood in the Ribble, October 25th, 1855.

The County Court at Settle used to be held monthly.

The "Oyster Patty" was published at Settle in 1835.

Giggleswick Workhouse now has under 40 inmates; in 1841 it had 180.

A Fire occurred in Chapel Square, Settle, June, 1853.

Mr. Carr, of Stackhouse, invented a Steering Apparatus.

The Banns of a Marriage were publicly forbidden at Giggleswick Church in October, 1842.

The Heating Apparatus at Giggleswick Church exploded in 1856.

Henry III granted Stockdale to Sawley Abbey.

The 5th of November is St. Alkelda's day.

Settle Cricket Club first played at Cammock.

The Rev. R. Ingram preached at Zion Chapel in November, 1854.

The Footbridge at "The Locks" was erected in 1857.

Lord Morpeth cut the first sod of the Little North Western Railway, at Cleatop, in 1846.

A Fire occurred at Langcliffe Place in May, 1857.

The Settle Choral Society was established in 1850.

Tom Thumb visited Settle in 1866.

The Settle Horticultural Society was founded in Oct., 1848.

The death-rate of Settle has steadily diminished during late years.

Settle and Stainforth Quakers' Meetings were licensed in 1689.

The Settle Almanac, containing 12 pages, was first issued in 1840.

Previous to 1856 Settle was lighted with "Vegetable-Gas."

Of several Local Pamphlets not a single known copy now exists.

The last conviction at Settle for "Profanely Swearing" was in 1857.

Settle Waterworks have been in operation nearly 150 years.

The Settle Literary Society was established in 1770.

The Area of Settle Township is 4490 acres.

The Settle Savings Bank was established in 1818.

Of the Main Road through Settle, 2 miles, 5 furlongs, 121 yards are in the Township.

The Annual Rental of the house property in Settle is estimated to be £6147 per annum.

Giggleswick Church is 132 feet long.

Only one Carriage was kept in Giggleswick Township in 1800.

Marshfield was burnt down about 90 years ago.

Six electors of Settle went to York to vote in 1708.

In 1792 beef was 4½d. a lb. in Settle.

Plans for restoring Giggleswick Church were prepared in 1852.

100 years since there were 800 acres of ploughed land in Giggleswick Parish.

There were 51 householders in Giggleswick in 1379.

In Burkill's " Reminiscences " the Ebbing and Flowing Well is stated to be " a sell."

The Percies owned " the town of Settle " in A.D. 1225.

In 1877 the Rainfall at Settle was 69·10 inches.

The Northern side of Settle Bridge is very ancient.

Furness and Fountains Abbeys owned much property about Settle.

E. Waddington was " Slayne in Settle " in December, 1642.

A Penny Bank was first established at Settle in 1857.

Giggleswick Sewing School was opened in 1859.

It was first proposed to light Settle with Gas in 1824.

Rope-making used to be carried on at Settle.

The first sod of the Settle and Carlisle Railway was cut at Anley, November, 1869.

The oldest Chalice of Giggleswick Church is dated 1585.

Henry III granted Settle Market to Hy. de Percy.

The old Talbot Inn used to be the headquarters of the Leather Dealers.

Walker's " Stenography " is one of the scarcest of local works.

The oldest known View of Settle is a drawing in the British Museum.

The Rev. R. Ingram published a work against duelling.

" Mischief Night" used to be annually observed at Giggleswick.

25 Giggleswick boys went to St. John's College, Cambridge, between 1631 and 1674.

The first Quakers' Meeting in Settle was held at Widow Armistead's.

Arthur Caterall, of Giggleswick, claimed £450 for damage done by the Parliamentary Troops.

In 1379 Settle Householders paid 17s. 10d. "poll tax"; Giggleswick, 21s. 8d.

In 1800 Mrs. Backhouse, of Giggleswick, paid £11 2s. 0d. for window tax.

The Registers of Giggleswick Church from 1627 to 1653 are lost.

Jackson and Troughton were two Settle Printers last century.

The Constables of Giggleswick made a general search for Rogues and Vagabonds, 24th April, 1784.

In 1773 Pennant said the Inn at Settle was the most comfortable one he was ever at.

Knitted Woollen Stockings used to be made in large quantities in Settle.

Many local persons are described in the novel called "Jabez Oliphant."

It has been suggested that the name "Bell Hill" is derived from " The Hill of Baal."

" The Folly " was never completed owing to lack of funds.

Giggleswick Church Tower is probably 100 years older than the body of the Church.

Bigland, in 1812, said the death rate of Settle " is about one in sixty."

In the " Northern Star " (1817), Giggleswick Tarn was described as "a large and beautiful Lake."

A number of Roman Coins were found near Giggleswick in 1783.

In 1822 the " Royal Union " Coach started from Settle, on its way from Kendal to Leeds, every day at noon.

Thomas Foster, by Will dated 1692, left £5 per annum to the poor of Giggleswick.

Dr. Windsor, the Botanist, was born at Settle, in 1787.

Dr. Lettsom was apprenticed to Dr. Sutcliffe of Settle.

Football was formerly played in Kirkgate every Shrove-Tuesday.

In West's "Antiquities of Furness" is a diagram of the supposed action of the Ebbing and Flowing Well.

Furness Abbey received £5 6s. od. rent from Stackhouse in 1535.

The Settle and Carlisle Railway was opened for passenger traffic, May 1st, 1876.

Settle has presented and endowed two Lifeboats.

The first confirmation at Settle Church was in 1866.

The first Agricultural Show at Settle was a "Sweepstakes Shew," in 1848.

The first burial (that of C. Edmondson) in Settle Church Yard was in January 1839.

The Rev. B. Waugh (of "Prevention of Cruelty to Children" fame) is a native of Settle.

The "Giggleswick School Olio" appeared in 1845.

Tom Twisleton's Poems have run through five editions.

The Craven Bank was established in 1791.

The Settle "Association for the prosecution of Felons" was formed in 1743.

King John confirmed the grant of Giggleswick Church to Finchale Priory, in 1208.

A pool of water suddenly appeared near Settle, in 1791.

The first marriage (James Hartley's) at Settle Church was in 1849.

Some people consider Giggleswick Church to be dedicated to "Hali-keld" or "Holy Well."

There were great festivities at Settle when the Crimean War ended.

Settle Agricultural Show was not held from 1866 to 1877.

The Friendly Societies of Settle used to have a "Club Walk" every Whit-week.

The Rev. R. Ingram laid the Foundation Stone of Settle Church.

The Wesleyans first began to preach at Settle in 1760.

The Children of Giggleswick Workhouse used to perform "St. George" as "pace-eggers," every Easter.

The 12th March used to be "potation day" at Giggleswick School.

Hutton published his "Tour to the Caves near Settle" in 1780.

There are 25 Faculty Pews in Giggleswick Church.

The first Catalogue of the Settle Library contains 46 Works.

A Consistory Court was held in Giggleswick Church in February 1890.

Giggleswick Church was reseated in 1822.

Giggleswick Grammar School was restored in 1851.

"Robin Hood's Mill" near Stackhouse is supposed to be an underground waterfall.

In 1749 there were legal proceedings respecting the Chancel of Giggleswick Church.

There used to be a Lime Kiln at the base of Castleberg.

Forty years since, Gas was 12s. per 1000 cubic feet in Settle.

The Rev. James Carr, founder of Giggleswick School, died in 1528.

There were 16 members of the Settle Literary Society in 1777.

There were 62 dances at Balderston's "Juvenile Ball" at Settle, in October, 1817.

J. Williams lectured on "The Advantages of Drunkenness," at Settle, in 1835.

Each Member of the old Benefit Societies of Settle used to expend 2d. in drink at every meeting.

A White Swallow was caught at Settle in 1793.

Marshfield formerly belonged to the Parkers of Browsholme.

Geo. Woods dedicated a volume of Poems to Dr Butterton.

Six Pamphlets were issued in the Giggleswick School controversy, 1861—1864.

In 1604 the only local Roman Catholic was Margaret Frankland, of Rathmell.

Her Majesty has only once passed through Settle Station, viz :--May 21st, 1891.

The boys of Giggleswick School used to scramble for figs every 12th of March.

A Purse of 200 guineas was presented to William Wildman, when he left Settle, in 1879.

The Settle Amateur Dramatic Society first performed in January, 1880.

Until 1817 the Craven Bank Notes had a view of Castleberg on them.

The Keighley and Kendal road was made about 1755.

There was a burglary at Mearbeck in 1842.

700 children had tea in the Snow Castle on the Green, on the 6th March, 1886.

300 years ago Giggleswick school-boys commenced work at 6-30 a.m.

1155 persons signed the pledge in the "Blue Ribbon Mission," at Settle, February, 1883.

Tom Twisleton and "Poet Close" wrote each others epitaphs in poetry.

The Hand-weavers of Settle were in great distress in 1828.

The old part of Giggleswick Workhouse was built in 1834.

The Settle Temperance Hotel Company (1883) had a capital of £3000.

It was proposed to re-make Giggleswick Tarn as a memorial of the Queen's Jubilee.

The Ebbing and Flowing Well is called "Giggleswicke Spring" in a very old map.

The Craven Bank used to issue (inter alia) both one pound and one guinea notes.

There was no funeral in all Giggleswick parish, for a period of 13 weeks, in 1788.

The Salvation Army "Attacked Settle," March 6th, 1886.

There were 32 Candidates at the first Settle Parish Council Election, in December, 1894.

Samuel Watson was fined for preaching "in the burying-place" at Settle, in 1670.

An Ancient Stone Circle formerly existed above Cleatop.

Many remains of the Red Deer have been found on High Hill.

A "Sociable" Society was established at Settle in 1781.

The present Bishop of Oxford (Dr. Stubbs) lived in Settle when a young man.

The "New Police" commenced their duties in Settle in 1857.

The old Bass Fiddle of Giggleswick Church still exists.

The Countess of Warwick gave Giggleswick Church to Henry de Pudsay, about 1160.

It is supposed that the Tumuli above Stackhouse are the burial places of Danes.

Giggleswick School Seal probably belonged to an old Religious House.

Edward VI endowed Giggleswick School with property worth £23 3s. 0d. per annum.

A Skirmish with the Highlanders is believed to have occurred near Gildersleets, in 1745.

The Rev. Rowland Ingram was the first president of the Settle Mechanics' Institute.

In 1678 the Husband family, of Rathmell, were the only local Roman Catholics.

Five regiments of Cavalry were at Settle, under General Lambert, in August, 1651.

The serial "Adventures at Sea" (Settle, 1841) was not a success.

The British Canoe, found in the bed of Giggleswick Tarn, is 8ft. 2in. long.

Mrs. Linnæus Banks, the Authoress, has close associations with Giggleswick.

The then Vicar of Giggleswick refused to allow a Memorial Sermon on Princess Charlotte to be preached in 1817.

T. B.

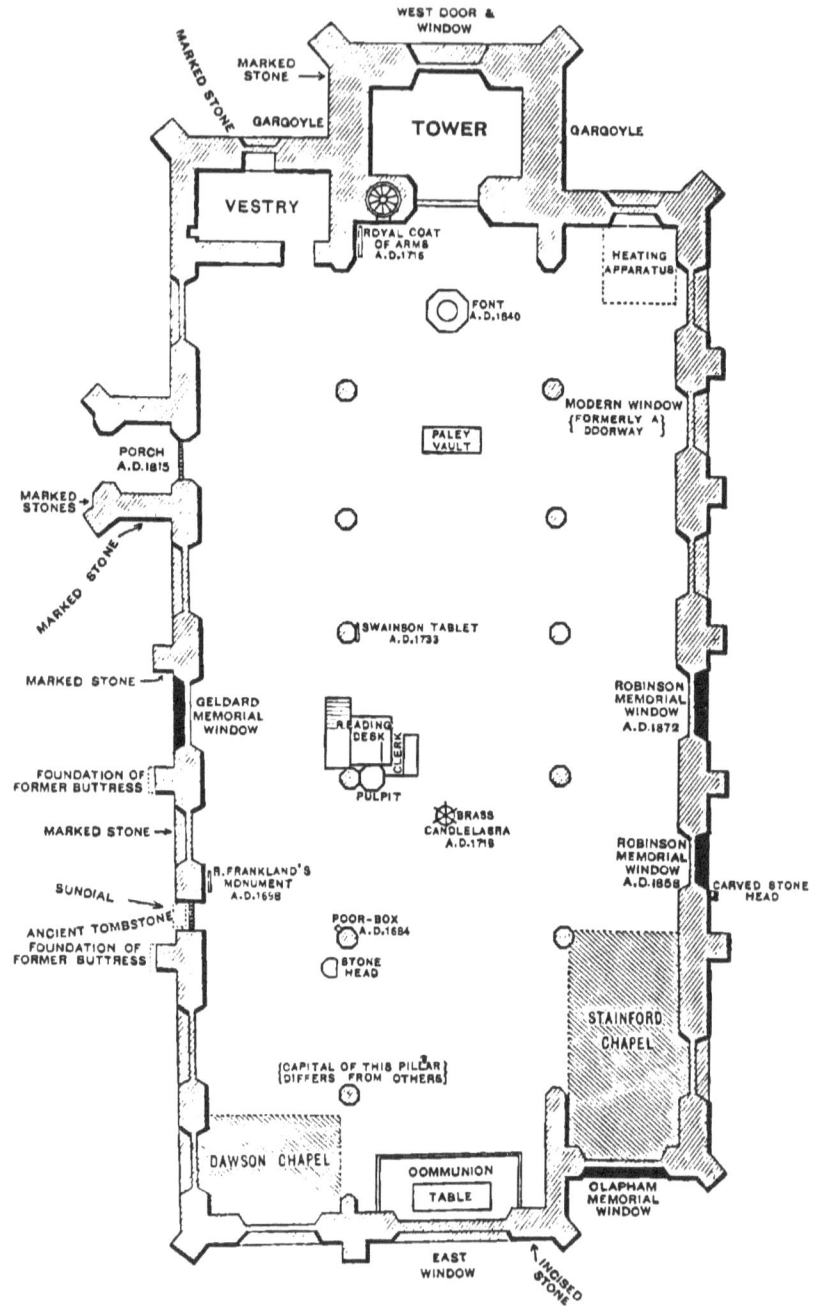

NOTES

ON

GIGGLESWICK CHURCH.

PART I.

WITH ILLUSTRATIONS.

EDITED BY

THOS. BRAYSHAW.

* * * * *

SETTLE:
PRINTED BY THE CRAVEN PRINTING COMPANY, LIMITED.

MDCCCLXXXV.

STACKHOUSE,

NEAR SETTLE,

AUGUST, 1885.

In No. 1 of this Series of "Local Tracts," I gave a list of the Churchwardens of Giggleswick from A.D. 1638 to the present time, together with extracts from the minute-books of the meetings of the "Twenty-four;" and in Tract No. 3 I printed the Charters and other early documents relating to the Church. In this number I give a series of miscellaneous notes referring to the history and fabric of the Church, and I hope to complete the subject at an early date. The photographic Illustrations to this number are permanent platinotypes by Mr. A. Horner, of Settle.

THOS. BRAYSHAW.

Twelve large and one hundred small paper copies printed for private circulation.

NOTES ON GIGGLESWICK CHURCH.

To a stranger, Giggleswick Church presents few points of interest ; but for almost every native of the parish it has some tender association. But independent of this it must, as the mother Church of, and the oldest building in, this large parish, be a centre of attraction to us, and when we survey the old grey walls, we involuntarily call to mind the great changes they have witnessed, not only in the village that clusters round them, but even in the form of worship followed in the building itself, for we must remember that the Church was built in pre-Reformation times, when Roman Catholicism was the national faith.

The earliest record of this parish extant is in the entry in Domesday Book, and there is no mention in it of a Church at " GHIGELESVIC " at that time, but this omission is by no means conclusive proof that such did not exist here ; indeed from the amount of land that was liable to taxation, and from the total absence of the word " waste " (which bore such dreadful testimony to the sufferings of the people in many parts,) I think that the place was in a fairly prosperous condition, and that in all probability there *was* one here.

The first mention of the Church that we can find is in one of Dodsworth's MSS. in the Bodleian Library, in a Charter of Matilda, Countess of Warwick, (daughter of William de Percy,) by which she gives and grants to Henry de Pudsay, his heirs and assigns, her town of Settle, and the rents of Giggleswick, *with the advowson of the Church there*, for fifteen marks in silver, and one palfrey, &c. The date of this Charter is probably about 1160 or 1170. From the attestation of a Lawrence, Parson of "Guckilswic," to a charter of William de Percy the younger, the Church evidently existed, and was unappointed, in the reign of Stephen (A.D. 1135—1154.) One Henry was a parson of "Gukleswic" about the year 1200.

In a previous number of these "Local Tracts" I have set out various charters and documents, and from these we see that Henry de Pudsay granted the church of "Gichellswick" to the Priory of Finchale, probably out of compliment to his father, Hugh Pudsay, (Bishop of Durham, from 1153 to 1166) and William de Percy granted the advowson of "Gyckleswic" Church to the same priory about the year 1227. This was confirmed by King John in the 9th year of his reign.

The prior and convent of Durham, as patrons of the subservient priory of Finchale, exercised the right of presenting to the Vicarage of Giggleswick, from the first institution which occurs in the registers of the See of York, to the Dissolution of religious houses in 1538, after which the Crown became the patron, until about the year 1600 when the Advowson was granted to a W. Brooke.

The living is now in the alternate presentation of the Hartley and Coulthurst families.

Let us now say a word or two as to the Parish of Giggleswick. It is a very extensive one, its area being 18500 acres. In addition to the Township of Giggleswick it comprises Settle, Stainforth, and Rathmell, in each of which places there is a church, the livings being perpetual curacies. The Vicar and Parish Clerk of Giggleswick consequently take their share of all fees paid for funerals, weddings, &c., at these churches. Langcliffe formed part of the ancient parish, but in 1851 it was made an independent one. The houses at the "Locks" still remain in Giggleswick however. The name of the street in Settle called "Kirkgate" reminds us of the time when it was the most direct route from the town to the (at that period) only church in the parish.

Dr. Whitaker, in his history of Craven, describes the Church as being "a large, uniform and handsome buliding, exactly in the style of the other churches in Craven, which are known to have been re-built in the reigns of Henry VII. and Henry VIII.

It consists of nave of four bays, with clerestory; chancel, with east window of six lights; north and south aisles to both nave and chancel; square west tower and south porch. The whole building appears to be of third Pointed style."

It is estimated that it will seat a thousand people, which is a small number considering the size of the building, but the square pews seem specially designed to afford accommodation for the smallest number of people in a given area. However, it is, for the present, amply sufficient for the wants of the scant congregation, for the great bulk of the population follow the example set them by their spiritual leader, the Vicar, and religiously abstain from attending the services of the church, or taking the slightest interest in it.

The Church is dedicated to St. Alkelda, and I can only find one other Church—Middleham—that is dedicated to the same saint, and strangely enough this Church also was appropriated to the Priory of Finchale. Of this Saint we can glean but little information, as her name does not occur in any of the best known martyrologies, but the following account is given by W. G. M. J. Barker (a Roman Catholic writer,) in his History of Wensleydale. Speaking of Middleham Church he says :—

" Saint Alkelda is said to have been the daughter of a Saxon Prince, or Earl, who, on account of her religion, was put to death by strangulation, by the Danes. In the east window of the chantry of our Blessed Lady, her passion was depicted in stained glass; portions of the representation are still there. She was shown in the act of being strangled by two females who had twisted a napkin round her neck. Possibly the scene of her suffering was the site of the present church or a little to the west of it; for it is certain that her sacred remains repose somewhere in the edifice, and a spring which rises not far off, is named St. Alkelda's Well. The water of this fountain was accounted beneficial for weak eyes, and the writer knew a Protestant lady, who died not long since at an advanced age, who, in early youth, was accustomed to repair to it, every morning, and who received much relief from its strengthening qualities. Certain fee-farm rents in Middleham are required to be paid upon St. Alkelda's Tomb, and were regularly deposited on a stone table (most probably an altar), in the middle of the nave, as also were some annual doles of bread, until the stone was removed, within the memory of persons recently living."

St. Alkelda's day is observed on the 5th of November. Lawton, in his "Collections relative to the Dioceses of York and Ripon" states that the Church is dedicated to St. Alkeld, who was a nephew of King Ina, and Bishop of Sherborne. He died A.D. 709. I think there is little doubt however that St. Alkelda is our real patron Saint, and not St. Alkeld.

In Pope Nicholas's first taxation, A.D. 1292, the church is valued at £33 6s. 8d.: but in A.D. 1318 a new taxation was made on account of the invasion of the Scots, and it was found that this parish had suffered so severely that the annual value was reduced to £14 3s. 4d., or considerably less than half its previous amount!

The Vicarage is valued in the King's books (26 Henry VIII) at £21 3s. 2d.; and in the Parliamentary Survey, vol. 18 it is stated: "Vicarage £50. The parish church is well situate for the most conveniency of the whole parish."

In "Notitia Parochialis," No. 809, the following return is given by the Rev. R. Ellershaw, who was appointed Vicar in 1686; "the Vicarage is endowed with the corn tithe of two small villages, called Langcliffe and Stainforth-under-Bargh, with Easter dues, small tithes and surplice fees. Endowment dated in 1249. The right to the advowson not well known but supposed to belong to the heirs or assigns of Josias Dockeray, D.D., late Rector of——— in the County of Northumberland. Above £30 per annum. Signed, Richard Ellershaw, Vic."

The living was augmented in 1732 with £200 to meet a benefaction of similar amount from Mr. Anthony Lister.

A decree in the Exchequer, in Michaelmas Term, 37th Eliz., as to tithes, is unreported. The following are the dates of the faculties that have been granted in connection with the fabric:

2nd February, 1738, Faculty to build a gallery.
5th March, 1742 ditto. ditto.
4th March, 1785 ditto. ditto.
9th February, 1810 ditto. and to re-roof the church.
17th December, 1819, faculty to re-pew the church.
12th March, 1822, confirmation of allotment of pews.

Additional burial ground was consecrated in 1817 and again in recent years, but there is every prospect that ere long, further enlargement, or a Cemetery, will become necessary.

The Registers of the Church commence in 1558, and go on to 1627. There is then an interval of $26\frac{1}{2}$ years, viz.: from the end of March, 1626 (*i. e.* 1627) to the end of September, 1633, of which we can find no records, and I fear they have unfortunately been destroyed like so many others, during the civil war.

They contain but few items of interest, as successive Vicars seem to have made their entries as brief as possible, and to have avoided making any memoranda in them relating to the parish, as was the practice in many other places.

In previous editions of the " Encyclopædia Britannica " there is the startling information that Giggleswick Church stands on the top of a rock 300 feet high, to which the ascent is by steps cut in the limestone rock! This is doubtless a confusion with Castleberg.

I propose in the first part of these " Notes" to confine myself almost exclusively to the fabric of the Church, leaving almost all the historical details, monumental inscriptions, &c., to a future part, and in order to describe the building more clearly, we may as well take an imaginary tour round it.

Let us first start at the old Market Cross (of which a plate and account are given in No. 2 of these Tracts). This is the sole remaining relic of the ancient importance of Giggleswick as a market town. At the base of it note the old pillar which is one of the two that formerly supported the stocks. Its sister post was broken off some time since and has several times been replaced by a poor and imperfect imitation, but this I am happy to say has lately been removed. We next come to the Lych-gate, which is of comparatively modern origin. The old Vicarage formerly stood close by this. It is commonly supposed that the portion of the Church-yard lying between the Lych-gate, and the "Black Horse" Inn is not consecrated ground. This Inn was formerly part of the buildings connected with the Church and several niches for the reception of statues of Saints may be seen in its exterior walls.

There is a *convenient* entrance from this Inn to the Church-yard, and dark tales are told respecting the Churchwardens, when it was the duty of these officials to leave the Church, whilst the sermon was proceeding, in order to see that all public houses were closed.

From the Lych-gate a good idea of the general exterior of the Church may be obtained. The building is a very long one and disputes with Kildwick the title of "The Lang Kirk of Craven". Near the West entrance to the Church yard may be seen a very ancient relic of our Parish in the old stone coffin which lies just under the wall. Its only use of late years has been to serve as a trough for watering the sheep which, until a few months since, used to pasture in the Churchyard. Of course we are entirely in the dark as to the person whose last resting place this coffin formed, but from the hollow being very narrow and only long enough to serve for a person of from 5 feet 3 inches to 5 feet 6 inches in height, it seems likely to have been that of a woman. It may indeed have been the coffin of one of the Monks formerly attached to the Church.

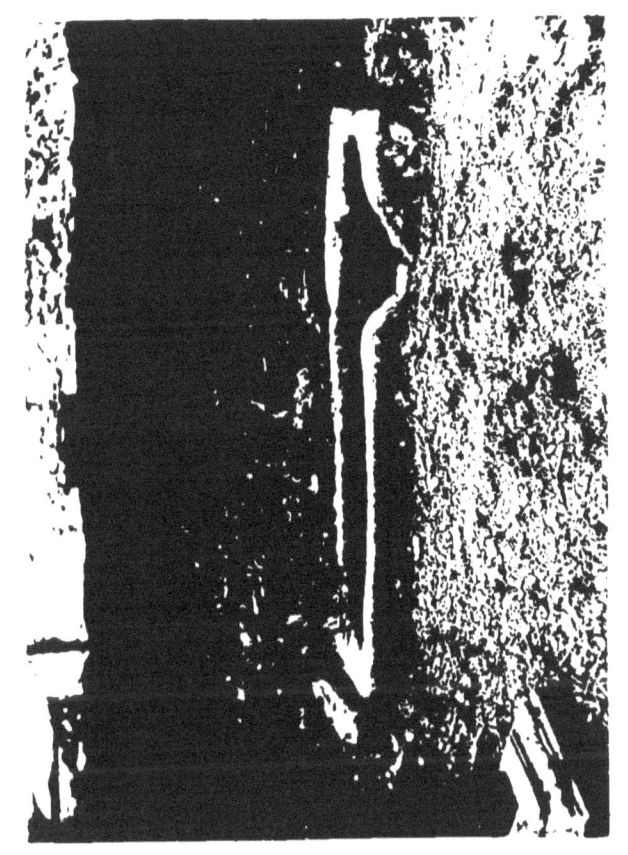

STONE COFFIN, IN GIGGLESWICK CHURCH YARD.

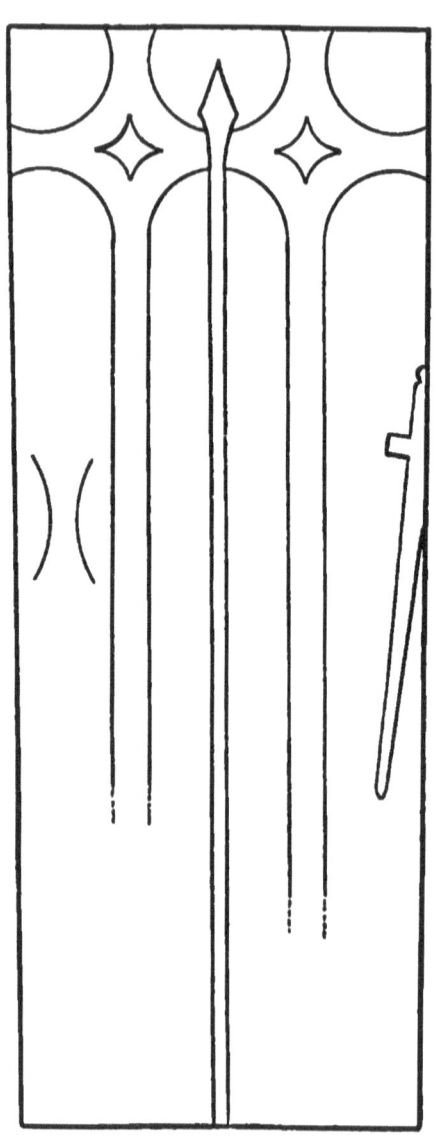

ANCIENT TOMBSTONE
IN GIGGLESWICK CHURCH YARD.

Nearly opposite the small porch is an old stone pillar. I fancy this has been the stand for a sundial, but it has been so worn away that it is imposible to say for certain.

On examining the East exterior wall of the Tower, we can see very plainly the former pitch of the roof, which used to be much higher than at present. The tradition is that the roofs of all the Churches in this neighbourhood were lowered owing to the one at Gargrave slipping down. The exterior of the Tower possesses little of interest; the gargoyles are curious, the clock has only one pointer, and is hardly a first class time-keeper, and the West window is the best feature of this part of the building. This is really a very nice little window and it is a pity that it is hidden from the view of the congregation by the " Singing Gallery ".

On many parts of the walls of the Church may be seen what are known as " Mason's Marks ". I give representations of four of these, which are found in different parts of the building. The third of these is the one most common.

The stones on which these are found were probably part of the Church which previously existed on the same site as the present one. These marks were made by the old Freemasons who assisted in the rearing of the edifice, when the members of that body were really operative.

Over the small South entrance to the Church note the sun-dial, one of the numerous ones in this locality. I fancy this has been an old work touched up in modern times.

At the base of the buttresses on each side of this porch there can still be seen the foundations of two of those of the former Church.

Just outside this porch there is a slab of stone, on which may be traced the outlines of a double cross. In the centre of the stone is a representation of a spear, on one side a sword, and on the other something that I fancy has been intended for a chalice. The lines on this stone are hardly discernible now, but Miss Sutcliffe made an accurate sketch of it more than forty years ago, when the markings on it were pretty clearly defined and it is from her sketch that I am enabled to give a representation of the stone. It is supposed to have marked the grave of some Ecclesiastic or Crusader, but what his name was or his deeds will never be known. May I respectfully hint to the Churchwardens that a few shillings would be well spent in the removal of this stone to some place where it would be less exposed, what with the constant wear and tear owing to people walking over it, and the cement with which some builders have carelessly smeared it, the figures on it are almost obliterated.

In going round the outside of the Church note the incised stone on the North side of the East window. This is a relic of the former Church and has evidently been part of a larger figure, but the stone has got broken or displaced when the Church was rebuilt; note also the carved stone head near the Robinson memorial window.

There are very few ancient tombstones remaining in the Church-yard. It is difficult to account for this unless it be that in early days the gravestones were composed of the soft stone found in the neighbourhood so that the inscriptions have been effaced by the hand of time.

Having completed our tour round the exterior let us go inside the Church. Here there is not very much of interest and the whole place is in a dreadfully dilapidated condition. Dirt, damp, decay and discomfort seen to reign here supreme, and the Churchwardens are totally unable to fight against these drawbacks, with the very limited means placed at their disposal by the congregation. In going round the inside of the Church we will commence at the North-east corner. Here note the stained glass window erected by the Executors of the late Miss Alice Atkinson, to the memory of the Revd. John Clapham. This window has a very odd effect at a short distance owing to the red wings of the angels. This part of the Church is the Stainford Chapel, and Dr. Whitaker states

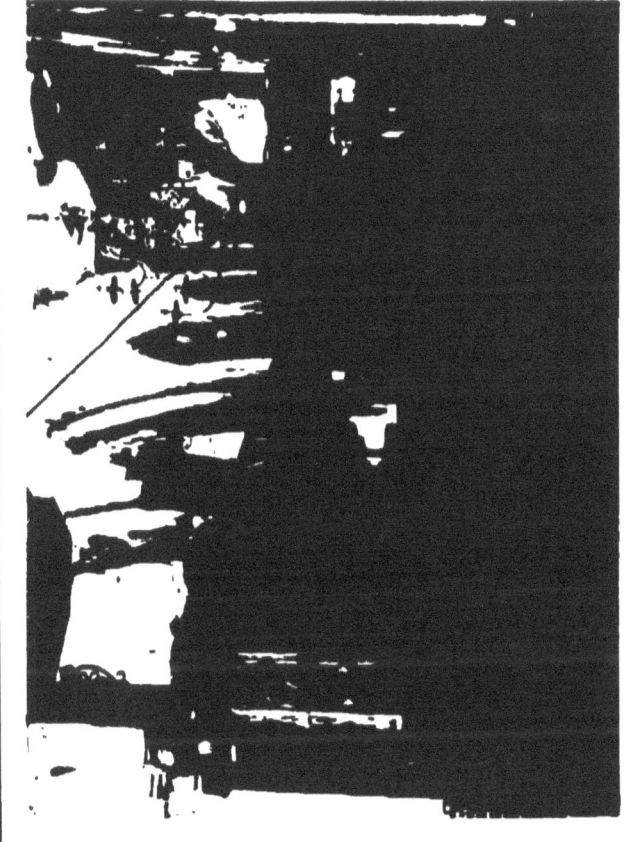

GIGGLESWICK CHURCH.—INTERIOR VIEW.

INSCRIPTION ON READING DESK IN GIGGLESWICK CHURCH.

"Stackhouse" Tract, No. 5.

that in it there were formerly two cumbent statues, undoubtedly of the Stainfords. This chantry was dedicated to our Lady, and was founded by Robert Stainford, the annual value being four pounds. Tempest's Chantry also was on the North side of the Church and probably adjoined the Stainford Chantry. The annual value of the Tempest Chantry was £4 13s. 4d. There also existed in the Church the Roode Chantry, founded by James Carr, Priest, the annual value of which was £6 1s. 0d.

On the north side of the church there are two stained glass windows; one in memory of Jane Robinson, 1858, the other in memory of William Robinson, 1872. The glaring colours of these windows are hardly considered to be in the best style of this branch of ecclesiastical art. Between these two windows is a very imposing Table of Charities, but this is now little less than a mockery as many of the benefactions left for the poor of this neighbourhood have been suffered to lapse, and others have been swallowed up by the Grammar School. The second window from the West in the North aisle is modern, there having been a doorway in its place until comparatively recent times. Many of the pews in the north aisle have the initials of their former occupiers carved in the woodwork. In the northwest corner we find the heating apparatus, which is admirably adapted for roasting part of the congregation and leaving the remainder to freeze. Until recently it was a favourite amusement of the parish clerk to diversify the service by "firing up" with great pomp and clatter just before the sermon, but this interlude is now dispensed with. The font was erected in memory of the Rev. Rowland Ingram, the following inscription running round it:

"Antiquum infra Fontem posuit ornabit Rowland Ingram, M.A., Vicarius Anno Domini mdcccxl.

The date is incorrectly given in Whitaker's 'Craven' as 1815. The pews near the font are found by the church officials to afford an excellent repository of wood for fuel. The bier generally ornaments this part of the church also, and this leads me to ask if some more appropriate place could not be found for these things. To the east of the font is the family vault of the Paleys, where lie the remains of the parents of the celebrated Archdeacon Paley.

Close to the tower is an old painting of the Royal coat of arms; the date of this work of art is 1716. This probably fit into the roof in former times, but I suppose that when the pitch of the roof was altered it became necessary to remove the painting, and in order to adapt it to its present position it was necessary to cut off the top.

The porch of the church was re-built in 1815; it is repairable by the owners of Close House.

In the south aisle note the Geldard memorial window and the monument to the memory of Richard Frankland, dated 1698. This monument is a plaster one and has evidently been cast in the same mould as that to the memory of General Lambert's son in Kirkby Malham Church. The heating pipes form the principal decoration of the wall of the south aisle. In the south-east corner of the church is the Dawson chapel, and it may be noted that the capital of the pillar nearest the east end in the south aisle differs from all the others. It is difficult to account for this, but probably the fact of its propinquity to the chapels may be the reason. There are two hatchments bearing the arms of the Dawson and Pudsay families in the Dawson Chapel.

On the wall opposite to the small porch may be seen a curious carved stone head, the hands of the figure being represented as trying to tear open the mouth. In the centre of the church is a handsome brass candelabra for twelve lights. This was put up in 1718, the inscription on it stating that Richard Brayshaw, John Armistead, Fran. Clapham, and Richard Lawson were the churchwardens at the time.

The pulpit is undoubtedly the principal object of interest in the church. The date of it is 1680, and it may be noticed that the capital of the pillar against which it rests is much cut about, probably to accommodate a previous construction. The pulpit is in the style known as a " three-decker," consisting of the pulpit proper, with sounding board above, the reading desk, and the clerk's snuggery. It is of fine old oak curiously and handsomely carved. On the panels are the names and badges of the Twelve Tribes of Israel, but in carving these badges the artist has obeyed the

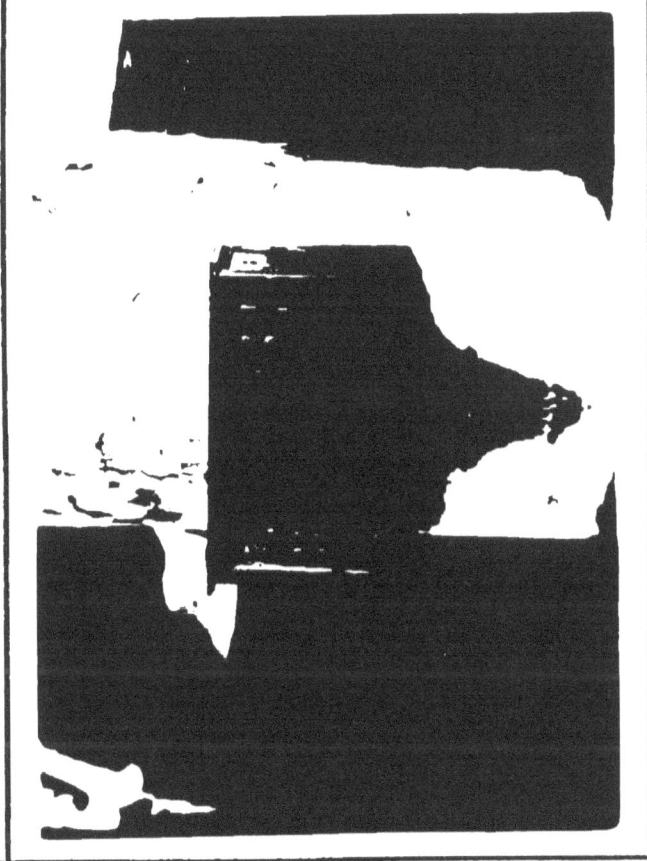

"POOR BOX," IN GIGGLESWICK CHURCH.

PANEL OF PULPIT, IN GIGGLESWICK CHURCH.

"Stackhouse" Tract, No. 5.

Biblical instruction not to make "the likeness of anything that is in heaven above, or in the earth beneath, or in the water under the earth." In front of the Reading desk is carved the inscription :

HEAR · IS · THE · STANDARDES · OF ·
THE · ISRAELITES · WHEN · THE · TO ·
CANAN · CAM · AGENEST · THE · CANANITES

This refers to the carvings above mentioned. On the side are carved the initials L.L, R.C, T.C, and W.K, these being the initials of Lawrence Swainson, Robert Carr, Thomas Clapham, and William Knipe, who were the churchwardens for the year 1680. The panels of which I give a photograph represent Reuben, Simeon, Levi, Gad, Naphthali, and Asher.

The badges and names of these tribes as carved are :

REVBIN. WAVES. ("unstable as water.")
SIM.   SWORD. ("Instruments of cruelty.")
LEV.   A SCROLL.
GAD.   FLAG OF BATTLE. ("He shall overcome.")
NAPH.   A HIND LET LOOSE.
ASH.   CUP. ("Royal dainties.")

On the pillar to the West of the pulpit is an old brass in memory of Lawrence Swainson, A.D. 1773.

One of my illustrations shows the old carved "poor box" with its quaint inscription " Remember the pore." The date of this is 1684, but the effect of it is spoilt by its being placed on a stand with the date 1844 conspicuously carved on it.

The Communion rails are probably the oldest pieces of work in the church. They bear the initials T.A., W.W., L.K., and T.S. These evidently refer to the Churchwardens for the year in which the rails were erected, and as they are not applicable to the holders of that office for any year for which we have a list of churchwardens, that is since A.D.

1638, they must be prior to that date. Within the communion rails are two fine old oak chairs. The flooring here is in a dreadful condition, earth and rushes being immediately below the carpet. The east window of the church is a very large and particularly ugly one. It is a disputed point whether it is of the original height or not. For my own part I venture to think that the top of it has been removed at the same period when the pitch of the roof was lowered.

In the Harleian M.S.S. in the British museum is a roughly drawn sketch of a coat of arms that was formerly emblazoned in one of the windows of Giggleswick Church. I give a copy of this shield. I believe it is intended to represent the arms of the Tennant family, and part of the pedigree of that family is given in the same M.S.S. It probably formed part of the window erected in the church in the year 1518, which bore the inscription :

"Orate pro bono statu Richardi Tennant et Margarete uxoris ejus de Byrkys procuratoris istius ecclesie et filiorum filiarumque eorum qui istam fenestram fieri fecerunt A.D. mccccc decimo octabo, et anno regis Henrici octabi post Conquesum octabo."

From a manuscript dated 1620 we find the east window of Giggleswick church was at that time ornamented with five figures "having shaven crowns and habited in blue coats," and this, taken in connection with the fact of the emblazoned coat of arms just mentioned, makes it seem probable that many of the windows of the church were formerly filled with stained glass.

In the view I give showing the general interior of the church some faint idea may be gathered of the unspeakable ugliness of the galleries. Just over the font is a large pew, ornamented with staves, which is sacred to the churchwardens. Behind that is the gallery where the singers hold forth and this is flanked on each side by galleries, consisting of Faculty pews. But for the fact that they *are* Faculty pews these hideous erections would probably have been removed ere this, but we can only live and hope. Some few years since an attempt was made to get them removed,

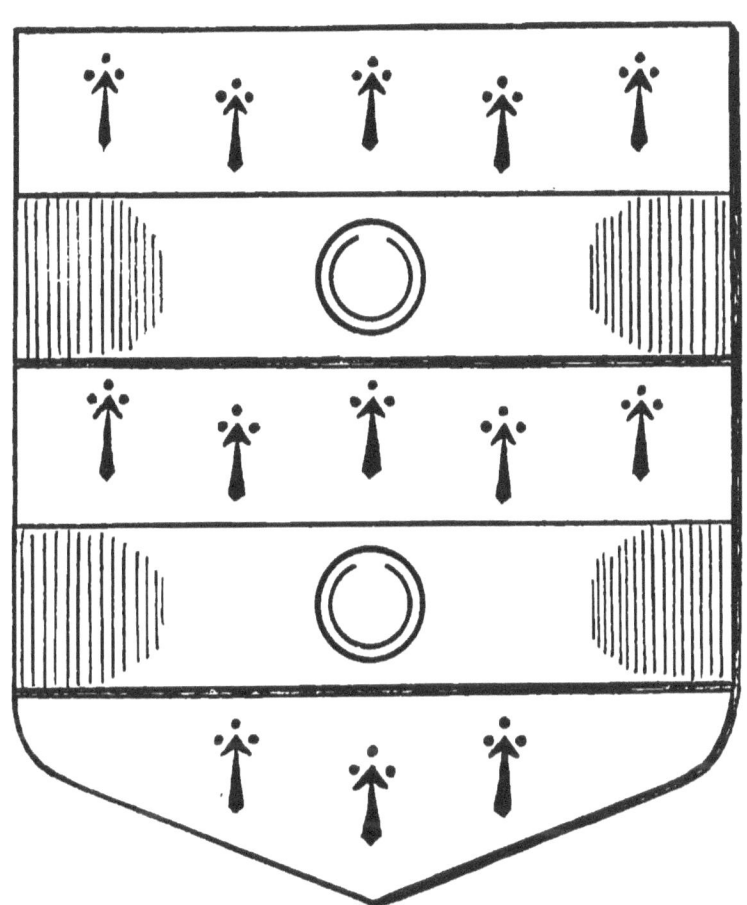

COAT OF ARMS FORMERLY IN ONE OF THE WINDOWS
OF GIGGLESWICK CHURCH.

and this was nearly successful, but the efforts of the promoters were frustrated by the firmness of a good old lady called Miss Lund, who declared that if any attempt was made to remove the gallery in which she sat, she would take her seat in her pew, and let them pull her down along with the gallery. The post of honour in the singing gallery is now occupied by a small but sweet organ. Before that a harmonium did duty here, and again prior to that a bass fiddle discoursed sweet sounds. Some people have the bad taste to think that the bass fiddle was by no means the worst of the lot. The congregation of Giggleswick church have rather a curious habit of turning round to the west during the singing of the hymns, so as to face the choir. The windows of the church are all leaded and it is curious to note that where a pane has been cracked it has been carefully repaired by putting a strip of lead along the fracture. The clerestory windows are worthy a passing glance. A great portion of the church is undermined with vaults. For sanitary reasons these have all been carefully cemented up.

Amongst the plate of Giggleswick church are three old chalices. Two of them bear the inscription " Giggleswick Communion Cup, 1731," but one of these has the Hall mark for 1652. The third chalice has the following inscription engraved round the rim of the bowl :

-|- THE · COMMVNION · CVPP · BELONGINGE · TO ' THE

PARISHE · OF · IYGGELSWICKE · MADE · IN · ANO · 1585.

The spelling " Iyggelswicke " is very curious. I can only hazard the conjecture that the I stands for J, so that the word would read " Jyggleswicke."

The services of the church are free from the least trace of Ritualism, but for my taste there is too much clerk and too little congregation audible, but as a rule the small number of the " Flock " accounts for the small noise they make. Except on Easter Sunday, when the volunteers attend church, a full congregation is rarely seen, and on this one occasion in the year they are not an unmixed blessing.

The mention of the volunteers reminds me that on the occasion of the funeral of one of their members, many years since, the firing party delivered a volley *inside the church*.

It is rather interesting to note the opinion of a stranger respecting the service at Giggleswick Church, so I extract the following from the " Reminiscences" of J. Burkill, whose very stupid book has had such a (deservedly) small circulation in this neighbourhood that it will probably be fresh to most of my readers:

"And what a study were those old musicians in the gallery (assuming to sing in parts). Their *music* (?) would have passed muster BEFORE "TUNES CAME UP." It would have afforded a splendid study for Thos. Faed, R.A. The Vicar was a rosy-faced man of middle-age, and in splendid condition. With a fine voice, which was well modulated, and a perfect pronunciation, every word he uttered could be heard distinctly in every part of the church. It was both solemn and impressive. I wondered if he were a Justice of the Peace as well as Vicar and a Reverend Father in God. If he were *not*, I thought he ought to have been, and then Shakespeare's lines would have been " *tres apropos* " :
" Then the Justice, with fair round belly
" With fat-capon lined——"
The late Charles Mathews was the model of volubility in "! Patter *versus* Clatter," but his Reverence at Giggleswick would " *beat him into fits.*" The rapid manner in which he hurried some of the Prayers suggested the idea that turkey and plum-pudding at the vicarage were ordered at a given time, and that he was " *making-running* " to be *in* at the feast. Such were my irreverent ruminations. The sermon which followed was *fully fifteen minutes* long by the parish clock, and the congregation were dismissed by *noon*, to go to their homes, and to feast upon the " bread that perisheth." I have no hesitation in pronouncing this *church* and *service* as *one* of the Natural " *Curiosities of Craven.*"

In concluding this part of my notes on Giggleswick church, may I, as an attendant at that church, express a hope that the time is not far distant when the building shall be restored and the abuses that at present exist shall be put an end to. In regard to the first point the galleries ought to be cleared away entirely, the roof raised to its former pitch, the east window restored, another form of heating apparatus in place of the present one, the lime and whitewash removed from the walls in the interior, and the height of the pews lowered. I fancy the nucleus of a fund for such work is already in existence. Will not some well-wisher of the old church take the matter in hand ?

REPRINT

OF

POEMS

ON THE

MEETING OF VOLUNTEERS AT SETTLE,

IN 1794,

AND ON

LORD NELSON'S VICTORY,

IN 1798,

BY

R. KIDD.

* * * * * *

STACKHOUSE,

NEAR SETTLE,

SEPTEMBER, 1885.

One of the scarcest of Local Works, and one that is known to but few of the present generation, is a little pamphlet by R. Kidd, formerly Assistant Master at Giggleswick School. This consists of two poems, the first being inspired by a meeting at Settle, in 1794, of some of the Yorkshire Yeomanry Volunteers who were enrolled in considerable numbers during the war panics at the end of the last century; the other being in commemoration of Lord Nelson's Victory of the 2nd August, 1798.

I have thought fit to reprint these poems, firstly, on account of their rarity; secondly, because the author was a local man; thirdly, because one of them relates to a matter of considerable local interest; and fourthly, because the poems themselves are so unlike anything else that ever has been, or in all probability ever will be written, that on this account I think them worthy of being reproduced and preserved. I have retained the errors in spelling as in the original.

THOS. BRAYSHAW.

Twelve large and one hundred small paper copies printed for private circulation.

A POEM

ON THE

MEETING OF THE GENTLEMEN

YORKSHIRE C VOLUNTEERS,

AT SETTLE, IN CRAVEN,

21st August, 1794.

BY R. KIDD.

Late Writing Master, and Teacher of the Mathematics, at the Free Grammar School, of Giggleswick, near Settle, now Land Surveyor.

SETTLE:
PRINTED AND SOLD [FOR THE AUTHOR] BY T. TROUGHTON, MAY BE HAD OF W. BAYNES, 55, PATER NOSTER ROW,
LONDON.

PREFACE.

WHENEVER an Author submits his Works to Public inspection, an invidious Critic will stigmatise every imperfection with malevolence, and reject Beauties highly meritorious.—Others again, actuated by a greater generosity in Criticism, will more impartially comment upon Faults, and in some measure approve of real Elegancies.

Regardless however, of such enmity; these Poems are humbly dedicated to gentlemen, as liberal in their sentiments, as they are patriotic in their services to the State; who I am persuaded will candidly read this work, and censure as it deserves. I am far from supposing that it is altogether irreprehensible, a Task to which I am by no means adequate: But as noble Actions in all ages have been the themes of Poetry, I was sensible the Subjects of the following verses, were deserving of celebration; for which reason, I have endeavoured to effect that, tho' I may have failed in the attempt, yet it detracts nothing from the intention of promoting valour: At least it may incite some abler pen to resume the subject, and to extol magnanimity of Spirit in more copious strains.

GENTLEMEN,

THAT YOU MAY INVIOLABLY MAINTAIN A FIRM ATTACHMENT TO THE KING'S MOST ROYAL PERSON, AN UNSHAKEN FIRMNESS TO THE BRITISH CONSTITUTION, AN UNRIVALLED FORTITUDE IN THE PROTECTION OF THE PUBLIC WELFARE, AN UNITED RESOLUTION IN REPELLING FOREIGN INVASION, AND REPRESSING INTERNAL COMMOTIONS; AND IN SHORT, AN HEROIC PERSEVERANCE, IN THIS YOUR GLORIOUS CAUSE, IS THE SINCERE PRAYER OF HIM, WHO HAS THE HONOUR TO SUBSCRIBE HIMSELF,

GENTLEMEN,

YOUR MUCH OBLIGED, MOST OBEDIENT, AND VERY HUMBLE SERVANT,

ROBERT KIDD.

THE YORKSHIRE VOLUNTEERS.

A NOBLE Subject now demands my Lays,
   Ye Volunteers! I'll sing your worthy Praise;
Oh! could my Muse do Justice to your Name,
Enroll'd in Lists of never-ending Fame;
Oh! would Minerva round my Brow entwine,
And could my Numbers equal my Design;
I'd cull Expressions in Miltonian Strain,
And Pope's sweet flowing Verse I'd strive to gain:
But ah! my Muse in vain attempts to rise,
Creeps low on Earth, nor mounts the lofty Skies;
I feel myself unequal to my Theme,
Tho Genius flags—accept my best Esteem;
I know your Prudence (for a gen'rous Mind,
Spurns at Contempt, when the Intent is kind;)
Will substitute the Wish, instead of Deed,
Mistakes forgive, while you with Candor read.
   Ye *Yorkshire* Gents! ye gallant *Volunteers!*
You stand distinguish'd—you have no Compeers!
You are Free-off'rings at Emergence' Voice,
You're led by Honour, and you act by Choice:
You have just Motives; may you gain your Ends,
Preserve yourselves, your Country and your Friends:
What conscious Pleasure must elate your Breast,
To quell Sedition, make your Kingdom blest;
T" extirpate Anarchs from a happy State,
To make them tremble with impending Fate;

To stem the Torrent of Confusions Tide,
And dire Effects of *Democratic* Pride;
To quash the Tumults, Riots, Mobs and Rage,
And disaffection of the present Age.
   All hail ye Gents! all hail this festive Day,
Success attend it, with propitious Ray;
May loyal Meetings your Importance spread,
You guard the Nation, and the King's your Head:
May Glory's Splendor with enliv'ning Beam,
Illume your Steps nor Shadows intervene;
May Emulation in the high'st Degree,
Excite your Souls to Intrepidity;
You are selected in one common Cause,
A Corps of Strength, a Standard of the Laws:
By Virtue's Buckler may you shield this Land,
Truth in your Heart, and Mercy in your Hand;
But if Protection should stern Justice call,
Unsheath the Sword and make the Rebel fall:
Let every Traitor of seditious Breath,
Be scourg'd with Rods, and let his Stripes be Death:
Keep stubborn Villains in profoundest Awe,
By *British* Pow'r, by *British* Arms and Law:
A Soldier's Merit, is a Soldier's Due,
And who is greater than a Soldier true?
Who serves his Country in contentious Days,
Shall wear the Garland of his Country's Praise;
Shall wear an Emblem of deserv'd Renown,
A deathless Laurel, an immortal Crown.
   Permit me Gents, a Question here to ask,
I'll give the Answer, and save you the Task:
What is't that prompts your valliant Souls to move?
'Tis manly Courage and your Country's Love;
'Tis not Ambition, that's an empty Name,
Which sinks degraded in the Lists of Fame;
'Tis genuine Merit of intrinsic Kind,
Much better felt, than by a Pen defin'd;
Let your own Hearts the brave Emotions know,
Unaw'd by Fear, and uncompell'd by Law;
You're Volunteers, and Volunteers I sing,
The Country's Bulwark, Chieftains to your King.
   But should you e'er be call'd to Action's Field,
The Cause itself will Satisfaction yield;

And should you not, the Exercise alone,
Will pay the Labour, and the Costs attone:
Be't as it may—'tis politic and just,
To've Corps defensive, of undoubted Trust;
To've Force internal, able to repel,
Invasive Foes, and all their efforts quell;
To crush Rebellion in the very Bud,
To save your own, but spill the Rebel's Blood.

   When Danger threatens, it's discreet to guard,
And be equipt impending Blows to ward;
The Object's glorious, and the Means are grand,
Gents deckt in Arms to save their native Land;
Not by Compulsion, not for Love of Gain,
You're Volunteers, and Volunteers of Fame!
Whose Bosoms glow, with patriotic Zeal,
With public Spirit and with public Weal;
The Work is noble, and the Call is great,
'Tis Constitution, Country, King and State;
Religion, Honour, Fortune, Wealth and Peace,
Call for Protection and for Health's Increase;
Whatever's dear, demands a saving Hand,
When fierce Invaders circumscribe a Land;
When dearest Relatives implore their Lives,
Our social Friends, our Daughters, Sons and Wives.

   Such is your Cause, your Bosoms swell with Rage,
When Galls usurp, and bloody Wars engage;
Your hearts untainted Loyalty display,
You rise to conquer—and you'll win the Day.

   Ye Sons of Mars! ye most heroic Sons!
Bestride your Steeds, erect your Swords and Guns;
Be clad in martial Armour, cap-a-pie,
And all the Terror of a Cavalry!

   Behold the Horse! with what tremendious Rush,
He plunges headstrong common Foes to crush;
With desp'rate Bounds he makes the Valleys smoke,
While Hills adjacent shudder at the Stroke;
He snorts at Danger and he mocks at Fear,
He meets hot Balls, the Cannon, Sword, and Spear;
Death, Fire, Destruction, cannot daunt his rage,
Nor all the Might that thund'ring Guns can wage;
While Rocks re-echo with the Din of War,
While Victor's Herald mounts his fi'ry Car;

Proclaims aloud with strong stentorian Voice,
These are the Gents who serve their King by Choice.
   With all this Horror, this majestic Dread,
Ye mighty Chiefs! by Honour still be led;
Go meet the French (by well-disciplin'd Law,)
Let them once feel a *British* Lion's Paw:
Go Volunteers! make but one bold Advance,
Down fall Convention, and the Hosts of France:
Shall a *Banditti* (void of King or Law,)
Bring royal Subjects into slavish Awe?
Forbid it Heav'ns, forbid it *British Tars*,
Ye *Howes* and *Hoods* and *Volunteers* of Wars;
Ye martial *Davids* now your Armour Try,——
Let proud *Monsieurs* in vanquish'd Numbers lie;
Let them confess, *Old England's* Pow'r and Might,
With all the Honours of a trophi'd Fight;
Let them confess, *Britannia* rules the Main,
And *George* the third, sole Monarch of the Plain;
Now let each Subject, give a cordial Cheer,
GOD save the *King*—GOD save the *Volunteer*.

A POEM

ON THE

GLORIOUS VICTORY

Obtained on the first and second of August, 1798.

BY REAR ADMIRAL

Sir Horatio Nelson, K. B.

BY R. KIDD.

Late Writing Master, and Teacher of the Mathematics, at the Free Grammar School, of Giggleswick, near Settle, now Land Surveyor.

SETTLE:
PRINTED AND SOLD [FOR THE AUTHOR] BY T. TROUGHTON, MAY BE
HAD OF W. BAYNES, 55, PATER NOSTER ROW,
LONDON.

PREFACE.

THE generality of Mankind have a constant propnesity to hearken to variety; for which reason I have ventured to make an Innovation from the common Mode of prefatory Introduction.

If the following Dedication should be so fortunate as to give any Satisfaction to the Public, and particularly to those Ladies and Gentlemen who have favoured me with their Subscriptions, there will be a mutual Gratification between the Perusers, and him who subscribes himself, with all due Deference and Respect, the Public's most devoted humble Servant.

R. KIDD.

DEDICATION.

WITH profoundest Veneration,
For the *British* Legislation;
The present Administration,
And each sound Denomination;
From the Head of Coranation,
To the lowest Situation;
I submit this Publication,
To their candid Approbation.
  May the brave English Nation,
In mature Delibration;
And Sapient Consultation,
With the noblest Animation;
And intrepid Co-operation,
In one firm Consolidation:
Put a total Extirpation,
To seditious Combination;
And rebellious Inflammation,
Through terraqueous Creation.
  That no desperate Invasion,
That no foreign Conspiration;
By illegal Violation,
Tyrannical Usurpation;
Imperious Depredation,
Perfidious Machination;
Most dreadful Depopulation,
Base horrid Strangulation;
Non-descript Assassination,
Satanic Annihilation;
May e'er find Perambulation,
Through Britannia's Habitation;
Is the humble Supplication,
Most constant Solicitation;
And the fervent Deprecation,
Of my daily Meditation.

Let men of ev'ry Persuasion,
In abject Subordination ;
With sincere Humiliation,
And devoutest Preparation ;
Christian-like Resignation,
And divinest Adoration ;
With a bodily Prostration,
But the Spirit's Exaltation ;
In the public Congregation,
And in private Ejaculation ;
With incessant Application,
And a pious Aspiration ;
A most ardent Cogitation,
Beatific Inspiration ;
The Heart's Examination,
With *Seraphic* Consolation ;
To our Lord's glorification ;
And the Truth's Manifestation ;
Pray for the War's Termination,
The bold Warriors Salvation ;
The poor Widow's Sustentation,
The Orphan's Accommodation ;
The Infidel's Illumination,
For the Gospel's Propagation ;
The whole world's Preservation,
And a lasting Pacification.

NELSON'S VICTORY
A POEM.

WAR seems a Curse to sympathizing Breasts,
And cut-throat Villains seem infernal Pests;
It strikes with Horror every Heart humane,
That human Blood should human Species stain;
That savage Man should Mankind make his Prey,
Destroy whole Nations, and vast Armies slay;
In one hot Battle most remorseless sweep,
A Group of Vessels to the briny Deep;
Ten thousand Spirits at one dire Behest,
Send to the regions of eternal Rest;
This seems ferocious, dreadful, cruel, base,
To make such Havock 'mongst the living Race;
But far from blaming the Decrees of Fate,
All's for the best in this uncertain State;
The Ways of Heaven (tho' now conceal'd in Night,)
Are strictly just, and consequently right;
But Man's short sighted, has a narrow View,
He seeks for Truth, not finding what is true;
And Hist'ries read, both sacred and prophane,
Evince War was—and is—and may remain;
It therefore follows, let us rest content,
With what is fix'd and what we can't prevent;
But what's the Cause? (the Querist here may ask)
I answer, Sir, too hard for me's the Task;
Whate'er's the Cause, th' Effect we plainly see,
Is Devastation and Calamity;
Hush! Causes and Effects are not my Theme,
My Muse displays a most victorious Scene;
I sing brave *Nelson* in this humble Page,
The greatest Warrior of the present Age;
The bravest Seaman Neptune e'er could boast,
In trackless Ocean, or extended Coast;

Behold the *Hero* of great *Egypt's Nile!*
The Scourge of France, the Glory of this *Isle;*
Let every Briton celebrate his Fame,
Extol his Merit—and revere his Name;
Proud Europe's Quarter of the spacious World,
Without his Aid had been in Ruin hurl'd;
Intrepid Valour doth his Soul inspire,
His naval Conquests ev'ry Seaman fire;
By vast Exertions, see, th' advent'rous Man,
Begin, continue, and complete his Plan;
Superior Stations, Numbers, Guns and Might,
Confess his Prowess, turn to shameful Flight
To naval Tactics, (that admired Art,)
He dedicates his Head, his Hand, his Heart;
No human Efforts can his Courage stain,
He fights through Bloodshed, and through Wrecks of slain;
Thro' roaring Oceans—midst tremendous Balls;
Where Groans re-echo, and a Squadron falls;
Where bolts of Thunder are incessant hurl'd,
Where dire Destruction sinks the *Gallic* World
The Sea enrag'd, with open Jaws of Death,
Unglutted gapes, and stops the En'mies' breath;
They're swept unpitied to the briny Urn,
(France feels the Shock, and all her Tyrants mourn;)
Where Foes, sworn Foes, and baneful Rancour cease,
Where e'en *Banditti* sleep in lasting Peace;
Where Heroes perish, and where Cowards lie,
Where Wars shall cease—where jarring Contests die.
  Who could subdue these Plagues and Pests of Mars,
But gallant *Nelson* and his *British Tars?*
No earthly Pow'r can such brave Vet'rans stand,
They rule the World by their all-conquering Hand;
And future Ages shall with Pleasure tell,
How *Nelson* fought! how Frenchmen fled and fell.
  Now Baron *Nelson*, wears the Victor's bays,
And every Tongue shouts joyful Cheers of Praise;
To save his Country—to preserve his Land,
He swam in blood, and lost his martial Hand.
He's full of Bruises, Sutures, Wounds and Scars,
The honour'd Emblems of Britannia's Wars;
No prox'y'd Coward, he fronts the Battles' Fire,
He'll sink, or swim, he'll conquer, or expire:

A Man so great, so brave, so bold, so true,
Demands our Praise—and public Thanks are due ;
Here Language fails in panegyric Verse,
His matchless Deeds in Numbers to rehearse ;
Here Genius fails and Words I cannot raise,
In ample Terms to equalize his Praise ;
Live *Nelson* live, an Honour to thy Cause,
A firm Protector of our Lives and Laws ;
Thy grand Atchievements fill the World with Fame,
Resound thy Worth—immortalize thy Name !
 In just Return for Battles fought and won,
Our gracious King rewards this gallant Son ;
Rewards his Offspring with Escutcheons grand
The royal Favor of his sovereign Hand :
Brave *Nelson's* Ensign, Coat of Arms shall be,
An *Argent Chief*, thereon the Waves of Sea ;
From which a *Palm Tree* shall appear in Sight,
Between a *Ship* disabled on the *right ;*
And on the *left* a ruin'd *Batt'ry* be,
All proper plac'd by Laws of Heraldry ;
Then for his Crest, on *Naval Crown* shall stand,
The *Plume* of *Triumph*, from the SIGNIOR's Hand ;
While this grand MOTTO shall his Name preserve,
" Let him wear PALMS—who doth the PALM deserve,"
Supporters true, a *Sailor* on the *right*,
And on the *left* a *Lion* fill'd with Might ;
A *palm Branch* fix'd in the *Sailor's* Hand,
A *palm Branch* in the *Lion's Paw* shall stand ;
A *Flag tri-colour'd* and a *Staff* shall be,
Plac'd in the *Lion's Mouth* with Dignity :
Thus *Baron Nelson* and his *Sons* shall shine,
In Herald's Office to the End of Time ;
And in Addition to the Stile of PEER,
A Pension neat *Three Thousand Pounds* a Year :
That Merit, still, should meet a Recompence,
Is moral Justice—and is common Sense :
Long may he live the Seaman's noble Toast,
Old ENGLAND's Chief—the *British* gallant Boast ;
Long may his Name the World's Expanse pervade,
Our great Deliv'rer—Safeguard of our Trade :
Long may he see his Country, Friends, and Wealth,
Enjoy his Sons, his honour, Peace and Health ;

Long may he soar as high as Fame can rise,
Beneath the Verge of pure celestial Skies;
So far as mortal Worth can shine and blaze,
So far may *Nelson* have the public Praise;
Nay, what is more, may he contented live,
Enjoy each Blessing that this World can give;
And when he quits this Scene of War and Strife,
Enjoy a Crown—enjoy eternal Life:
Remov'd from Egypt's coast, to Canaan's Shore,
And reign in peaceful Bliss for evermore.

→ SUBSCRIBERS. ←

SETTLE.
Mr. Peart
,, Horner, 2 Copies
,, Fate
,, W. Birkbeck, Jr.
,, J. Birkbeck, Jr.
,, N. Birkbeck
,, E. Birkbeck
Mrs. W. Birkbeck
,, Parker, Marsh Field
Miss A. Birkbeck
,, Lawson
Mr. Aggs
,, Moffat
,, Sutcliff, 2 Copies
,, Hartley
,, Salmon
,, Carr
,, Hall, Y. W. R. Y. C.
,, Oldfield
,, Redmayne
,, Robinson
,, Tristram
,, Calvert
,, Thornber
,, Overend
,, Hampston
,, Wilman
,, Holgate
,, Windsor
,, Ellison
,, Hunter
,, Dale
,, Waddington
,, Dodds
,, Duckit
,, Preston
,, Wilson
,, Halpike
,, Whittam
,, Greenwood
,, Hardacre
Mrs. Foster

Mrs. Williams
,, Harger
Miss Addison
,, Slinger
,, Harrison

GIGLESWICK.
Revd. N. Wood
Revd. O. Clayton
Revd. T. Paley
A. Lister, Esq. 2 Copies
Mr. J. Holden
,, A. Taylor
,, Shires
,, Hardacre
,, T. Wilkinson
,, P. Hargraves
,, S. Wilkinson
,, Slinger
Mrs. Hargraves
Mr. J. Smith
Revd. J. Melissent, M.A.
Mr. F. Thornton
,, J. Kidd
Miss E. Paley, Jr.
,, Settle
Mr. J. Kendal
,, J. Steel
,, Brayshaw
,, Waller, W. R. Y. C.
,, F. Bolland
,, Howson
,, Kirkley, W. R. Y. C.
,, Brennand
,, Hutton
Miss E. Barrow
Mr. I. Gifford
J. Foster, Esq. 3 Copies

STACKHOUSE.
Mr. Carr, 2 Copies
,, J. Carr
,, Lund

LANGCLIFFE.

Mr. Clayton, 2 Copies
,, I. Wolfenden
,, J. Wolfenden
T. Paley, Esq.
Capt. G. Paley
Mrs. Starkie
Mr. J. Slater
,, W. Slater

STAINFORTH.

Mr. J. Bradley
,, Jackman
,, Winder
,, Walker
,, Foster
Miss Foster
,, E. Preston
Mr. Brown
,, Pearson
,, Minto
Miss Stackhouse
Mr. Stackhouse
,, Iveson
,, Hey
,, Bickerstaff
,, Scott
,, Bateson

HORTON.

Revd. G. Holden, L.L.D.
Mr. Hesleden
,, Howson
,, Jackson
,, Metcalfe
,, Wilson
Miss Moor
,, E. Moor
Mr. Carr
,, Bolland
,, Germain
Miss Wilson
Mr. Proctor
Mrs. Metcalfe
Mr. Shepherd
,, T. Shepherd
,, Green
Miss Lister
Mr. Lister
,, Germain
,, Germain

Mr. Mitton
,, Morphet
Miss Foster
Mr. Redmayne
,, Burton
,, Baxter
,, Jackson
,, T. Carr
Miss Mallison, Hornby
J. Marsden, Esq.
G. Wright, Esq.
Mrs. Wright
Mr. Proctor
,, Cook
,, Wilson
,, Thompson
,, Kilshaw
,, Townson
,, Wildman
,, Williamson
,, Wright
,, Marshal
,, Layfield
Miss Coulston
,, Lambert
,, Clapham
Mr. Robinson
,, Abbotson
,, Rutherford
,, Kirkham
,, Warbrick
,, Coultherd
,, Kitson
Miss Bracken
Mr. Sawrey
Revd. J. Worswick
Revd. M. R. Hall
Miss Croft
Mr. Foster

LANCASTER.

Mr. Charnley
Revd. I. Widditt
Mr. J. Atkinson
,, R. Bagott
Revd. R. Bowstead
J. Moore, Esq. Mayor
Revd. J. Rowley
Mr. Rolinson
,, W. Swainson
,, A. Shepherd

Mr. T. Addison
,, J. Addison, Sr.
,, T. Burrow
,, H. Walmsley
,, P. Bell
,, B. Dawson
,, W. Dalrimple
,, J. Fearenside
Capt. T. Kidd
Mr. W. Kitson
,, G. Little
,, Mashiter, 2 Copies
,, J. Overend
,, R. Swainson
,, H. Walker
,, W. White
Miss Williams
Mr. J. Welsh, Jr.
,, T. Woods
,, Dowbiggin
,, Baldwin
J. Bradshaw, Esq.

ULVERSTON.

Mr. Burton, 2 Copies
,, Thompson
,, W. Jackson
,, Witterage
,, Butcher
,, Sands
,, Ingleby
J. Yarker, Esq. 3 Copies
Mr. Dickinson
J. Harrison, Esq.
Revd. J. Burns
Mr. R. Parker

CARTMEL.

Mr. W. Field
,, R. Buttle
,, E. Barrow, Alithwaite
,, Toulmin, Flookburgh
,, Bryers,   Ditto
,, J. Butler,   Ditto
,, Carter, Carter House
Revd. R. Fell, Flookburgh
Mr. Gibson,   Ditto
,, Galfert, Cark
,, R. Harrison, Ditto

Mr. Jackson, Flookburgh
,, B. Jopson, Ditto
,, T. Kellet, Ditto
,, Raby,   Ditto
,, J. Troughton, Ditto
,, J. Bailiff, Ditto
,, J. Taylor, Ditto
Revd. Mr. Taylor, Bolton
Mr. J. Statter,   Ditto
,, R. Whitehead, Slyne
,, I. Mosan, Kellet
,, Jenkinson, Bolton
W. Buyshop, Esq. Ditto
Mr. Overen
,, J. Asquith, W. R. Y. C.
,, J. Asquith, Sr. Steeton
,, J. Asquith, Jr. Ditto
,, J. Hartley
,, J. Meeber
,, Mount
,, Wilkinson, Winterburn
,, Preston, Hanleth
,, Tattersall, Blackburn
,, Dixon, Sutton
,, Preston, Hanleth
,, Wrathall, W. R. Y. C.
,, J. Hartley, Settle
,, Preston, Paley Green
,, Wilkinson, Otley
,, Redmayne, Blackburn
,, Ellershaw, Tunstall
,, H. Wood, Gildersleets
,, W. F. Paley, Leeds
,, J. Holdsworth
Miss Waddilove, Rilston
,, Howson, Studfield
,, French,   Ditto
,, Morphet, Ditto
Mrs. Brown
,, Rimington, Scosthorp
Miss Preston, Ditto
Mr. R. Brown, Thornton
,, W. Cookson, Holy Plat
,, J. Wilson, Ditto
,, J. Faraday, Ditto
,, C. Wilson, Ditto
,, A. Thompson, Ditto
,, C. Johnson, Ditto
,, J. Redmayne, Ditto

The above Subscribers are inserted, simply as they came to hand, upwards of 1000 *more we acknowledge, which our Limits prevent Inserting.*

Parliamentary Electors

OF THE

PARISH OF GIGGLESWICK,

A.D. 1708 - 1849.

COMPILED BY THOS. BRAYSHAW.

* * * * * * *

STACKHOUSE,

NEAR SETTLE,

July, 1886.

Just now political matters occupy a large share of our time and attention, and for this reason I thought that lists of the voters in the various Townships comprising the ancient Parish of Giggleswick, shewing which candidates they supported, might be of some little interest. I therefore give lists of the electors in this parish at those contests which have taken place in the last and present centuries, up to the time of the Ballot Act coming into force, for which I can find the Poll-Books.

It is, of course, impossible to say for what candidates the "free and independent" electors have cast their suffrages since the method of voting was changed.

I am indebted to the Rev. CANON RAINE, of York, for courteously supplying me with the list for 1708, the M.S.S. Poll-Book for that election being in his possession.

THOS. BRAYSHAW.

Twelve large and one hundred small paper copies printed for private circulation.

VOTERS IN THE PARISH OF GIGGLESWICK.

At the commencement of the eighteenth century the County of York was an undivided constituency, being represented in the Imperial Parliament by two Knights of the Shire.

The first contested election for the County during that Century was in 1705, Sir John Kaye, the Marquis of Hartington, and Thomas Wentworth being the candidates. Mr. Wentworth, however, finding his candidature hopeless ,withdrew from the contest.

In 1708 another contested election took place, the candidates being Lord Viscount Downe, Sir William Strickland, Bart., Colonel D'Arcy, Sir Arthur Kaye, Bart., and Mr. Wentworth.

After a contest lasting four days, the result of the poll was that Viscount Downe and Sir W. Strickland were elected. The numbers polled were—

DOWNE	4737
STRICKLAND	3452
D'ARCY	3257
KAYE	3139
WENTWORTH	958

The following list shews who were the electors from this Parish who journeyed to York on this occasion, and how they voted.

	Downe	Strickland	D'Avy	Kaye	Wentworth

SETTLE.

	Downe	Strickland	D'Avy	Kaye	Wentworth
Bolland, Leonard				1	1
Baley, Thos.				1	
Carr, Thos.				1	1
Richardson, Miles				1	1
Rawson, Peter			1		
Wainwright. Joseph				1	

GIGGLESWICK.

	Downe	Strickland	D'Avy	Kaye	Wentworth
Ellershaw, Richard				1	1
Gill, Henry				1	1
Lawson, Thos.					1
Wetherell, Mathias				1	1
Whitehead William			1		

RATHMELL.

	Downe	Strickland	D'Avy	Kaye	Wentworth
Naylor, Anthony				1	

LANGCLIFFE.

	Downe	Strickland	D'Avy	Kaye	Wentworth
Clarke, Joseph			1		
Lawson, Richard		1			
Richardson, John		1		1	

STAINFORTH.

	Downe	Strickland	D'Avy	Kaye	Wentworth
Benson, John			1		1
Ellis, John				1	
Elwick, John, Gent.		1			
Kelham, Thos.		1			
Mallison, John		1	1		1
Newsom, Robert		1	1		
Pashley, Geo.					1
Rogers, John			1		
Reeder, Robert		1		1	

The next contested election for the County was in 1727, on the occasion of the death of Sir Arthur Kaye. The result was that Mr. Cholmondeley Turner defeated Sir John Kaye.

In 1734 Sir Miles Stapylton and Mr. Cholmondeley Turner were the successful, and Sir Rowland Winn and the Hon. Ed. Wortley Montague the unsuccessful candidates, the poll at this election lasting six days.

Of these two last elections I am sorry to say I cannot succeed in finding any copies of the Poll-Book.

In the year 1740 Sir Miles Stapylton and Lord Morpeth were returned without opposition. In consequence of the death of Lord Morpeth a contested election took place in December, 1741, the candidates being Cholmondeley Turner, Esq., and George Fox, Esq. The poll was open eight days, and the result was as follows—

CHOLMONDELEY TURNER 8003

GEORGE FOX 6949

The polling took place at York, and the Freeholders of this Parish who exercised their electoral privileges on that occasion were the following—

Supporters of Mr. Fox, with their places of Freehold—

GIGGLESWICK.
Bolland, Robert, Bolton
Carr, Richard, Rathmell
Clapham, Thomas, Horton-in-Ribblesdale
Morley, Josias, Rathmell
Taylor, William
Rawson, Tho.
Warkinson, Mathew, Langcliff and Rathmell
Banks, William, Rathmell
Knowles, Mathew, Malham Moor

KNIGHT STAINFORTH.
Armistead, John
Hargrave, John

LODGE, BY SETTLE.
Greenbank, John, Dent
Armistead, Roger

RATHMELL.
Atkinson, Robert
Brown, John
Clarke, Thomas
Dobson, Robert
Dugdale, John
Houghton, John
Jackson, Thomas
Knowles, Richard

Settle, John
Settle, Thomas

SETTLE.
Armistead, James
Armistead, Robert
Carr, Allen
Carr, Robert
Clapham, Christo., Horton-in-Ribblesdale
Dale, William
Hall, Hugh
Hall, John, Little Settle
Hall, William
Hammond, Edmond, Helwick Bridge
Higgins, Christopher, Barnoldswick
Maud, Edward
Peart, William, Horton
Peart, William, sen.
Preston, Howard, Dipdale
Procter, John, Rathmell
Richardson, John
Roberts, Robert, Langcliffe
Sigsworth, James
Town, Henry
Twisleton, Thomas
Windsor, John

WINSKILL.
Stackhouse, Christo.

Supporters of Mr. Turner with their places of Freehold.

GIGGLESWICK.

Weatherhead, Mathias

LANGCLIFFE.

Andrews, Nathaniel, Barnsley
Andrews, William
Vellans, Samuel
Whittel, Benj., Drax & Longcliffe

RATHMELL.

Marley, John
Moore, Paul
Moor, Samuel
North, John
Sedgwick, Leonard
Todd, Francis, Wakefield
Wrigglesworth, Tho.

SETTLE.

Binns, John
Tatham, Robert, Kt. Stainford
Ward, Roger, North Coates

STAINFORTH.

Aaron, Robert
Marsden, John, Wath
Painthorpe, Richard

STOCKDALE.

Thompson, William

WIGGLESWORTH.

Broadley, Richard
Leach, John, Tosset
Midleborough, Christ., Paythorn
Smith, Edward
Smith, Stephen
Smith William

This shews that whilst 46 Freeholders of the Parish supported Mr. Fox, only 25 recorded their votes in favor of Mr. Turner.

From 1741 to 1807 the constituency was not contested, but in the latter year there was fought one of the most celebrated contests in the history of electioneering, the candidates being William Wilberforce, Esq., Lord Milton, and the Hon. Henry Lascelles, afterwards Earl of Harewood. The real struggle was between Milton, the Whig candidate, and Lascelles, the Tory one, for Wilberforce was an old servant in whose election both parties concurred. The poll was open for fifteen days, the County being in a state of violent agitation the whole time, party spirit was wound up to the highest pitch by the friends of the two noble families, and everything was done that money or personal exertion could accomplish. The result of the poll was as follows—

  WILBERFORCE (Tory) ... 11806
  MILTON (Whig) ... 11177
  LASCELLES (Tory) 10989

This election is said to have cost the three candidates not less than half a million of money! A lovely contrast to these days of "Corrupt Practices Acts." The voters from this Parish who polled at York on this occasion were as follows—

SETTLE.

Name and Description. Freehold.	Wilberforce	Lascelles	Milton
Adamthwaite, William, Clerk, Sedbergh	1	1	
Birkbeck, John, Esq.	1		
Birkbeck, William, Esq.	1		1
Bolland, William, Esq., Kettlewell	1	1	
Bowskill, John, Butcher, Langcliffe		1	
Bowskill, William, Yeoman, Langcliffe		1	
Bowskill, Wm., Whitesmith		1	1
Brennand, Robt., Cottonspinner, Gisburn		1	
Buck, William, Yeoman	1	1	
Ellison, James, Farmer		1	
Houlden, Thomas, Farmer, Gisburn Forest	1	1	
Herd James, Husbandman	1	1	
Harger, Richard, Glazier, Horton	1		1
Holdgate, William, Tallow Chandler	1		1
Marsden, Wm., Saddler			1
Preston, Richard, Glazier	1		
Procter, Thomas, Farmer	1		1
Procter, Christopher, Farmer, Merebeck	1		1
Peart, John, Gent.	1		
Parkinson, Edw., Cordwainer			1
Ralph, John, Cooper, Langcliffe		1	
Salmon, Henry, Papermaker, Langcliffe	1	1	
Swale, David, Esq., Hebden			1
Town, William, Yeoman, Langcliffe		1	
Tristram, Henry, Gent.	1	1	
Thornber, James, Cottonmanufacturer		1	
Wilson, Thos., Ironmonger	1	1	
Wilman, John, Yeoman	1	1	

GIGGLESWICK.

	Wilberforce	Lascelles	Milton
Clapham, Wm., Esq.	1	1	
Clapham, John, Clerk	1	1	
Dawson, Stephen, Farmer, Rathmell	1	1	
Hardaker, Alexander, Farmer	1	1	
Ingram, Rowland, Clerk, North Cave	1	1	
Kidd, John, Cordwainer, Lawkland	1	1	
Lund, John, Gent., Malham	1	1	
Lister, Anthony, Esq.	1	1	
Maudsley, Thomas, Farmer	1	1	

GIGGLESWICK (Continued.)

Name and Description.   *Freehold.*

	Wilberforce	Lascelles	Milton
Procter, William, Farmer	1	1	
Wood, Henry, Farmer	1	1	
Wildman, Wm., Farmer	1	1	

RATHMELL.

	Wilberforce	Lascelles	Milton
Brown, Anthony, Farmer		1	
Buck, Thomas, Farmer, Wigglesworth		1	
Butler, Henry, Farmer		1	
Clark, Henry, Farmer		1	
Geldart, John, Gent.	1	1	
Geldart, Robert, Farmer		1	
Knowles, Thomas, Farmer		1	
Kendall, William, Yeoman		1	
Tomlinson, John, Weaver		1	

STAINFORTH.

	Wilberforce	Lascelles	Milton
Armistead, John, Farmer, Halton Gill		1	
Brown, Christopher, Farmer, Langcliffe	1	1	
Foster, William, Farmer, Horton	1	1	
Hey, Thomas, Farmer	1	1	
Stackhouse, Thomas, Farmer, Langcliffe	1	1	
Stackhouse, John, Farmer	1	1	
Shepherd, Robert, Farmer, Dent	1	1	

LANGCLIFFE.

	Wilberforce	Lascelles	Milton
Hill, Robert, Farmer			1
Howson, Francis, Farmer, Horton	1	1	
Jackman, Mathew, Slater		1	

At the elections in 1812, 1818, and 1820, there were no contests, the seats being held by a nominee of each of the two great political parties.

In 1826, for the first time, four Knights of the Shire were elected at York. Five candidates were nominated, but one of them withdrew previous to the election. As there was no contest the expenses of the four successful candidates (two Whig and two Tory) only amounted to the trifling sum of £150,000!

In 1830 the accession of King William IV. caused a general election. The Whig candidates were Lord Morpeth and Henry Brougham (who afterwards became the celebrated Lord Chancellor). The Tory candidates were the Hon. W. Duncombe and Richard Bethell, and a Mr. Stapylton was an independent candidate, proposed by himself. Mr. Brougham's seconder on this occasion was Mr. William Birkbeck of Settle.

The poll was only open two days when it became evident that the contest was a farce, the numbers polled being—

MORPETH	1464
BROUGHAM	1295
DUNCOMBE	1123
BETHELL	1064
STAPYLTON	94

So the High Sheriff peremptorily closed the poll without any objection being raised.

As no poll-list was issued, I am unable to say how the freeholders of this parish voted on this occasion.

In November, 1830, Mr. Brougham's elevation to the woolsack caused a vacancy, and a contest commenced between Sir John Johnstone and George Strickland, Esq. At two o'clock, however, Mr. Strickland retired, the state of the poll being—

JOHNSTONE	361
STRICKLAND	104

By the Reform Act of 1832, the representation of the County was divided, two members being allotted to the West Riding. The two Liberal candidates, Lord Morpeth and George Strickland being returned unopposed.

In May, 1835, Lord Morpeth was appointed Chief Secretary for Ireland, which necessitated his seeking re-election.

His seat was contested by the Hon. J. S. Wortley, on behalf of the Conservatives, the result of the poll being—

MORPETH 9066
WORTLEY 6259

The qualified electors of this Parish on this occasion were the following, but it will be seen that some of them did not vote.

SETTLE.

Names of Electors. Residence.	Morpeth	Wortley
Armistead, Richard, Settle	1	
Atkinson, Robert, Settle	1	
Birkbeck, William, Settle	1	
Birkbeck, Henry, Kiswick Hall, Norfolk		
Birkbeck, John, Anley House	1	
Bilton, William, Settle...	1	
Bolland, William, Settle		1
Bamford, Walker Robert, Sherburn House		1
Calvert, William, Settle		
Charnley, Thomas Armistead, Lancaster		
Dawson, Pudsey, Marshfield		
Duckett, Charles, Settle	1	
Ellison, James, jun., Settle	1	
Hallpike, Vincent, Settle		
Harger, Eli, Settle	1	
Harger, Joseph, Settle...	1	
Harger, Robert, Settle...	1	
Harger, William, Settle		1
Hargreaves, Stephen, Stockdale...		1
Hartley, John, Settle ..		
Hutchinson, John, Settle	1	
Holroyd, John, Giggleswick	1	
Ibbotson, Robert, Settle	1	
Marsden, William, Settle	1	
Moffat, John, Settle	1	
Nixon, Thomas, Settle...		
Oldfield, Samuel, Cleatop	1	
Parkinson, Edward, Settle	1	
Parker, Stephen, Lodge	1	
Preston, John, Mearbeck	1	
Procter, Richard, Clerk, Laxton	1	
Procter, Robert, Mearbeck		
Procter, Thomas, Settle		
Read, John, Settle,	1	
Redmayne, Mathew, Langcliffe ...		
Stackhouse, Anthony, Settle		1

SETTLE (Continued.)

Names of Electors.   Residence.

Shepherd, Richard, Settle ...
Snell, Henry, Settle ... ...
Silverwood, James, Settle ...
Tatham, John, Settle ... ...
Thornber, John, Runley Bridge
Turner, William, Settle ...
Waddington, John, Settle ...
Whittam, Mathew, Settle ...
Wildman, Mathias, Settle ...
Wilkinson, John, Settle ...
Wilman, John, Settle ... ...
Wilman, Stephen, Settle ...

GIGGLESWICK.

Clapham, Rev. John, Giggleswick
Clapham, Thomas, Giggleswick
Clapham, John, Settle ... ...
Carr, Richard, Stackhouse ...
Clark, Thomas, Giggleswick ...
Dale, David Hall, Paley Green...
Garstang, Robert, Giggleswick ...
Howson, Rev. John, Giggleswick
Hartley, John, Catteral Hall ...
Ingram, Rev. Rowland, Giggleswick
Leech, William, Swabeck ...
Maudsley, Thomas, Grain House
Maudsley, John, Grain House ...
Maudsley, Henry, Rome ...
Procter, William, Close House ...
Parker, Cuthbert, Giggleswick ...
Robinson, William, Giggleswick
Smith, Elias, Giggleswick ...
Tatham, John, jun. Settle ...
Tatham, Thomas, Settle ...
Wildman, William, Close House
Wildman, Christopher, Roustroth
Wildman, William, Giggleswick

RATHMELL.

Burrow, Thomas Dixon, Settle ...
Clark, Henry, Rathmell ...
Clark, John, Sheepwash ...
Dawson, Stephen, Gildersleets ...
Dawson, John, Bank ... ...
Geldard, John, Cappleside ...

RATHMELL (Continued.)

Names of Electors.   Residence.

Geldard, Robert, Rathmell
Hays, Thomas, Cappleside
Knowles, Richard, Hesley Lane
Kendall, William, Low Folds
Kendall, William, New Hall
Newhouse, Edward, Halton, late of Sheepwash
Towler, George, Holling Hall
Towler, Joseph, Holling Hall
Tomlinson, John, Hensley Hill...
Wolfenden, George, Rathmell
Wolfenden, Robert, Crosskeys

STAINFORTH.

Armistead, John, Stainforth Hall
Armistead, Richard, Sannat Hall
Batty, John, Stainforth
Brotherton, John, Stainforth
Brown, Christopher, Stainforth
Brown, Thomas, Stainforth
Holgate, Thomas, Neals Ing
Hudson, Miles, Stainforth
Iveson, James, Hidon...
Metcalfe, John, Stainforth
Parker, Thomas, Sherwood House
Redmayne, Marmaduke, Stainforth
Redmayne, Thomas, Stainforth
Sedgwick, Charles, Sherwood House
Stackhouse, Anthony, Stainforth

LANGCLIFFE.

Clayton, William, Langcliffe Place
Constantine, John, Cowside
Hill, Robert, Langcliffe
Holden, Richard, Winskill
Jackman, Jonathan, Langcliffe ...
King, William, Langcliffe
Kitchin, William, Westside House
Lofthouse, Mathew, Langcliffe...
Maudsley, Joshua, Winskill
Robinson, John, Langcliffe
Wright, Christopher, Langcliffe
Yeadon, Thomas, Langcliffe
Yeadon, James, Langcliffe

In 1837 a general election took place, Mr. Wortley again endeavoured, without success, to wrest one of the seats from the Liberals.

The declaration of the poll shewed the result to be—

MORPETH 12576

STRICKLAND 11892

WORTLEY 11489

The local electors were as follows—

SETTLE.

Name and Residence.	Morpeth	Strickland	Wortley
Armistead, Rd., Settle	1	1	
Atkinson, Robert, Settle	1	1	
Birkbeck, Wm., Settle	1	1	
Birkbeck, H., Kiswick Hall, Norfolk	1	1	
Birkbeck, John, Anley House	1	1	
Birkbeck, Thos., Settle	1	1	
Bilton, Wm., Settle	1	1	
Bolland, Wm., Settle			1
Bamford, W. R., Sherburn House			1
Bowskill, John, Settle			
Bowskill, Wm., Settle			1
Bullock, John, Settle	1	1	
Calvert, Wm., Settle			
Charnley, Thos., A., Lancaster			
Dawson, Pudsey, Marshfield			1
Dawson, Fred, London			
Dawson, Henry, Hopton, Norfolk			
Duckett, Charles, Settle	1	1	
Duckett, Charles, Mearbeck	1	1	
Edmondson, Chris., Settle			
Ellison, James, jun., Settle	1	1	
Ellis, Francis, Settle	1	1	
Ellison, James, Settle			
Ellison, Thomas, Settle	1	1	
Foster, John, Walthamstow			
Foster, Thomas, E., Gargrave			1
Hallpike, Vincent, Settle			
Harger, Eli, Settle	1	1	
Harger, Joseph, Settle	1	1	
Harger, Robert, Settle	1	1	
Harger, Wm., Settle			1
Hargreaves, Stephen, Stockdale			1

SETTLE.

Name and Residence.

Hartley, John, Settle...
Hardacre, William, Settle
Harrison, John, Settle
Heseltine, Francis, Kilnsay
Holroyd, John, Settle
Hutchinson, John, Settle
Hurtley, Thos., Settle
Lawson, Robert, Thorns, Sedbergh
Marsden, Wm., Settle
Moffat, John, Settle ...
Moore, John, Bolton-le-moors
Nixon, Thomas, Settle
Oldfield, Samuel, Cleatop
Parker, Stephen, Lodge
Parkinson, Edward, Settle
Prest, Wm., Blackburn
Preston, John, Mearbeck
Procter, John, Settle...
Procter, Richard, Laxton
Procter, Robert, near Gargrave
Procter, Thomas, Settle
Ralph, Luke, Settle ...
Ratcliffe, Charles, Settle
Read, John, Settle
Redmayne, Mathew, Langcliffe
Sagar, Edward, Alston Hall
Stackhouse, Anthony, Settle
Snell, Henry, Settle ...
Silverwood, James, Settle
Spencer, Henry, Settle
Tatham, John, Settle
Thornber, John, Runley Bridge
Turner, Wm., Settle...
Waddington, John, Settle
Whittam, Mathew, Settle
Wildman, Mathias, Settle
Wilkinson, John, Settle
Wilman, John, Settle
Wilman, Stephen, Settle
Windsor, John, Manchester

GIGGLESWICK.

Beckwith, John Batty, Wham
Brayshaw, Thos., Giggleswick
Clapham, Rev. John, Giggleswick

GIGGLESWICK (Continued.)

Name and Residence.

Clapham, Thos., Stackhouse
Clapham, John, Settle
Carr, Wm., Giggleswick
Carr, Richard, Stackhouse
Clark, Thos., Giggleswick
Dale, David Hall, Paley Green
Dixon, John, Giggleswick
Fell, John, Crawridge
Garstang, Robert, Giggleswick
Green, Thos., Lum
Howson, Rev. John, Giggleswick
Hartley, John, Catteral Hall
Ingham, Rev. Rowland, Giggleswick
Leech, Wm., Swabeck
Lawson, Thos., Stackhouse
Maudsley, Thos., Grain House
Maudsley, John, Grain House
Maudsley, Joshua, Little Bank
Maudsley, Thos., jun., Rome
Newsholme, Geo., Wham
Procter, Wm., Close House
Parker, Cuthbert, Giggleswick
Preston, Samuel, Stackhouse
Parker, John, Rome
Robinson, Wm., Giggleswick
Smith, Elias, Giggleswiick
Tatham, John, jun., Settle
Tatham, Thos., Settle
Taylor, John, near Clitheroe, Lancashire
Twisleton, James, Settle
Towler, George, Sandford Brow
Wildman, Wm., Close House
Wildman, Wm., Giggleswick
Wildman, Chris., Routsworth
Waller, John, jun., Giggleswick

RATHMELL.

Armistead, John, Ragged Hall
Armistead, Wm., Tatham
Ayrton, Wm., near Malham
Burrow, Thos. Dixon, Settle
Brown, Ralph Horner, Rathmell
Butler, Henry, Winterskill Bank
Clark, Henry, Rathmell

RATHMELL (Continued.)

Name and Residence.

Dawson, Stephen, Gildersleets
Dawson, John, Gildersleets
Geldard, John, Cappleside
Geldard, Robt., Rathmell
Holden, Thomas, Rathmell
Hayes, Thos., Cappleside
Kendall. William, Lowfoulds
Kendall, Wm., New Hall
Knowles, R., Horton-in-Ribblesdale
Newhouse, Edward, Halton
Newhouse, John, Hesley Lane
Parker, Thos., Lower Winterskill Bank
Parker, Joseph, Lawkland
Redmayne, Wm., Rathmell
Robinson, John, Green
Standing, Wm., Hesley Lane
Standing, Wm., jun., Laddy Green
Tomlinson, John, Hensley Hill
Towler, George, Hollin Hall
Towler, Joseph, Hollin Hall
Taylor, James, Hesley Lane
Taylor, Jon, Huggon House
Tatham, Thos., Settle
Wolfenden, Geo., Hollin Hall
Wolfenden, Robert, Cross Keys

STAINFORTH.

Armistead, John, Stainforth Hall
Armistead, Rd., Sannat Hall
Batty, John, Stainforth
Brotherton, John, Stainforth
Brown, Chris., Stainforth
Brown, Thos., Stainforth
Foster, Thos., Stainforth
Hudson, Miles, Stainforth
Iveson, James, Hidon
Metcalfe, John, Stainforth
Metcalfe, Wm., Stainforth
Parker, Thos., Sherwood House
Redmayne, Marm., Stainforth
Redmayne, Thos., Taitlands
Redmayne, Thos., Taitlands
Sedgwick, Charles, Sherwood House
Stackhouse, Anthony, Stainforth
Wildman, Stephen, Stainforth
Winder, Thos., Stainforth
Witts, Fras. Edward, Gloucestershire

LANGCLIFFE.

Name and Residence.	Morpeth	Strickland	Wortley
Clayton, William, Langcliffe Place		1	1
Hill, Robert, Langcliffe		1	1
Holden, Richard, Winskill			1
Hunter, Thos., Cowside		1	1
Jackman, Jon., Langcliffe		1	1
Jackman, Mathew, Langcliffe			1
King, William, Langcliffe			1
Kitchin, Wm., West Side House			
Lofthouse, Mathew, Langcliffe		1	1
Madgsley, Joshua, Winskill		1	1
Robinson, John, Langcliffe			1
Salmon, Henry, Melburn, Kent			
Wright, Chris., Langcliffe		1	1
Yeadon, Thos., Langcliffe		1	1
Yeadon, James, Langcliffe		1	

At the General Election in 1841, the efforts of the Conservatives were at length rewarded with success, their two candidates, the Hon. J. S. Wortley and Mr. Denison, being returned at the head of the poll. The numbers were—

HON. J. S. WORTLEY (Con.) ... 13165
EDM. B. DENISON (Con.) ... 12780
Lord MILTON (Lib.) ... 12080
LORD MORPETH (Lib.) ... 12031

The following list shews how the local voters distributed their favors—

SETTLE.

Names of Electors. Residence.	Wortley	Denison	Milton	Morpeth
Armistead, Richard, Settle			1	1
Atkinson, Robert, Settle			1	1
Ayrton, Henry, Settle			1	1
Birkbeck, Henry, Kiswick Hall, Norfolk				
Birkbeck, John, Anley House			1	1
Birkbeck, Wm. Lloyd, Southampton Buildings, London			1	1
Birkbeck, Thomas			1	1
Birkbeck, John, jun., Anley House			1	1
Bilton, William, Settle			1	1
Bowskill, William, Settle	1	1		

SETTLE (Continued.)

Names of Electors. Residence.

	Wortley	Denison	Milton	Morpeth
Bullock, John, Settle			1	1
Bullock, John, Duke Street			1	1
Bentley, Authony, Anley House			1	1
Bentley, Robert, Settle Green			1	1
Calvert, William, Settle				
Charnley, Thomas A., Lancaster				
Charnley, William, Birkby, Lancaster				
Dawson, Pudsey, Marshfield		1	1	
Dawson, Frederick, Pump Court, Temple, London				
Dawson, Henry, Hopton, Norfolkshire				
Duckett, Charles, Settle			1	1
Ellison, James, Upper Settle			1	1
Ellis, Francis, Settle			1	1
Ellis, John, Settle			1	1
Foster, John, Walthamstow		1	1	
Foster, Thomas Edward, Settle				
Foster, Thomas Edward, Settle		1	1	
Gifford, John, Settle		1	1	
Hallpike, Vincent, Settle				
Harger, Eli, Settle				
Harger, Joseph, Settle			1	1
Harger, Robert, Settle			1	1
Harger, William, Settle				
Hargreaves, Stephen, Stockdale		1	1	
Hartley, John, Settle				
Hardacre, William, Settle		1	1	
Harling, Thomas, Settle			1	1
Heseltine, Francis, Elysee, Island of Jersey		1	1	
Higginson, William, Settle				
Holroyd, John, Settle			1	1
Howson, John Saul, Inverary Castle, Argylshire		1	1	
Hutchinson, John, Settle			1	1
Hurtley, Thomas, Settle			1	1
Ingram, Rowland, jun., Giggleswick		1	1	
King, John, Settle			1	1
Lawson, Robert, Chadburn		1	1	
Moffat, John, Settle				
Moore, John, Bolton, Lancashire		1	1	
Nixon, Thomas, Settle				
Oldfield, Samuel, Cleatop		1	1	
Ormrod, Oliver, Yorkshire St., Rochdale			1	1
Parker, Stephen, Lodge				
Parkinson, Edward, Settle			1	1
Preston, John, Mearbeck		1	1	
Preston, Thomas Ellison, Upper Settle			1	1
Procter, Richard, Laxton, Nottinghamshire		1	1	
Procter, Thomas, Settle			1	1

SETTLE (Continued.)

Names of Electors. Residence.

Procter, James, Bedford St., Liverpool
Procter, Robert, Mearbeck
Procter, John, China Lane, Lancaster
Ralph, Luke, Settle
Ratcliffe, Charles, Settle
Read, John, Settle
Redmayne, Mathew, Langcliffe and Stainforth
Stackhouse, Anthony, Settle
Snell, Henry, Settle
Silverwood, James, Settle
Spencer, Anthony, Settle
Spencer, William, Settle Green
Sutcliffe, Henry, Belle Hill, Giggleswick
Tatham, John, Settle
Thornber, John, Runley Bridge
Thomson, James, Settle
Turner, William, Settle
Town, Augustus Francis, Fenton St., London
Waddington, John, Settle
Whittam, Mathew, Upper Settle
Wildman, Mathias, Settle
Wilman, Stephen, Settle
Windsor, John, Piccadilly, Manchester
Wildman, John, Settle
Wildman, James, Settle

GIGGLESWICK.

Brayshaw, Thomas, Giggleswick
Clapham, Thomas, Stackhouse
Clapham, John, Giggleswick...
Carr, Wm., Giggleswick
Carr, Richard, Stackhouse...
Clark, Thomas, Giggleswick
Dale, David Hall, Paley Green
Dixon, John, Giggleswick
Fell, John, Crawridge
Fletcher, John, Wham
Garstang, Robert, Giggleswick
Green, Thomas, Lum
Green, Thomas, Giggleswick
Howson, John, Giggleswick
Hartley, John, Catteral Hall
Ingram, Rowland, Giggle wick
Jackson, John, Settle
Leech, William, Swawbeck
Maudsley, Joshua, Little Bank
Maudsley, Henry, Rome

GIGGLESWICK (Continued.)

Names of Electors. Residence.

Maudsley, Thomas, Stainforth Hall
Moorby, John, Giggleswick...
Metcalfe, John, Austwick ...
Maudsley, John, Grain House
Newsholme, George, Wham
Parker, Cuthbert, Giggleswick
Preston, Samuel, Stackhouse
Parker, Joseph, Rome
Procter, John, jun., Long Preston
Procter, John, Close House
Robinson, William, Giggleswick
Smith, Elias, Giggleswick ...
Tatham, John, jun., Settle...
Tatham, Thomas, Settle
Taylor, John, Twiston, near Clitheroe
Taylor, Thomas, Twiston, near Clitheroe
Taylor, Robert, Twiston, near Clitheroe
Twisleton, James, Settle
Towler, George, Sandford Row
Wildman, Christopher, Routsworth
Waller, John, jun., Giggleswick
Wildman, William, Close House

RATHMELL.

Armistead, William, Robert Hall, Tatham
Armistead, William, Low Bentham...
Ayrton, Stephen, Higher Sheepwash
Armistead, John, Crakemoor
Brown, Ralph Horner, Rathmell
Butler, Henry, Winterskill Bank
Barrow, Thomas Dixon, Settle
Clark, Henry, Rathmell
Charnley, Robert, Far Cappleside
Dawson, Stephen, Gildersleets, Giggleswick...
Dawson, John, Gildersleets, Giggleswick
Geldard, John, Cappleside...
Geldard, Robert, Rathmell
Geldard, Chris. J., Cappleside
Holden, Thomas, Rathmell
Higson, John, Waddington Lane, Clitheroe
Hardacre, Henry, Rathmell
Knowles, Richard, Crag Hill, Ribblesdale
Kendall, William, Lowfoulds
Kendall, William, Lowfoulds
Newhouse, Edward, Aughton, Lancashire
Parker, Joseph, Black Bank, Lawkland
Robinson, John, Green
Standing, William, Hesley Lane
Standing, William, Laddy Green, Wigglesworth

RATHMELL (Continued.)

Names of Electors. Residence.	Wortley	Denison	Milton	Morpeth
Towler, George, Hollin Hall	1			
Towler, Joseph, Hollin Hall	1			
Taylor, James, Hesley Lane			1	1
Tomlinson, John, Rathmell			1	1
Taylor, Jonathan, Huggon House	1	1		
Tatham, Thomas, Settle			1	1
Towler, John, Blackleach			1	1
Wolfenden, Robert, Cross Keys				

STAINFORTH.

Armistead, Richard, Sannat Hall	1	1		
Batty, John, Knight	1	1		
Brotherton, John, Stainforth-under-Bargh			1	1
Brown, Thomas, Stainforth-under-Bargh			1	1
Brown, Christopher, Ludgate Street, London	1	1		
Brown, James Batty, Settle	1	1		
Foster, Thomas, Stainforth-under-Bargh	1	1		
Foster, James, Stainforth-under-Bargh	1	1		
Hudson, Miles, Stainforth-under-Bargh	1	1		
Iveson, James, Hedon, East Riding	1	1		
Johnson, John, Stainforth-under-Bargh			1	1
Metcalfe, William, Stainforth-under-Bargh				
Metcalfe, Christopher, Neals Ing	1	1		
Parker, Thomas, Sherwood House	1	1		
Redmayne, Marmaduke, Stainforth-under-Bargh				
Redmayne, Thomas, Taitlands			1	1
Sedgwick, Charles, Sherwood House	1	1		
Stackhouse, Anthony, Stainforth-under-Bargh	1	1		
Wildman, Stephen, Stainforth-under-Bargh			1	1
Winder, Thomas, Stainforth-under-Bargh			1	1
Witts, Francis Edward, Morton-in-Marsh, Gloucestershire				

LANGCLIFFE.

Clayton, William, Langcliffe Place			1	1
Foster, William, Settle	1	1		
Hill, Robert, Langcliffe			1	1
Holden, Richard, Winskill	1	1		
Hunter, Thomas, Cowside				
Hartley, John, Catteral Hall, Giggleswick				
Jackman, Jonathan, Langcliffe			1	1
Jackman, Mathew, Langcliffe	1	1		
King, William, Langcliffe			1	1
Lofthouse, Mathew, Langcliffe			1	1
Maudsley, Joshua, Winskill				
Pratt, James, sen., Westside House	1	1		
Pratt, James, jun., Westside House	1	1		

LANGCLIFFE (Continued.)

Names of Electors. Residence.	Wortley	Denison	Milton	Morpeth
Pratt, William, Westside House	1	1		
Preston, Thomas, Langcliffe	1	1		
Robinson, John, Langcliffe	1	1		
Rugg, Henry, Giggleswick...	1	1		
Salmon, Henry, Melburn, near Maidstone, Kent				
Swale, Hogarth John, Langcliffe Hall	1	1		
Wright, Christopher, Langcliffe			1	1
Yeadon, Thomas, Langcliffe			1	1

In 1848, in consequence of the elevation of Lord Morpeth to the House of Lords, on the demise of his father, a vacancy occurred in the representation of the West Riding. The candidates who sought to fill Lord Morpeth's place were Mr. Edmund Denison, on behalf of the Conservatives, and Sir Culling Eardley, on behalf of the Liberals.

The poll resulted in the return of Mr. Denison, the numbers being—

DENISON 14743
EARDLEY 11795

The local voters were—

SETTLE.

Name and Residence.	Denison	Eardley
Armistead, Richard, Settle		
Atkinson, John, Settle...		1
Atkinson, Joseph, Wigglesworth	1	
Atkinson, Robert, Settle		1
Ayrton, Henry, Settle...		1
Bateson, Thomas, Settle	1	
Bentley, Anthony, Anley House Lodge		1
Bentley, Robert, Green	1	
Bilton, William, Settle...	1	
Birkbeck, Henry, Kiswick Hall, Norfolk		
Birkbeck, John, Giggleswick	1	
Birkbeck, Thomas, Settle	1	
Birkbeck, William, Lloyd, London		
Bullock, John, Settle ...		
Calvert, William, Settle		

SETTLE (Continued.)

Name and Residence.

	Denison	Eardley
Charnley, T., Armistead, Lancaster	I	
Cork, William, Settle	I	
Dale, David Hall, Cleatop	I	
Dawson, Frederick, London		
Dawson, Henry, Hopton, Norfolk		
Duckett, Charles, Settle	I	
Dunn, Thos. Rowlandson, Lancaster	I	
Ellis, John, Settle		
Ellison, James, Settle		I
Foster, John, Walthamstow		
Foster, Thos. Ed., Constitution Hill	I	
Gardner, Ed., Halton, near Lancaster	I	
Hallpike, Vincent, Settle		
Hardacre, Thomas, Settle	I	
Hardacre, William, Settle	I	
Harger, Joseph, Settle...		
Harger, Robert, Settle...		
Harger, William, Settle		I
Hargreaves, Stephen, Stockdale	I	
Harling, Thomas, Settle		
Hesletine, Francis, Kilnsey	I	
Horner, James, Settle ...		
Howson, Jno. S., Trentham Hall, Staffordshire		
Ingram, Rowland, jun., Giggleswick	I	
King, John, White Horse Inn		
Lancaster, Daniel, Settle Green		I
Marsden, John W., Clitheroe	I	
Nixon, Thomas, Settle...	I	
Parker, Stephen, Lodge	I	
Parkinson, Edward, Settle		
Preston, John, Mearbeck	I	
Procter, Christopher, Mearbeck		I
Procter, John, Lancaster	I	
Procter, Robert, Malham	I	
Ralph, Luke, Settle		
Ratcliffe, Charles, Settle	I	
Read, John, Settle		
Robinson, John, Duke Street		
Robinson, Robert, Chapel Street		I
Robinson, William, Settle	I	
Rogers, William, Kendal		
Roper, James, Liverpool	I	
Roper, Richard, Kirkby Lonsdale		
Snell, Henry, Square, New Road		
Spencer, Anthony, Settle	I	
Spencer, William, Settle Green...	I	

SETTLE (Continued.)

Name and Residence.

Stackhouse, Anthony, Settle Green
Turner, William, Settle Green ...
Twisleton, James, Upper Settle...
Waddington, John, Settle ...
Walker, John, Lancaster ...
Walker, William, Haslingden ...
Whittam, Mathew, Upper Settle
Wildman, John, Settle... ...
Wilman, James, Settle... ...
Wilman, Stephen, Settle ...

GIGGLESWICK.

Armistead, Richard, Field Gate
Armistead, Thomas, Field Gate
Brayshaw, Thomas, Giggleswick
Burton, Edward, Kendal ...
Butterton, George Ash, Craven Bank
Carr, Richard, Stackhouse ...
Carr, William, Giggleswick ...
Clapham, Thomas, Stackhouse...
Clark, Adam, Lower Wham ...
Ellis, Francis, Settle ... ...
Fell, John, Crawridge ... ...
Green, Thomas, Giggleswick ...
Hartley, John, Catteral Hall ...
Howson, Rev. John, Giggleswick
Ingram, Rev. Rowland, Giggleswick
Jenkinson, Charles, Giggleswick
Johnson, John, Paley Green ...
King, Henry, Giggleswick ...
Leech, William, Swawbeck ...
Maudsley, Henry, Rome ...
Maudsley, John, Grain House ...
Maudsley, Joshua, Little Bank...
Maudsley, Thomas, Stainforth ...
Metcalfe, John, Giggleswick ...
Moorby, John, Giggleswick ...
Parker, Cuthbert, Giggleswick ...
Parker, Joseph, Rome... ...
Pollard, John, Rome .. ...
Preston, Samuel, Stackhouse ...
Procter, John, Settle ... ...
Rhodes, Samuel, Kendal ...
Robinson, William, jun., Settle...
Smith, Elias Smith, Giggleswick
Tatham, John, Settle ... ...

GIGGLESWICK (Continued.)

Name and Residence.

Taylor, John, Croft Closes
Taylor, Thos., Twiston, near Clitheroe
Thompson, William, Kendal
Waller, John, Giggleswick
Wildman, Christopher, Routsworth
Wildman, William, Thames Cottage
Woods, Thomas, Lancaster

RATHMELL.

Armistead, John, Airton
Armistead, William, Low Bentham
Battersby, Barnabas, Rathmell
Burrow, Thomas Dixon, Settle
Butler, Phineas, Winterskill Bank
Charnley, Robert, Far Cappleside
Clark, Thomas, Giggleswick
Dawson, John, Gildersleets
Dawson, Stephen, Gildersleets
Geldard, Chris., John, Cappleside
Geldard, John, Cappleside
Geldard, Robert, Rathmell
Helm, Robert, Swainstead
Holden, Thomas, Rathmell
Kendall, William, New Hall
Kendall, William, Lowfoulds
Knowles, Rd., Horton-in-Ribblesdale
Knowles, Richard, Rathmell
Newhouse, Edward, Aughton, Lancashire
Robinson, John, Green
Schofield, Abraham, Todmordon
Standing, William, Hesley Lane
Taylor, James, Gisburn Forest
Taylor, William, Rathmell
Tomlinson, James, Hensley Hill
Towler, George, Hollin Hall
Towler, George, jun., Cross Keys
Towler, John, Lawkland
Towler, Joseph Hollin Hall
Wilson, William, Long Preston
Wolfenden, James, Ragged Hall

STAINFORTH.

Armitstead, Richard, Airton House
Atkinson, Thomas, Sandwith
Dawson, Pudsey, Hornby Castle
Foster, Thomas, Stainforth

STAINFORTH (Continued.)

Name and Residence.					Denison	Eardley
Hesletine, Benjamin, Knight Stainforth	...	...	...	...	1	
Hodgson, John, Stainforth	...	...	...	...	1	
Hodgson, John Parker, Stainforth	...	...	...	...	1	
Hodgson, Joseph, Stainforth	...	...	...	...	1	
Hudson, Miles, Stainforth	...	...	...	...	1	
Metcalfe, Christopher, Neals Ing	...	...	...	...	1	
Parker, Thomas, Sherwood House	...	...	...	...	1	
Redmayne, Marmaduke, Stainforth	...	...	...	...		
Redmayne, Thomas, Taitlands	...	...	...	...		
Richardson, William, Knight Stainforth		...	...	...	1	
Stackhouse, Anthony, Stainforth	...	...	...	...	1	
Wildman, Stephen, Stainforth	...	...	...	...		
Winder, Thomas, Stainforth	...	...	...	...		1
Witts, F. E., Morton-in-Marsh, Gloucestershire	...	...	...			

LANGCLIFFE.

Armistead, Christopher, Langcliffe	...	...	...	...		1
Brown, Christopher, London	...	...	...	...	1	
Buller, Joseph, Langcliffe	...	...	...	...	1	
Clayton, William, Langcliffe Place	...	...	...	...		
Forrester, Joseph, Settle	...	...	...	...	1	
Foster, William, Settle	...	...	...	...	1	
Hill, John, Langcliffe	...	...	...	...	1	
Jackman, Jonathan, Langcliffe	...	...	...	...	1	
Jackman, Mathew, Langcliffe	...	...	...	...	1	
Longbottom. John, Holme Head	...	...	...	...		
Maudsley, Joshua, Winskill	...	...	...	...	1	
Pratt, James, jun., Westside House	...	...	...	...	1	
Pratt, James, sen., Westside House	...	...	...	...	1	
Preston, Thomas, Langcliffe	...	...	...	...	1	
Robinson, John, Langcliffe	...	...	...	...	1	
Sedgwick, William, Giggleswick	...	...	...	...	1	
Swale, Hogarth John, Settle	...	...	...	...		
Twisleton, Francis, High Winskill	...	...	...	...	1	
Wilson, Charles, Langcliffe	...	...	...	...		1
Wilson, Richard, Langcliffe	...	...	...	...		1
Wilson, William, Langcliffe	...	...	...	...		1
Wright, Christopher, Langcliffe	...	...	...	...	1	
Wright, Thomas, Langcliffe	...	...	...	...	1	
Yeadon, Thomas, Langcliffe	...	...	...	...	1	

The Conservatives held both seats until 1852, when one representative of each party was chosen, and this arrangement continued until 1859, when the Liberal candidates were Sir John Ramsden, and Mr. Frank Crossley; and the Con-

servative candidate was Mr. J. S. Wortley.
The result of the polling was—

RAMSDEN	15978
CROSSLEY	15401
WORTLEY	13636

The local votes were as follows—

SETTLE.

Name and Residence.	Ramsden	Crossley	Wortley
Armistead, John, Settle	1		
Atkinson, John, Settle	1	1	
Bentley, Anthony, Runley Bridge	1	1	
Bilton, William, Settle			1
Birkbeck, John, Giggleswick			1
Bradley, John, Mearbeck			1
Charnley, Richard, All Saints' Street, Bolton-le-Moors	1	1	
Dale, David Hall, Cleatop			1
Davenport, Michael, Hardmans-in-the-Fields, Bury			1
Ellison, James, Settle	1	1	
Foster, Edward Thomas, Settle			1
Gardner, Edward, Halton, Lancaster			1
Hardacre, William, Settle			1
Harger, John, Settle	1	1	
Harger, Joseph, Oxton, Birkenhead, Cheshire			
Harger, Joseph, Settle	1	1	
Hargraves, Robert, Stockdale			
Hartley, John Johnson, Market Place			
Jackson, Joseph, Back Lane	1	1	
King, John, Naked Man Inn	1	1	
King, Joseph, Augerholme, Mallerstang, Kirkby Stephen, Westmorland	1	1	
King, Lawrence, 63, Whitehead Bridge, Bury, Lancashire	1		1
King, Thomas, 3, Kaye Street, Little Bolton, Lancashire			1
Lancaster, Daniel, Settle Green	1	1	
Laytham, Joseph, Upper Settle			1
Ormerod, Thomas, 16, St. George's Terrace, Little Bolton Street, Bolton-le-Moors	1	1	
Pierson, William Frederic, Parsonage			1
Preston, John, senior, Merebeck			1
Preston, William, Duke Street	1	1	
Procter, Christopher, Mearbeck	1		
Robinson, Henry, The Terrace, Settle	1	1	
Robinson, John, Duke Street			
Robinson, Robert, Chapel Street	1	.1	
Robinson, William, Settle			1
Rogers, William, Calne, Wilts.			1
Roper, Richard, Kirkby Lonsdale, Westmorland			1

SETTLE (Continued.)

Name and Residence.

Slater, John, Upper Settle
Snell, Henry, Square, New Road
Spencer, William, Settle Green
Stackhouse, Anthony, Settle ..
Twisleton, James, Upper Settle
Walker, John, 136, St. Leonard Gate, Lancaster
Walker, William, High Street, Haslingden, Lancashire...
Waugh, James, Market Place
Wilkinson Newsholme, George, Settle
Wise, John, Swan Inn, Clitheroe
Wood, Samuel, Bolton Street, Bury

GIGGLESWICK.

Birkbeck, Joseph, Stackhouse
Bolland, John, Close House ...
Bolland, Thomas, New Hall, Rathmell
Carr, William, Giggleswick ...
Carr, William, Stackhouse ...
Clapham, William, Giggleswick
Clark, Adam, Lower Wham ...
Fell, John, Craven Ridge
Harrison, Joseph, 14, Chapel Street, Lancaster
Hartley, John, Catteral, Hall
Jenkinson, Charles, Giggleswick
Johnson, John, Paley Green ..
Johnson, John jun., Gildersleets
Langhorne, John, Giggleswick
Leach, William, Swabeck
Littlefair, Thomas, Field Gate
Lowcock, George, Close House
Maudsley, John, Grain House
Maudsley, Joshua, Little Bank
Maudsley, Thomas, Grain House
Moorby, John, Giggleswick ...
Parker, Cuthbert, Giggleswick
Parker, Joseph, Rome
Preston, Samuel, Stackhouse
Proctor, John, Settle
Rhodes, Samuel, Bank Top, Kendal, Westmorland
Robinson, Wm. jun., Duke Street
Tatham, John, Settle
Thompson, William, Highgate, Kendal
Waller, John, Giggleswick ...
Wildman, Christopher, Routsworth ...
Winder, Thomas, Claughton, Lancaster
Wray, Michael, Giggleswick ...

RATHMELL.

Name and Residence.	Ramsden	Crossley	Wortley
Armistead, John, Crakemoor, Airton	1	1
Armistead, Thomas, Ragged Hall	1	1
Battersby, Barnabas, Rathmell	1	1
Butler, Phineas, Winterskill Bank			1
Dawson, John, Bank		1
Geldard, Chris. John, Bankwell, Giggleswick			1
Geldard, Robert, Rathmell			1
Helm, Robert, Swainstead			1
Higson, John, Hesley Lane			1
Kendall, William, Lowfoulds			1
Knowles, Richard, Hanlith			1
Mercer, Richard, Rathmell			1
Morley, Thomas Wilson, Birkby Rectory, Northallerton			1
Schofield Abraham, Know Top, Todmordon			1
Standing William Huggon House			1
Taylor, William, Far Cappleside			1
Towler, George, Hollin Hall			1
Towler, George, jun., Cross Keys			1
Towler, Joseph, Hollin Hall			1
Wigglesworth, Thomas, Rathmell			1

STAINFORTH.

Armitstead, Robert, Airton House | 1 | 1 |
---|---|---|---
Charnley, Robert, Stainforth | | | 1
Foster, James Halliday, Stainforth | | | 1
Hesleton, Benjamin, Knight Stainforth | | | 1
Hodgson, John, Stainforth | 1 | 1 |
Hodgson, Joseph, Stainforth | | | 1
Maudsley, Thomas, Stainforth | | | 1
Metcalfe, Christopher, Neals Ing | | | 1
Parker, James, Sherwood House | | | 1
Redmayne, Thomas, Taitlands | 1 | 1 |
Richardson, William, The Parsonage | | | 1
Sedgwick, Christopher, Sherwood House | | | 1
Stackhouse, Thomas, Stainforth | | | 1
Witts, Edward Francis, The Vicarage House, Stanway, Winchomb | | | 1

LANGCLIFFE.

Bashall, Richard, Langcliffe Place, Lostock House, Preston			1
Brown, Christopher, Stainforth			1
Graham, Mathew, Kirkgate, Settle	1	1
Jackman, Jonathan, Langcliffe	1	1
Pratt, James, jun., Westside House			1
Preston, John jun., Mearbeck			1
Twisleton, Francis, High Winskill			1
Wright, Christopher, Langcliffe			1
Yeadon, Thomas, Langcliffe		1

In 1861 an Act was passed dividing the West Riding into two divisions—the Northern and Southern—each to return two members, and at the election in 1865, Sir F. Crossley, Bart., and Lord F. Cavendish (Liberals) were returned unopposed. They represented the division until the death of Sir F. Crossley in 1872, when his place was taken by Mr. F. Powell (Conservative) who defeated Mr. I. Holden.

The Liberals recovered the seat in 1874, when Lord F. C. Cavendish and Mr. (now Sir) M. Wilson defeated Messrs. Powell and Fison.

Lord Frederic and Sir M. Wilson, held their seats until the murder of the former in 1882, when Mr. Holden was elected in his place.

By the " Redistribution of Seats Act" the old Northern Division of the West Riding was split up into five divisions, Settle being in the Skipton Division.

Sir M. Wilson was the first member, but in the present year lost the seat to Mr. Walter Morrison, a " Unionist " Liberal, who now holds it.

The following tabulated list shews how the voters from this Parish distributed their favors at the elections from 1807 to 1859—

1807.	Voted.	Gigg'wk.	Lang.	Rath.	Set.	Stain.	TOTAL
		12	4	9	28	7	50
WILBERFORCE (Tory)	...	12	1	1	15	6	35
LASCELLES (Tory)	...	12	3	9	18	7	49
LORD MILTON (Whig)	...	—	1	—	9	1	11

1835. On List of Voters.	G. 24	L. 13	R. 17	S. 50	St. 15	119
MORPETH, L.	Voted { 10	9	6	26	5	56
WORTLEY. C.	12	3	8	12	7	42

1837.	Voters.	G. 38	L. 15	R. 32	S. 72	St. 20	177
MORPETH, L.		16	9	11	39	6	81
STRICKLAND, L.	Voted	16	8	10	37	6	77
WORTLEY. C.		18	4	17	18	10	67

1841.		G. 24	L. 21	R. 33	S. 82	St. 21	199
WORTLEY, C.		19	10	17	21	12	79
DENISON, C.	Voted.	19	11	14	21	12	77
MILTON, L.		18	6	11	41	6	82
MORPETH, L.		17	7	11	41	6	82

1848.	Voters.	G. 41	L. 24	R. 31	S. 71	St. 18	185
DENISON, C.	Voted.	21	13	22	35	13	104
EARDLEY, L.		12	8	7	15	1	43

1859.	Voted.	G. 33	L. 9	R. 20	S. 47	St. 14	123
WORTLEY, C.		22	6	16	26	11	81
RAMSDEN, L.		11	2	3	23	3	42
CROSSLEY, L.		11	3	4	19	3	40

The votes given by adherents of the two political parties at the contests this century are—

	1807	1835	1837	1841	1848	1859
CONSERVATIVES ...	49	42	81	79	104	81˙
LIBERALS	11	56	67	82	43	42

At present there are about 700 voters in the five townships, the Liberals being in a considerable majority, having a preponderance of supporters in Settle, Giggleswick, and Langcliffe, whilst the Conservatives are in a majority in Stainforth and Rathmell.

"COLLECTANEA GIGGLESWICKIANA."

PART II.

WITH ILLUSTRATIONS.

COMPILED BY THOS. BRAYSHAW.

* * * * * * * *

STACKHOUSE,
NEAR SETTLE,
July, 1887.

In the hope and belief that a few more miscellaneous items relating to this parish, collected together into one pamphlet from various sources, may be acceptable to my friends, I issue a second part of "Collectanea Giggleswickiana."

THOS. BRAYSHAW.

Twelve large and one hundred small paper copies printed for private circulation.

"COLLECTANEA GIGGLESWICKIANA."

DOMESDAY BOOK.

The earliest written records of our parish remain in the pages of Domesday Book, and I give a facsimile of some of the entries relating to this neighbourhood.

[Facsimile of Domesday Book entries beginning "TERRA ROGERII PICTAVENSIS."]

Set out at full length the above would be roughly translated as follows :

LAND OF ROGER OF POICTOU.

Manor. In Ghigelesvvic (Giggleswick) Fech had four carucates to be taxed. In Stranforde (Stainforth) three carucates. In Rodemele (Rathmell) two carucates. In Chirchebi (Kirkby Malham) two carucates. In Litone (Litton or qy. Linton) six carucates. These berewicks belong to the above-mentioned manor. Roger of Poictou now has them.

In Cuningestone (Coniston) William de Percy held two carucates to be taxed, but Roger de Poictou has it.

Manor. In Bernulfesuuic (Barnoldswick) Gamel had twelve carucates to be taxed. Berenger de Todeni held it, but now it is in the Castellate of Roger de Poictou.

Manor. In Prestune (Long Preston) Ulf had three carucates to be taxed, and one church. In Stainforde (Stainforth) three carucates. In Wiclesforde (Wigglesworth) one carucate. In Helgefelt (Hellifield) one carucate and a half. In Neuhuse (Newsome) half a carucate. In Padehale (Painley) one carucate. In Ghiseburne (Gisburn) two carucates. In Hortone (Horton-in-Ribblesdale) one carucate and a half. In Cheuebroc (Kelbrook) six oxgangs. In Croches (Crooks) two oxgangs to be taxed.

Manor. In Chetelwelle (Kettlewell) Ulf had one carucate to be taxed. In Hubergheham Hubboram) half a carucate. In Stamphotone (Starbottom) half a carucate.

Manor. In Anele (Anley) Burun had three carucates of land to be taxed. Setel (Settle) three carucates to be taxed.

Manor. In Witrebvrne (Winterburn) Torfin had three carucates of land to be taxed. In Leuetat (Leslat) three carucates. In Flatebi (Flasby) four carucates. In Geregraue (Gargrave) two carucates. In Neutone (Newton) two carucates. In Hortune (Horton) two carucates. In Selesat (Selside) one carucate.

Manor. In the same Torfin had two carucates of land to be taxed.

Other entries in Domesday Book are as follows :

Manor. In Rodemare (Rathmell) Carl had two carucates to be taxed. In Winchelesuurde (Wigglesworth) ten oxgangs. In Helgiflet (Hellifield) two carucates and a half.

Manor. In Lanclif (Langcliffe) Fech had three carucates to be taxed.

Manor. In Stacuse (Stackhouse) Archil had three carucates to be taxed.

In Geregrave (Gargrave) three carucates. In Otreburn (Otterburn) three carucates. In Scotorp (Scosthrop) three carucates. In Malgon (Malham) three carucates. In Anlei (Anley) two carucates. In Coningeston (Coniston) three carucates. In Hœlgefeld (Hellifield) three carucates. In Hanelif (Hanlith) three carucates. These all belong to Bodeltone (Bolton).

LAND OF THE KING.

Soke. Anleie (Anley) two carucates. Hangelif (Hanlith) three carucates. They are waste.

As to the dimensions of a carucate, I feel I cannot do better than quote Canon Isaac Taylor, who says:

" In the Domesday survey of the northern shires two phrases occur in the account of almost every manor. These are the *carucata ad geldum*, the " geldable carucate," which was the fiscal unit for purposes of taxation ; and the *terra ad unam carucam*, the " arable carucate," which was the unit for agricultural purposes. This arable carucate is that which is so often mentioned in contemporary documents, the geldable carucate being used chiefly in Domesday, which was a record for fiscal purposes. Naturally, these two measures of land have been confused. Fleta, a writer on English Agriculture, who lived in the reign of Edward I., only two hundred years after Domesday, gives an account of the carucate which is the key to the Domesday mensuration. He says that if the land lay in three arable fields—that is, if a three-year shift were adopted, the whole carucate consisted of one hundred and eighty acres, sixty acres in one field for Winter tillage, sixty acres in another for Lent tillage, and sixty acres in a third for fallow; whereas in a two-year shift, when the land lay in two fields, the carucate consisted of one hundred and sixty acres, eighty for tillage and eighty for fallow.

From the actual measurements of manors which have remained unchanged to modern times it is possible to recognise the two-field and the three-field manors, and to show that in three-field manors the Domesday *carucata ad geldum* was normally sixty acres, the land tilled in one field in one year by one plough, while the *terra ad unum carucam* was one hundred and twenty acres, the land tilled in both fields in one year by one plough, and the whole carucate, including fallow, was one hundred and eighty acres. In two-field manors, both the *carucata ad geldum* and the *terra ad unam carucam* were eighty acres, and the whole carucate including fallow, one hundred and sixty acres, by the reckoning locally used, either the Norman hundred of five score, or the English hundred of six score."

It seems strange to us that eight hundred years ago, Anley, now consisting of a single house, should have been a hamlet or township.

A LIST OF THE SOLDIERS UNDER CAPTAINE PARKER, 1661.

RATHMELL.

Charles Nowell
John Armistead
Robt. Settle
John Armistead, jun.
Tho. Knowles
Will. Bankes
Richard Preston
Gyelse Hoghton
Richard Husband

UNPAID POLL TAX.

A pticular Note of what Money is behinde and unpaid of the Pole money wthin the severall pishes of Gigleswicke, Gysborne & longe Preston, the pties upon whome the same were assessed some of them have billeted souldiers & were not assessed above xij^d a piece some have paid in other places and some were gone out of their services & some dead betwixt the tyme of the assessinge & collectinge of the said pole money as by seuall certificates under the pettie Constables & assessors hands doth appeare.

	s.	d.
ALLOWED to billiters of souldiers not assessed above 12^d a man	23	0
Mort 2	2	0
paid in other places........................	9	0
gone out of their services so many psns as were asse^d	9	6
	43	6

LETTER OF PROTECTION
Granted by General Lambert whilst encamped with the Parliamentary Army at Giggleswick.

To all Captaines Lieutenants and all other Officers and Souldiers wthin the liberties of Craven.

Theise are to Charge and require yo^u and everie of yo^u that you forbear to enter the house of Edward Parker of Brousholme Esqr by night, or to take anie horses or other goods from him, eyther wthin the house or wthout the house, Eyther by day or by night, wthout speciall Command from mee : as yo^u and everie of yo^u will Answer the Contrarie at yor pills.* Giuen at Gigleswicke vnder my hand the Nyneteenth daie of December, 1643.

JOHN LAMBERT.

LADY BURLINGTON'S RENTS.

From the Clifford Papers at Bolton Hall we find that in the year 1651, the first lady Burlington's rent-roll included property in Giggleswick of the annual value of £48 16s. 3d., in Settle £56 1s. 9d., and in Long Preston £31 19s. 0d.

BRITISH CANOE.

In June 1863, as some workmen were draining the fields which were formerly covered by the waters of Giggleswick Tarn, they came upon an ancient canoe, buried some five feet below the surface, and evidently of Celtic or British workmanship. It had been hollowed out of the trunk of a large oak tree, and when found was in an excellent state of preservation. The dimensions of the boat are as follows :

Length over all	8ft. 2in.
Breadth, inside	1ft. 9in.
,, including two " washboards	3ft. 0in.
Depth, inside	1ft. 2in.
,, outside	1ft. 5in.

* " Perils."

The Canoe was presented by Mr. Hartley, the owner of the property, to the Museum of the Leeds Philosophical Society, where it may now be seen.

It has unfortunately, in process of drying, shrunk and cracked very much, and one of the " washboards " is missing, which reduces its present breadth to 2ft. 6in.; and these " wash boards " are not the least curious parts of the canoe, they were fastened to the sides by round plugs of wood, and were evidently intended to steady the boat.

Through the stern end of the canoe is a round hole, possibly intended to thrust a pole through, for the purpose of steering or paddling; tho' this was found plugged up with a conical piece of wood.

Two iron crooks, each about eighteen inches long, and fastened together by a ring of iron, were found near it and looked as if intended for a rude anchor.

The sight of this old boat calls up many reflections as one thinks of the old savage who owned it, paddling about where are now fertile pastures, at times enticing the wily trout to his hook, and at other times, it may be, taking the " trippers " of that day for " an hour's row on the lake." And one wonders whether the dream indulged in by many at the present time of seeing the sign

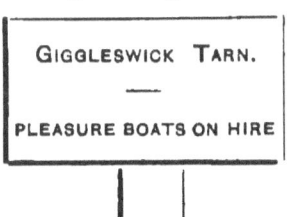

will ever be realized.

I may add that our illustration is from a photograph I had specially taken by the kind permission of the Leeds Philosphical Society.

AN OLD ACCOUNT OF SETTLE.

In Cox's History of Yorkshire the following notices are given of Settle and Giggleswick. I think them worth reprinting on account of the scarcity of the book.

"*Giggleswick*, a village situate on the River *Ribble*. At this Town is a noted School, founded by one Mr. *Bridges*, and well endowed."

"*Settle* hath its Market weekly on Tuesday, and Fair yearly on - - - - -. It is a good town and the Lordship very early belonged to the Piercy's, at length earls of Northumberland. Richard the son of Josceline of Levaine, who by his Contract of Marriage with the Heriess of William de Percy, named Agnes, was to assume the name of Piercy, was in Possession of her Estates, of which this was a part; and left it at his death to his youngest Son Henry; but not enjoying it quietly by Reason of some Claim, his other Brother, William, had to it, he gave him the Manor of Hesset in Sussex to release his Title to it. Henry seems either to have left no issue, or that they were extinct in the Reign of Edw. II Reg. 4 for then we find Henry, the Descendant from William his elder Brother, in Possession of this Manor of Settle, and procuring the King's Charter of Free Warren for all his Demesne Lands here, and elsewhere, in this and other Counties; and after him Idomea, the Widow of another Henry, who lived in King Edward III's Reign, Anno 20, was assigned this and some other Estates for her Dowry."

HUTTON'S TOUR.

A little more than a hundred years ago the Rev. John Hutton made an Excursion to Settle, and he published a little book detailing his experiences. Our author broaches the astounding theory that the marine shells which are to be found at the tops of the hills, are there, *owing to the impact of a comet with the earth.*

The following is extracted from his book—

"At Stainforth, which is about three miles from Horton, and two from Settle, we were entertained with two cascades, one in the Ribble near the road, about 6 or 8 yards high, and another, a little above the village, perhaps 20 or 30 yards perpendicular.

About a quarter of a mile before we arrived at Settle, we turned to the right, along the road towards Kirkby Lonsdale, about a mile, under the high and romantic rocks called Gigleswick-scar; in order to see the well by the way side which ebbs and flows. We were in luck, seeing it reciprocate several times while we were there, and not staying above an hour. We could not however learn with any degree of certainty, by what intervals of time, and to what depths and heights, the reciprocation was carried on. We were informed that if the weather was either very droughty or very wet, the phænomenon ceased. I have seen some philosophical attempts to solve this extraordinary curiosity on the principle of the syphon, but in vain; as on that hypothesis, if the syphon is filled by the spring it will flow on uniformly for ever. We are told by 'drunken Barnaby' that it puzzled the wits of his age.

Two country gentlemen, about 30 or 40 years ago, promised something more successful in the issue of a paper war that was carried on between them, to the great amusement of the neighbourhood. Nothing however was determined or contended for about this well, so famous in History, whether it was a natural curiosity or not.

Settle is irregularly built, has a large and spacious market place but not many good houses in it. Though by no means an inconsiderable town either for trade, riches, or number of inhabitants, it has no church or chapel. The church is at Giggleswick, about a mile off, which appeared to be the court end of the parish.

From Settle we proceeded eastward over the moors and mountains about half a dozen miles, to Malham or Maum, in order to see some other natural curiosities of the precipice and cataract kind. We had indeed seen so many, that our wonder could not easily be excited, except they were more great and terrible. As such we had them represented at Settle, or else we should scarce have left the turnpike road; and when we saw them we were not disappointed, for great and terrible they were."

DR. BURTON'S ARREST.

The following account of his adventures at Settle is from the narrative of Dr. Burton, in his pamphlet entitled " British Liberty Endangered."

This Dr. Burton was the celebrated author of the " Monasticon Ebor.," and his account gives us a good idea of the unsettled times in which he lived.

" On Friday November 22, 1745, about Noon, an Express arrived at the Guild-Hall in the City of York, to acquaint the Lord Mayor, that the Van Guard of the Highland Army was arriv'd at Kendal ; but that it was uncertain, whether they would take the Yorkshire or the Lancashire Rout. If the first then they must have march'd thro' the Lordship of Nuby, in which Manor, my two estates of Birkwith and South-House lie, where I had Rent to the amount of £120 Sterling, due to me from the Michaelmas Day preceding.

As at this Time the City Gates were lock'd up at Ten o'Clock at Night, and not open'd again 'till a little before Sun-rise in the Morning, ; and as the Place I was to go to was distant 48 computed miles from York, the Roads bad and Days short ; I could not pretend to go it in one Day, unless I set out before the usual time of opening the City Gates, and as that could not be done without an Order from the Lord Mayor, I publicly desir'd that favour of him (who as well as others had heard the Reasons of my going) and my Request was granted ; and the Lord Mayor then sent one of the domestic Officers to the Officer who was to be upon Guard that night, with Orders to permit me to go out of the Gates, at what hour I pleas'd next Morning.

As I knew several sersons in York had Dealings in Settle and Skipton I offered if they had any letters, or small Parcels, that my Man should carry 'em ; but by good Luck (as Things turn'd out afterwards) they had none to send.

I accordingly set out next Morning, being Saturday the 23rd; but not so soon as propos'd on account of the heavy Rain, which continu'd 'till near Seven o'Clock, and did not quite cease till after Sun-rise.

It would be needless to relate all the Particulars of my Journey 'till I got to Settle, which was between nine and ten o'Clock in the same Evening, when and where an Express just went thro' the town, for the West of Yorkshire, and brought the account of the Highlanders having taken the Rout towards Lancaster. Upon this I wrote to the Recorder and my Wife, by next Morning's Post, to acquaint 'em therewith; and that I propos'd to be at Home on Tuesday or Wednesday following if I could get my Tenants and Workmen together.

This very Day I went to Hornby, which is the nearest Market Town to my Estate; where I could have any tollerable Accommodation. But as ill Luck wou'd have it, here was I taken Prisoner as my Barber was shaving me at my Inn, by a Party of the Highland Army, who had conducted Lord Elcho and other Gentlemen to Hornby Castle, to dine and see the Place. It cou'd not be Curiosity that led me hither, because the Express of the Night before did assure me, that the Highlander's Rout was at least 12 miles from that Place—And I cou'd prove, if requir'd by the Oaths of several honest Men, that I had not the least Intelligence of this Party.

I then returned to Settle that Night, where my Tenants and Workmen were waiting for me according to Order, at my Inn. The Workmen who had been building and repairing the Houses and Out-Houses were all paid, and Mr. William Hall, my Tenants, and I, then settled Accounts, and I had the whole of the Ballance, to the Amount of about 60 Pounds, in either Bills or Money from Mr. Hall. These Bills I had Money for, from several Inhabitants of York, after my Return from Settle, which I left next Morning, and got to York that Night about nine o'clock.

I have been a little more particular about my Tenants and Workmen, because some here, according to their usual

Candour, gave it out, that I had no legal Business in that Country. But if this had been the Case, or my enemies had suspected any ill Design; as my Return was publickly known, Why was I not seized on the Road, or as soon as I arriv'd.

Upon my being seen (altho' a Prisoner) with the Highlanders, a Quaker, one B-rb-k of Settle (who abounded more with the evil Spirit and Malice, than with Meekness and Truth) sent the News Express to York, which not a little surpris'd every one; my Friends with Concern lest the Highlanders should hurt me; and my Enemies with Joy, in Hopes that now they should have a Pretence of doing me an Injury with Impunity.

This Piece of News made my Wife apprehensive, that an Order might be given to the Guards at Micklegate Bar to seize me as I should enter the City; and as she had often heard me declare that, were those people to use me in the same illegal Manner they had used other People, that I would shoot the first man who should attack me; and as she also saw me change my Pistols before I went (according to my Custom when I go a journey) and knew my resolute Disposition; she was afraid if these Men should attempt to stop and seize me, that I should be as good as my Word; and therefore sent a person out of the Bar to desire in Case of such an Attempt, that I would not offer to make any Resistance.

At my return Home, my Wife and some Company she had with her, told me the Report and Hurry that was occasion'd by this Quaker; upon which I sent to acquaint the Recorder with my Arrival; who said he desir'd to see me that Night, if convenient; and notwithstanding I was so wearied, I went, and over a Bottle of Wine, told him every Thing which had befell me, and further agreed to go with him the next Morning to our then Archbishop, Dr. Thomas Herring."

SETTLE BEAUTIES.

Montagu, in his " Gleanings in Craven " proves that he had an eye for the beautiful, not only of the inanimate, but of the animate ; and I reproduce some of his remarks which are as applicable today as when written :

" I was much struck with the appearance of Settle and the neighbourhood of Giggleswick, which is, as it were sprinkled with beautifully detached villas, and seems as if respectability and wealth had selected this part of Craven for its head-quarters ; and I was likewise forcibly reminded when here, of a truth which has perplexed all my " philosophy," that, towards the most mountainous countries, small feet and delicately turned ankles invariably abound ; and as an anatomical sequiter—the best figures ; the former being inseparable from the latter. Yorkshire women and pretty feet, are so prettily associated in my mind that I shall never think of them apart, and I shall think of them continually. A beautiful face certainly bequeaths a sweet legacy to the memory, (if not to the heart,) but the codicil affixed by observation greatly affects the will, if the face be unsupported by small and beautiful feet and ankles. A pretty face and bad feet and ankles is like a Dutch-built vessel with an elegant figure head."

CELTIC WALL.

There are few places in the Parish of Giggleswick more interesting to the Archæologist than Smearside and its immediate locality. Here may be found traces of old earthworks, circular dwellings, tumuli, &c., and several parts of a Celtic Wall yet remain in fair condition. It is probable that this wild spot has been the scene of many a contest in olden times, and doubtless when the neighbouring tumuli come to be examined, some interesting discoveries will be the result.

I give an engraving of one of the best preserved portions of the wall above mentioned. It runs along the top of the hill opposite Smearside, parallel to its steepest side; the measurements of this particular piece being 26 yards in length, about 5ft. 6in. in height, and 5ft. 3in. in breadth at the base. The weather-beaten old stones, which have stood here undisturbed for centuries, bid fair to stand for ages more, as they are well and skilfully laid, altho' no mortar or lime binds them together; and very possibly they may see the time when the inhabitants of our valley will consider us of the present generation to have been as uncivilized as we regard the builders of the old wall; and it is devoutly to be hoped that no farmer, finding these stones ready to his hand, may use them for walling and such like purposes.

A little to the south of the part of which I give a view, another portion of the wall, about 17 yards in length, may be seen. This however is not in so good a state of preservation as the former, indeed for about half its length there is nothing more to be seen than the foundations peeping just above the surface.

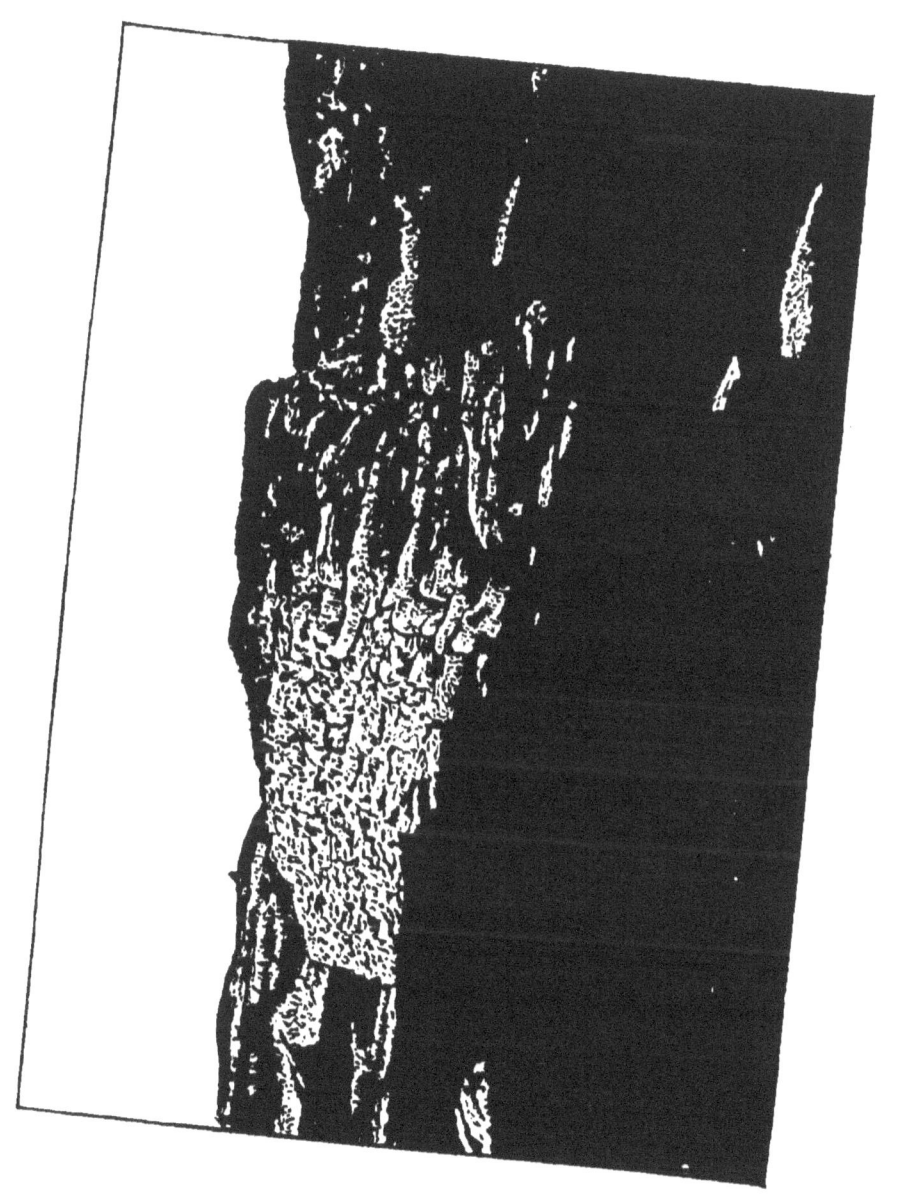

SETTLE IN 1773.

In the year 1773 the well known Antiquarian and Botanist, Thomas Pennant, visited Settle whilst on a Tour from Downing to Alston Moor. After leaving Malham, he says:

" Cloud Berries are found plentifully on the Moors between Malham and Settle. They take their name from their lofty situation. I have seen the berries in the Highlands of Scotland served as a dessert. The Swedes and Norwegians preserve great quantities in autumn to make tarts and other confections, and esteem them as excellent antiscorbutics. The Laplanders bruise and eat them in the milk of reindeer, and preserve them quite fresh till spring by burying them in the snow.

I descended an exceedingly tedious and steep road, having on the right a range of rocky hills with broken precipituous fronts. At the foot of a monstrous lime-stone rock, called Castleberg, that threatens destruction, lies Settle, a small town in a little vale, exactly resembling a shabby French town with a 'place' in the middle. Numbers of coiners and filers lived about the place, at this time entirely out of work, by reason of the recent salutary law respecting the weight of gold.

I dined here at the neatest and most comfortable little inn I ever was at, rendered more agreeable by the civility and attention of the landlady. This is a market town, and has a small trade in knit-worsted stockings, which are made here from two to five shillings a pair. The great hill of Penygent is seen from hence, and is about six miles distant.

Settle is destitute of a Church; its parish is that of Giggleswick, higher up the vale, which I passed after crossing the Ribble, which hurries from its source a few miles higher, on the back of Wharnside-hill between Blea-moor and Snaysfell.

This parish was one of the most ancient manors of the Percies. I believe it to have been included among the eighty-six in this county granted by the Conqueror to William de Perci, one of his Norman followers : but the first time I find mention of the Manor of Settle, as their property, is in 1230, the fifteenth of Henry III.

A little beyond the village, the road is continued on the right side of the vale, beneath a long and lofty scar of the same name. It runs for a mile in length ; the height decreases with the ascent of the road, but preserves a level on its top the whole way. This scar is of white limestone, finely overgrown with ivy, has a mineral appearance, and bits of lead ore, found in forming the turnpike-road, give earnest of important discovery.

The famous flowing spring lies on the road side beneath this scar. It is a well of small size, which ebbs and flows once in a quarter of an hour, and sometimes with that force as to rise a foot high. I watched it for some time, but it happened to be quiescent ; my patience was exhausted, and I pursued my journey.

The " Potentilla verna " or " Vernal Cinquefoil," Fl. Sc. 1,270, is found near this well ; and those who delight in mosses, may discover, on the adjacent rocks, the " Lichen crinitus " and " polyrhizos," Fl. Sc. 11,860 and 864.

From this spot I had a fine view of Pendle hill which appeared quite insulated.

On gaining the summit of the road, the Apennines of England appeared full in view; the tops often rise into little mounts, and the sides very rocky. On the left is a flat bounded by heathy hills, and intermixed with dreary moors."

SETTLE MARKET IN 1813.

The following 'poem' on Settle Market seventy-four years ago is said to have been written by an officer of a detachment of troops who were passing through the town. Altho' written in a sarcastic vein it contains a good deal of truth, and is not wholly inapplicable to the present time.

> The shades of night returned the morning fair,
> When to the market wonderous crowds repair,
> Anxious to gain the busy bustling place
> They now and then increase their eager pace;
> What mercy 'tis to pass the crowded road,
> And have no accidents their feelings goad.
> Then having reached the wide and spacious square,
> Surprised you meet the great assemblage there.
> There's twice ten men and twice ten women too,
> At one wide look you have them all in view.
> Behold three carts with fine potatoes filled,
> Produced from fields that industry has tilled;
> You men of Settle this a favour view,
> For you have long làid by the useful plough;
> No teams in spring to cultivate your fields,
> You reap alone the verdour nature yields.
> Think not potatoes here alone are sold,
> There's what makes Yorkshire men so strong and bold,
> Oatmeal, the grand supporter of his frame,
> Which gives him strength to gain a mighty name,
> Oh! great supporter, we, deprived of thee
> Of smaller stature every one would be.
> Yorkshire for oatmeal, Yorkshire is the place,
> Her sons rise up like Hog's gigantic race:
> Their Riddle-bread gives them baath strength and mettle,
> For proof look round and view the men of Settle.
> Ten slaughtered sheep, and pigs in number three
> You in the great and mighty market see,
> So great a market scarce from pole to pole,
> Six pecks of apples makes the wonderous whole.

SETTLE OLD STOCKS.

With the progress of civilization we have discarded many of the punishments which our ancestors inflicted—or suffered —as the case may be, amongst these being confinement in "the stocks." Without doubt many of these punishments were barbarous, and their disuse is a matter of congratulation, but as to the stocks I venture to think there is much to be said in their favor, and altho' some tender-hearted humanitarians will doubtless howl at me, I must say that I should not be sorry were their use to be revived in certain cases. For instance " Five shillings and costs " is all very well in a case of simple drunkenness, but it is possible that three hours' quiet meditation in the stocks would be a more effective deterrent, whilst the six hours reflection that a man caught in the act of gambling on a Sunday, was constrained to indulge in, would surely induce him to forswear that bad habit.

At Giggleswick there may yet be seen, at the foot of the old market cross, the remains of the parish stocks. One post has been broken off and the moveable upper wooden beam is missing, but the other post still remains, whilst the lower stone, into which the ancles fitted and on which the upper wooden part rested, still acts as a silent monitor.

At Settle the stocks consisted entirely of wood, and have been moved bodily away. I give an engraving of them, as they are rapidly going to decay, and will probably soon be numbered amongst the "have-beens." The honour of having been the last person to occupy them involuntarily lies between Messrs. " Tal Bradley " and " Jimmy Carr "; but one thing is certain,—that " Tal," who was a fruit hawker, used to sell more oranges whilst in durance than at any other time.

SETTLE IN 1796.

In the year 1796 the Hon. Mrs. Murray Aust passed through Settle in the course of a tour, and penned the following as her impressions of the place:

" From Chapel-in-the-Dale, by Horton, to Settle is 10 miles; but I think not a carriage road. At Horton are many curiosities. On the road to the right is a curious stone quarry.

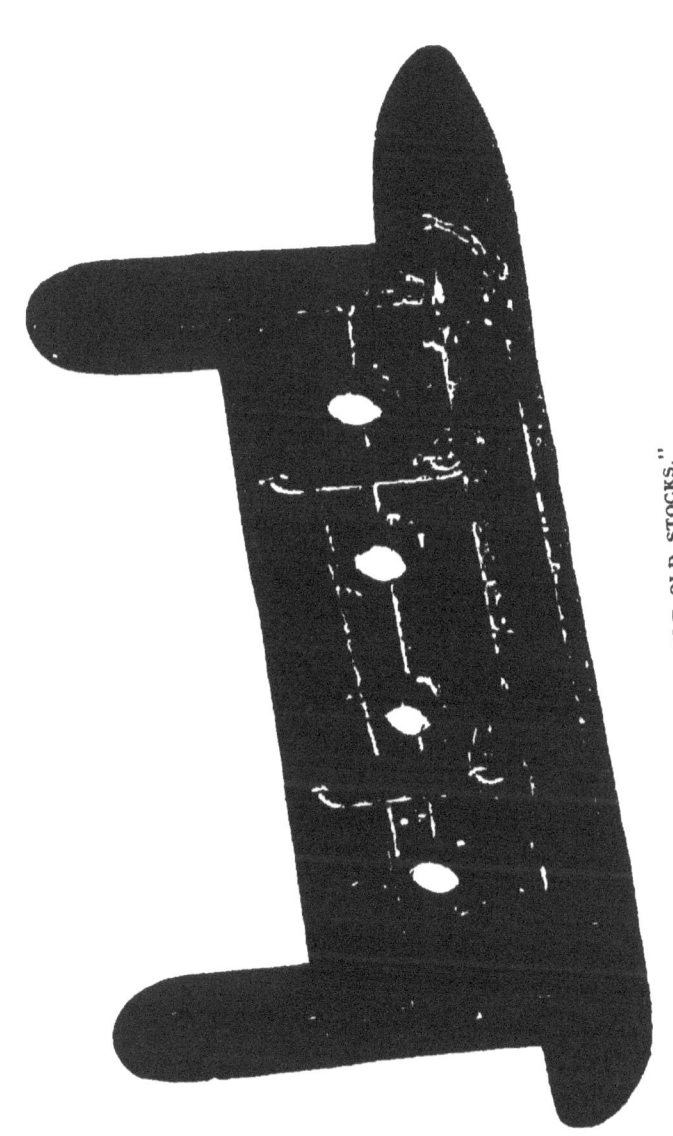

"SETTLE OLD STOCKS."

At Stainforth two waterfalls on the river Ribble. The vale of Horton is so shaded from the sun, and so cold, nothing ripens in it, not even potatoes. It consists of sheep farms, and I was told at Settle, that notwithstanding the climate of Hortondale, there are many farmers living in it possessing from two to three hundred pounds a year.

From Ingleton to Settle, by the turnpike road is 10 miles ; that drive is delightful, from the great variety of mountains, wood, crags, and water. The town of Clapham is delightfully situated, and the Clapham Scars are fine ; but·Crowness Scars, on the left in ascending the mountain, before the descent to Settle, are very singular, and particularly grand ; being, as it were, a long range of fine castles in ruins, with Gothic Gateways, pillars, &c. Just after Crowness Scars, and a short way distance from Settle, are the magnificent Giggleswick Scars, under which, close on the road's side, is the well which ebbs and flows.

The situation of Settle is under vast mountains, and crags. A whiteish rock, like towers, called Castleberg rises almost perpendicularly from the houses at the back of the town; it has zig-zag walks made up it, and from the top is an extensive view over Ribblesdale : this rock is walled round to prevent cattle or man from injuring it ; it now belongs to the town of Settle. The river which runs by Settle is the Ribble. The bed-rooms at the inn are middling ; the parlour is very good, and the Fausets, who kept it in 1796, were very civil, accommodating, intelligent people.

The distance, over the moors and mountains, from Settle to Gordale, is 6 miles."

Mrs. Aust went from Settle to Malham, and altho' her opinion of the natives of the latter place is very uncomplimentary, it is amusing on account of her prejudice.

" The alehouse at the village of Maum affords no entertainment for man, and but little for horses: the people too are the most stupid I ever met with : I could procure no information ; and it was with difficulty I got a guide, who at last was only a lout of a boy, who could just lead the way to the left, a mile to Gordale Scar ; and to the right afterwards, half a mile, to Maum Tor."

LOCAL GLEANINGS

(Reprinted from the Settle Household Almanack for 1898.)

Compiled by Thos. Brayshaw.

SETTLE:
THE CRAVEN PRINTING AND STATIONERY COMPANY, LIMITED.

LOCAL GLEANINGS.

CHANTRIES IN GIGGLESWICK CHURCH.

Towards the close of King Henry VIII's reign a Commission was appointed to make an enquiry into all the Chantries attached to the various Churches throughout the country. The first set of the following notes is from the Report of these Commissioners. The King's death however interrupted the work, and in the first year of King Edward VI. the Archbishop of York, Robert Chaloner, Thomas Gargrave, and Henry Savyll, by virtue of the King's Commission to them of the 14th Feb. 1548, granted the second set of certificates, relating to the same Chantries as the previous ones.

THE CHAUNTERIE OF OUR LADY IN THE PAROCH CHURCH OF GYGLESWYKE, CALLED STANFORD CHAUNTERIE.

Richard Somerskayle, incumbent. Of the foundacion of Robert Stanford, esquier, to pray for the sowle of the founder and all Christen sowles, who did gyve certen landes to the late monastery of Salley, for the intent that the first incumbent herof and his successors for ever shulde have one annuytie of iiij*li* yerlie, goynge furth of the possessions of the said monasterye.

The same is in the saide paroch Church, and used accordinge to the foundacion. Ther is no landes alienate sithens the statute.

Goodes, ornamentes, and plate belonginge to the same, as apperyth by inventory, viz. :—goodes valued at xjs. viij*d*., and plate, nil.

The sayde incumbent haith and receyvyth yerlie one annuytie of iiij*li*., goynge furth of the possessions of the late monastery of Salley, payd by thandes of Sir Arthure Daryce.

Wherof
Paiable to the Kynges Majestie yerelie for the tenthe, viijs. And so remanyth, lxxijs.

THE CHAUNTERIE OF THE ROODE
IN THE SAME PAROCH CHURCH OF GYGLESWYKE.

Thomas Husteler, incumbent. Of the foundacion of James Skarr', prist. To th' intent to pray for the sowle of the founder and all Cristen sowles, and to synge masse, every Friday, of the Name of Jhesu, and, of the Saterday, of Our Lady. And further that the said incumbent shulde be sufficientlie sene in playnsonge and gramer and to helpe dyvyne service in the same churche.

The same is in the saide churche and used accordinge to the foundacion. Ther is no landes aliened sithens the statute.

Goodes, ornamentes, and plate perteynynge to the same, as apperyth by the inventorye, viz.:—goodes valued at xixs. ij*d*., and plate, xlijs.

First, one mesuage with th' appurtenances in Oterbourne, in the tenure of Cuthberte Carre, xxiiijs.; Christopher Tompson, ijs.; John Smyth, one cotage, ijs.; Henry Atkinson, one mesuage with th' appurtenances ther, xviijs.; the wyff of Thomas Atkinson, one mesuage and one oxgang of land, xs.; Thomas Atkinson, one mesuage with th' appurtenances, xvs.; Christopher Thompson, one cotage, vs.; Richard Thompson, one cotage, vs.; Henry Swier, j mesuage with th' appurtenaunces, xvs.; Richard Patenson, one mesuage with th' appurtenaunces, xvs.; and William Haroo', one mesuage with th' appurtenaunces in . . . ., xs. In all, vj*li*. xij*d*.

Whereof
Paiable to the Kinges Majestie yerlie for the tenthes, viij*s.* viij*d.*; and to John Smyth yerlie for his annuytie durynge his lyffe, vj*s.* In all, xiiij*s.* viij*d.*

And so remanyth, cvj*s.*, iiij*d.*

THE CHAUNTERIE IN THE NORTH SIDE OF THE SAID CHURCH CALLED TEMPEST CHAUNTERIE.

Ther is none incumbent therof. The same was founded by Sir Richarde Tempest, knight, as it is allegied. To th' entent to pray for the soule of the founder and all Cristen sowles. And ther is yerlie goinge furth of the parsonage of Kirkby Mallondale one annuall rent of iiij*li.* xiij*s.* iiij*d.* for the mantennce of the same, payd by thandes of Sir John Tempest, knight, fermor of the same to the Kinges Majestie. Which parsonage is part of the possessions of the late dissolved monasterie of Derham in the county of Norffolk.

The same is in the saide paroch church, yet this day vacant. Ther is no landes solde or aliened sithens the statute.

Goodes, ornamentes, and plate perteynyng to the same as apperyth by inventory, viz.:—goodes valued at xxxix*s.* iiij*d.*, and plate xlviij*s.*

Ther is belonging unto this same chauntrie one annuytie or annuall rent of iiij*li.* xiij*s.* iiij*d.* goinge furthe of the parsonage of Kirkby Mallendale payd by thandes of Sir John Tempest, knight, fermor of the same, iiij*li.* xiij*s.* iiij*d.*

Wherof
Payable to the Kinges Majestie yerlie for the tenthes viij*s.* viij*d.*

And so remanyth, iiij*li.* xiij*s.* iiij*d.*

The following are the returns of King Edward's Commissioners:—

GYGGLESWIKE PARRYSHE.
THE CHAUNTRY OF OUR LADY IN THE PARYSHE CHURCHE THERE.

In the parysh of Gyggleswike is one preist found to serve the cure, besyde the vicar, the nomber of houslyng people is xijc* and the seyd parysh is wyde.

Rychard Somerskayle, incombent, lx yeres of age, somewhat learned, hath none other lyving then the said chauntrie.

Goods, xs. ijd. Plate, x onces di., parcell gylte.

The yerely value of the seyd chauntrie paide in annuall rent, iiijli. Coppiehold, nil.

Wherof
Resolutes and deductions by yere, nil.

THE CHAUNTRY OF THE RODE IN THE SEYD PARYSHE CHURCHE.

Rychard Carr,† incombent, xxxij yeres of age, well learned, and teacheth a grammer schole there, lycensed to preache, hath none other lyving then the proffitts of the seyd chauntrie.

Goods, vjs. viijd. Plate, nil.

The yerely value of the freehold land, vjli. xijd., Coppiehold, nil.

Wherof
Resolutes and deductions by yere, vjs.
And so remayneth clere to the Kinges Majestie by yere cxvs.

---

* Every person over 14 years of age would be achounted a "houseling" person, or one who received the sacrament; it is therefore estimated that the 1200 "houseling people" would represent one half the total population of the parish, which would therefore probably be about 2400.

† This Richard Carr was the nephew of James Carr, priest, who founded Giggleswick School in 1507.

THE CHAUNTRY CALLED TEMPEST CHAUNTRIE IN THE NORTH SYDE OF THE SEID PARYSHE CHURCHE.

Thomas Thomson, incombent, LXX yeres of age, unlerned, hath receyved and had one annuitie of iiij*li*. xiij*s*. iiij*d*. by yere, unto hym payd by Sir John Tempest, knight, out of the parsonage of Kyrkby in Malehome Dale, which he hath not receyved by the space of three yeres last past.

Goods, xiiij*s*. iiij*d*., Plate, xij onces, parcell gylte.

The yerely value of the seyd chauntrie payd in annuall rent, iiij*li*. xiij*s*. iiij*d*.
Wherof
Resolutes and deduccions by yere, nil.

A SOME OF MONEY GYVEN FOR THE MEYNTENANCE OF A PREIST FOR YERES IN THE SEID CHURCH.

John Malhome, preist, disseassed, dyd gyve and bequeth by his last will and testament, as apperith by the certificat of Gyggleswike aforeseyd, the some of xxxiij*li*. vj*s*. viij*d*., wherof one Thomas Edon, prist, hath ben founde by the space of VIJ yeres and di. last past, and hath receyved every yere for his stypend after the rate of iiij*li*. iij*s*. iiij*d*. amounting to the some of xxxj*li*. v*s*. And so remayneth xl*s*. xx*d*.

Of the Chantries above referred to the Stainford Chapel was situate in the North Aisle, where the organ now stands, the Tempest Chapel was to the east of this, on the site of the present vestry, whilst the Carr Chapel was in the South Aisle of the Chancel.

The following certificate as to the continuance of Giggleswick School is from the Return, dated 11th Aug. 1548, by Sir Walter Mildmay and Robert Kelway, to the Commission directing them to enquire what Schools, &c. should be maintained, and the Supplementary Report to the Commissioners by Henry Saville, the Crown Surveyor.

Carr's School being thus favourably reported on was endowed a few years afterwards out of the property of the less fortunate Priory of Acester.

GIGGLESWIKE.
SCOOLE MAYNTEYNED WITH A SOMME OF MONEY.

Memorandum: that in the seide Parishe one John Malhome, prest, and Thomas Husteler, diseased, did give and bequethe by their last will and testament, as apperith by the certificat of Giggleswike, the some of £24 : 13 : 4 towardes the maytenaunce of a scoole master there for certyn yeres, whereupon one Thomas Iveson, priest, was procurid to be Scolemaster, which hathe kept a Scole there these three yeres paste, and hathe receyved every yere for his stipende after the rate of £4 the yere, the hole £12, and so remayneth £12 : 13 : 4.

Continuatur Scole per quantitatem pecuniæ.
Examinatur per Henricum Savill, Supervisorem.

"SEXTON DICKY'S" POEMS.

Between 60 and 70 years ago, Richard Hardacre of Long Preston, better known as "Sexton Dicky," but who described himself as "The celebrated Ribblesdale Poet," issued an annual sheet of Rhymes, printed at Settle, which contain many local illusions. As specimens I print a few verses culled from various issues of these "Poems."

> The Cotton-Weavers do complain,
> Their wages are so low again;
> And bread is now so very dear,
> Is the complaints of the last year.
> (1828).

> Unions they are a help to poor,
> We never had one here before;
> A few poor men they do subscribe,
> A penny a week for to provide.
> (1829).

Times do not mend that I can see,
They are as bad as need to be;
Provisions now are quite as dear
As when I wrote for you last year.
                                    (1830).

For Trade is bad now every where,
And some things are exceeding dear;
The Cotton Weavers do complain,
Their Wages now are bad again.
                                    (1832).

There is one thing I have to tell,
Settle Town's Hall, looks very well;
It sets the town out I declare,
Useful for market or for fair.

It's ornamental to the town,
It's usefulness is yet unknown;
The architect must be clever,
In planning it altogether.

It's topping, gallant, noble, fine,
And has been building two years' time;
About it now I'll say no more,
I ne'er saw such a place before.
                                    (1833).

A Poor-house built at Giggleswick,
And everything likewise made fit;
It is intended for the poor,
I thought there was plenty before.

It is designed for good ends,
As poor people have but few friends;
So then I hope that none will rue,
If all accounts I hear be true.
                                    (1834).

At Rathmell a New Church you'll find,
That old and young who hath a mind;
May find a place of worship there,
For all who choose to go next year.

At Settle, they also expect,
Quite a New Church there to erect;
It's been talk'd of many a year,
So now I think the time draws near.
(1835).

Settle Town's Hall looks very well,
For now they've got both clock and bell;
And the New Church will look quite grand,
The plan I do not understand.
(1836).

At Skipton a new Church you'll see,
A handsome large one it will be;
At Stainforth one they do expect,
But have not begun to erect.
(1837).

Settle New Church is now complete,
And it does look exceeding neat;
They have built a handsome spire,
The steeple should have been higher.
(1838).

The seventh of January last,
There was an exceeding great blast;
It blew up many trees by root,
And many buildings did un-roof.
(1839).

There! I think that's quite enough of Dicky's "poetry."

Dr. COOKSON.

Died May 8th, 1836, aged 79. Ambrose Cookson, M.D., for many years the principal practitioner in York, and senior physician in the County Hospital, Lunatic Asylum, and other public Institutions. He was a native of Yorkshire and was educated at Giggleswick by the father of the late Dr. Paley.

(Gentleman's Magazine).

Mr. WILLIAM BIRKBECK.

Died Jan. 6th, 1838, at Linton, aged 66. William Birkbeck, Esq., banker, of Settle. He was the first member of the Society of Friends who qualified as a justice of the peace. He was courteous and gentle in his transactions with all, faithful in the discharge of his duties, and persevering almost to a proverb. His interest in the success of Mechanics' Institutes was scarcely less than that of his brother, Dr. Birkbeck, of London.

(Gentleman's Magazine).

OLD PLAYBILL.

The people of Settle have for many years shown a keen appreciation of Dramatic Art, and in the early part of this century many travelling Theatrical Companies visited the place, usually performing in some barn either at Settle or Giggleswick. I possess a number of their early Playbills, and the following one (A.D. 1821), will give a good idea of the fare our ancestors were treated to.

NEVER ACTED HERE,

THEATRE SETTLE.

On Friday Evening 21st February 1821,
will be performed the celebrated Play (never acted here), called

The Foundling of the FOREST,

Or, the Unknown Female.

Written by William Dimond, Esq., author of 'The Hero of the North,' 'Adrian and Orilla,' 'Hunter of the Alps,' &c. and performed to brilliant and overflowing houses at the Theatre Haymarket, with unbounded applause.

The incidents and natural situations pourtrayed throughout this admirable Play, are calculated to fix the attention and call forth the sympathy of every feeling heart, when accompanying the Foundling in his hair-breadth escapes from the murderous bravoes employed by the enemy to deprive him of life; particularly when the unknown female is represented as a lunatic, to answer the cruel ends of ambition. The subsequent denouement in the third act, between Florian and the unknown female, is allowed to be one of the finest incidents ever introduced on the English stage.

Florian the Foundling - - Mr. Taaffe
Count de Valmont - Mr. Smythson
Baron Longueville - - Mr. Hall
Gaspard - - - - Mr. Lardner
Bertrand - - - - Mr. Cooper
Sanguine - - - - Mr. Rowlatt
Lenoir - - - - Mr. Leyland
Henrie - - - Master Stanley
Phillip L'Eclair (with the Song of 'The Bandy Leg'd Captain') Mr. Lardner, Jun.
Eugenia (the unknown Female)......Mrs. Aldis.
Geraldine......Mrs. Cooper.
Monica......Mrs. James. Rosabella......Mrs. Smythson.

Incidental to the Play,
A Pas de deux, by Master Stanley & Miss Cooper.

End of the Play,
A Comic Song by Mr. Taaffe. and A Hornpipe by Mr. Lardner, Jun.

To conclude with the laughable Farce of

FORTUNE'S FROLICS,
OR THE
Ploughman turn'd Lord.

Old Snacks......Mr. Lardner. Frank......Mr. Hall.
Rattle......Mr. Taaffe. Country Boy......Master Stanley.
Hob......Mr. Rowlatt. Robin Rough Head......Mr. Cooper.
Nancy......Mrs. Cooper. Dolly......Mrs. Smythson.
Margery......Mrs. James.

Tickets to be had of Messrs. Smythson & Cooper, & of W. Walker, Printer.

Doors to be opened at 6 and to begin precisely at 7 o'Clock.

Pit 2s.----Gallery 1s.
No children in arms admitted.

No admittance behind the Scenes.

THOMAS DENNY.

The first Church in the ancient parish of Giggleswick, of which we have certain proof, was a Saxon one, built on or close to the site of the present Church of St. Alkelda.

For centuries the adjacent Churchyard was the only one in a wide district, and until 60 years ago the whole of the burials from the townships of Giggleswick, Settle, Rathmell, Stainforth, and Langcliffe (with few exceptions), took place there. I should estimate therefore that the earthly remains *of at least fifteen thousand persons* have been laid to rest there, probably far more.

Amongst this multitude many are worthy of commemoration, not the least of them being the well-known character, Thomas Denny, the classical scholar, who was buried on the 7th September, 1748.

An account of this eccentric, yet talented man, is to be found in Whitaker's "Craven," where there is also printed a Latin epitaph on Denny, composed by Major Dawson, but this epitaph was never inscribed on a gravestone,—indeed none was erected to mark his last resting place. In the "Gentleman's Magazine" for 1779 is to be found an article on Denny, in which his burial place is wrongly stated to be Melling, as well as a translation of the above-mentioned epitaph.

The parish registers prove however that Denny was buried in our village Churchyard, and the following extract from an interesting memorandum, made in the year 1826, points out the exact place of burial:—

"There is not, nor ever was, any monumental inscription put up to record the place of his interment. That place was pointed out to me by old Gilbert Johnson (who well remembered this most extraordinary man and was present at his funeral), as being close to the wall of the Churchyard, about two paces to the left of the principal gates."

It may be noted that Denny died on the 4th Sept., 1748. As his birthplace is not known (it is supposed to have been at Halton, near Lancaster), his age cannot be ascertained. The entry in the parish register, of his burial, is written in larger characters than usual, as tho' to point out that the person it referred to was not of an ordinary type.

It must be noted, in determining the site of Denny's grave, that the "principal gates" stood a little to the north-east of their present site.

A SETTLE SYSTEM OF SHORTHAND.

A few years ago some anonymous friend sent me by post a most curious little pamphlet, the Title of which runs

Stenography,
OR

INSTRUCTIONS
for the meanest capacity
IN SHORT HAND WRITING,
and attainable in a few hours so as it
may be used
By Tradesmen in all common concerns,
proving a saving of Time and Paper, and
many other advantages, &c.

By C. WALKER, P.D.

Settle: Printed for the Author by Wm. Walker.

(Price 3 shillings.)

I have never found out who sent me the book, but I would here express my sincere thanks to him or her, as it is one of the most treasured of my collection of local works.

The Author was a genius in his way, but the person who could use the system of shorthand here taught, would —in my humble opinion—be even more clever, as this is a sample of the "instructions":—

"I shall begin by saying that you must first write the characters of No. 1, upon a slate, or what you please, 'till you get them of by art, and be careful about the form and size of them at the beginning and in a little time you will be expeditious, after this gained you then proceed *getting* your paper or slate ruled as you see in the specimen, then you proceed to get the places of the LETTERS by art so when this is done you proceed to work," &c., &c.

"The next is sh all words that begin with sh you call that sh and so write short, as for instance you would write shall you set L in that place and then it will stand thus shl which Stenographers read shall, but supposing it to be shortness you set the character T in the place and the character S in the place of N then with the places they stand thus shtns .which is read shortness, and so by two characters marked in their proper places you have five letters for the word," &c., &c.

As the whole of the above extracts are merely *part* of one involved paragraph, I gave up in despair an attempt to solve our Author's meaning, and who "C. Walker, P.D." was, and who succeeded in learning his system "of by art" is a mystery I have not yet fathomed.

A SETTLE SYSTEM OF "AIDS TO MEMORY."

I have above given a short note on a local system of shorthand, but it must not be supposed that an improvement in that art was the only science on which the geniuses of this place exercised their ingenuity, as in the year 1827 a Mr. Joseph Broader (who was the first Master at the Settle National School), brought out a book entitled "A New Method of Artificial Memory, applied to General History, Chronology, &c., Ancient and Modern : containing twenty-seven large-octavo Copperplates."

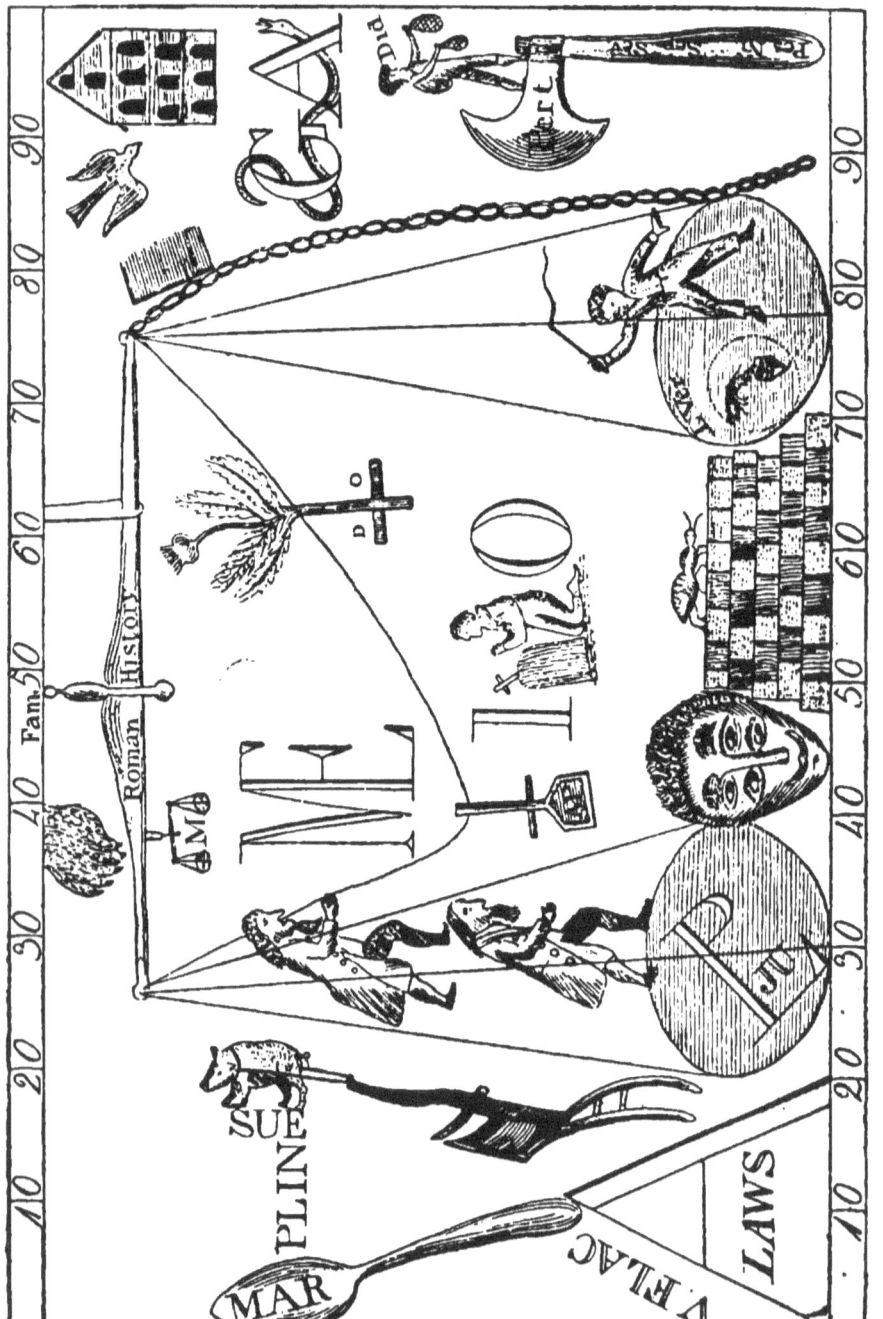

It would be difficult to clearly describe Mr. Broader's system in a short article, so I re-produce one of the illustrations that accompanied his work in order to make the matter clearer.

The events here depicted represent those occurring in the 2nd century, A.D., and the first thing the learner must do is to study the plate until he carries in his memory all the symbols figured thereon. When that is done he can recall to his mind that the first thing pictorially represented at the era in question is the word MAR in a *spoon*. Mr. Broader intends by this to remind you that *Martial* the poet, of *Spain*, flourished at this period. But the connection between *spoon* and *Spain* is striking compared with other of our Author's allusions, for instance the casual observer might not remark the close resemblance of *plough and hog* to *Plutarch*, whilst his symbols of a *tall M.E.* to represent *Ptolemy*, and a head with *double e'en* (eyes) to denote *Dublin* are sufficient to account for the limited success that the ingenious Mr. Broader's efforts to smooth the path of youth, met with. Amongst other objects depicted the reader may note the praying man (the emperor *Pius*), the ant on the wall (*Antoninus's wall*), a boy making a top *reel* (Marcus *Aurelius*), &c., &c.

There can be no doubt but that Broader was a singularly clever man, as can easily be judged from his other works, but his system of Artificial Memory seems to be a monumental example of misplaced ingenuity.

JAMES DOWNHAM, Poet.

Although the late lamented "Jimmy" Downham was a very well-known man, comparatively few persons are aware that one of his ambitions was to shine as a poet and hymn-writer.

A collection of his published "hymns" now lies before me and forms pathetic reading, as one cannot refrain from smiling at the oddity of the rhymes and sentiments, whilst the obvious sincerity of the writer and his struggles to put his feelings into verse compel one to take a friendly interest in his efforts.

It would be out of place to make fun of such well-intentioned effusions, but as I believe few people know Downham's literary compositions I content myself with quoting, without comment, the two concluding verses of one of his hymns:—

> If that your sins be red,
>   And doth a crimson dye;
> Come to the fountain hope amid,
>   And wash them white as snow.
>
> Manasseh, he did so,
>   And Paul and Peter too;
> And to this fountain they did run,
>   And came out pure and clean.

GALLOWS IN SETTLE.

In A.D. 1278, King Edward I. directed writs of "Quo Waranto" to be issued enquiring as to the right of particular individuals to exercise certain rights and privileges.

Previous to this, returns had been made as to who were holding Manors formerly belonging to the Crown, who had turned waste land into game preserves, who exacted illegal tolls, who oppressed their neighbours, &c. These returns are printed in the "Rotuli Hundredorum," and in them we find the following significant entry:—

Wapentake of "Stayncliffe."

"Setel." Two (or more) gallows lately erected by persons unknown.

It must of course have been perfectly well known to the local juries, to whom the enquiries had been submitted, who had erected these gallows, but they doubtless stood in fear and trembling of their oppressive Lords and dare not speak freely. Indeed, altho' the gallows at "Setel" were the only ones returned under the "Rotuli Hundredorum" in the Wapentake of Staincliffe, others were discovered at Letherston, Carleton, Appletreewick, and Burton-in-Lonsdale, under the more searching enquiries of "quo waranto."

The mere fact of there having been *two* gallows at Settle throws a grim light on the state of affairs here in the "good old times"—600 years ago.

THOS. BRAYSHAW.

LOCAL EXTRACTS.

LIEUT. ARTHUR CATERALL.

The following is a copy of a document which is in the Public Record Office, and is very interesting as throwing a vivid light on the troublous times in this locality 250 years ago. It is a claim by Arthur Caterall of Giggleswick, a lieutenant in the Royalist Army, for losses sustained by him during the great Civil War. The total amount of the claim is £454 10s. 0d., a very large sum in those days.

"A p'ticuler of the losses and sufferinges of Arthure Caterall of Gigelsweecke in Craven and in the County of Yorke, gent., and Leefetennant of Horse under the Earle of Newcastle is in Ma^{lis} servics.

	£	s.	d.
Inprimis I had takne from me per Captayne John Lambert's troope of horse and Maios Eaden's five dayes plowing of Oats out of my barne to the value of tenn pownds in the year 1644 ...	10	0	0
My wife payed to Thomas Carr and Thomas Knowles, Sepuest^r or Agents for the Parlament one pownd and six shillinges in the year 1646	1	6	0
She payed to the aforesayed sequestrators in the year 1647 the some of four pownds	4	0	0
She pd. to John Hodgson of Broughton Agent 1648 six pownds	6·	0	0
Pd. to Agent in Gigelsweeçke at Hugh Stackhouse house in 1648, but the acquittance is lost, four pow'	4	0	0

Anthony Foster of Rathmell farmed my estate thre yeares of the Committy at Yorke and plowed my grownd when Beanes was sould for four nobles a bushill and receaved my rents to the value for forty pownds 40 0 0

Goods taken by Captayne Ripon's souldgers in the yeare 1648 to the value of twenty-nine pownds 29 0 0

I had a bullocke and a heffer taken per John Paley Agent when Maior Rippon's souldgers kept Ingleton Hall to the value of sevven pownds... 7 0 0

Captayne John Lamber's souldgers did take from me four kine and thre horses to Thorneton Hall in the year 1645 to the value of twenty.eight pownds 28 0 0

William Bradley a souldger of Colonel Bridge's did take from my man in Austweeck one bay nag of the value of four pow' ten shill' 4 10 0

Collonell Bellingiam's souldgers did take from me goods to the value of ten pownds in 1645 ... 2 0 0

I had had taken in pewther bras and lining by Captayne Rippon's men to the value of aleaven pownds 11 0 0

I was taken prisoner by Maior Yeaden's troope of horse and soare wounded that I lay in the perill of death seaven weeckes the losse of my horse armes and cloths and chargis in my sicknes I was damnified twenty pownds and lame of one of my hands 20 0 0

I was forced to fly into the Scots Armie when his Matie was with them at Newcastle and they stole two horses from me worth forty pownds 40 0 0

Upon his Ma^{tis} goeing from the Scots to the English I marched into Scotland and wthin six weeckes into France and theire I was two yeares my chargis cost me forty-five pownds 45 0 0

And coming home agayne I was taken prisoner at
sea and I lost in money and cloths tenn pownds
and I was set a shore at Yarmouth in Norfolke
a begging home 10 0 0
And upon Sr Marmaduke Langdall's and the Scots
coming to Preston in Lanckisheere I was taken
prisoner to Shefeeld Castle and lost my horse
armes cloths and to the value of twenty pownds 20 0 0
And after Preston Battell upon Olliver's returne out
of Scotland he beate up our quarters in Cumberland and I was taken prisoner by Reybe
|Raby?| Castle men and there I lost horse
armes money and apparill to the value of sixteen pownds ... ...'16 0 0
All that time my wife and six smale children could
naither keep horse nor cow nor close fit to
weare upon Sunday but by conveying them to
nightbour houses.
And when Olliver set forth his Ac of grace as there
was unt (?) much in it I came home and one
Mr. Johnsons Justice of the peace sent for me
and tould me I was a dangerus person ag^t the
Common weale and wthout good bondsmen he
would commit me and soe I stud bound from
one Sessions to another that it cost me six
pownds 6 0 0
And 4 yeares since when Olliver committed the Officers to Yorke I was one of the number and
their it cost me tenn pownds 10 0 0

"SUFFERINGS" OF THE QUAKERS.

In another article in these "Extracts," I have discussed the Rectorial Tithes of Giggleswick. But it must not be imagined that the impropriators or owners of these tithes got in their dues without considerable trouble. The old Quakers especially used to decline to pay, and regularly had their goods seized. A M.S. volume is still carefully preserved enumerating the goods taken from these sturdy old non-conformists, which shows that the members of the Society of Friends suffered from many other causes as well. The following extracts from this old volume are of interest in these days of religious equality, many of them being entries in the handwriting of Samuel Watson himself.

1658. "Samuell Watson of Staineforth upon ye 18th day of ye 10th month 1659 went into ye parish publick place of worshipp in Gigleswick and walked into his own Quire which of right belonged to him and after a while spake amongst ye people as he was moved of God. But after a litle some of ye rudest sort pulled him down and brok his head upon ye seates and haveing haled him out threw him downe upon ye ice. Is not this the state of a synagogue and not of ye true Church of X^t"

Samuel got into trouble the following year because he went one Sunday "into a Steeplehouse in Leedes, and beginning to speak a few words to ye people, was violently haled out and sent to prison." He was imprisoned eight days, but the day after his release he preached in the market-place at Leeds.

1670. "Samuell Watson of Knight Stainforth in the Parish of Giglesivick for praying in a Meeting 12 of 4 mo. 1670 was informed against by John Read and John Thompson before Jno. Ashton and William Drake, Justices of the peace, was convicted and fined the sum of £20 : 0 : 0.

The said Samuell Watson for haveing a meeting at his house the first day of next week after and declaring of matters of faith and salvation in the assembly then mett together, being ye 19 day of ye said month was informed against by ye afforesaid Jno. Read, before Tho. Parker, John Ashton and William Drake, Justices, and was convicted and fined £60 : 0 : 0.

The said Samuell Watson for being at a Meeting in Settle ye next first day after, being ye 26 of ye said month was before Tho. Parker, John Ashton and William Drake, Justices of the peace, informed against by Robert Banks and Thomas Kidd for speaking of the things of God in ye said meeting and was convicted and fined for ye same £40 : 0 : 0.

For which said Fines the afforesaid Justices of the peace issued out their warrants to ye Constables and ovverseers for ye poor of ye afforesaid parish of Gigleswick, who came to ye house of ye said Samuell Watson distrained and drove 28 head of cattle, 9 horses, and an 130 sheeps, which apprised and sould for ye afforesaid fines of £120 : 0 : 0.

1670. Jno. Hall of Setle for being at two meetings was convicted and fined as afforesaid 15s. 0d., and had 4 pair of shows (shoes) taken from him.

Jno. Robinson of Setle for being at 3 meetings was fined £1 : 5 : 0 for which ye officers distreaned a cow and sould her which was worth £3 : 0 : 0.

John Kidd of Setle for being at two meetings was fined 15s. 0d for which the officers took 2 coats and covercloth, part of an hide of leather, and one paire of shooes worth £1 : 0 : 0.

Christopher Armestead of Setle for being at two meetings was fined 15s. 0d. for which he had taken from him by ye officers goods of the vallue of £1 : 3 : 0.

Richard Armesteade for being at two meetings was fined 15 shillings for which ye officers took 7 pair of shoos worth £1 : 0 : 0.

Mathew Wildman of Selside in Horton parish for being at same meetings was fined for himself and his wife 40s. and alsoe haveing the fines of others laid upon him of the vallue of 20 shillings, for which fines distress was made by ye officers of his houshould goods and hay to the value of £4 : 15 : 0.

Note that all ye afforementioned suffering persons, and upon ye statute made against conventicles, belonged to ye particular meeting of Settle and places adjacent, all convicted by all or some of ye afforementioned Justices, and upon ye information of all or some of ye afforesaid persons, informers, upon some whereof the hand of the Lord eminently appeared in judgment against them at or before their dying day, as may be hereafter more particularly made mention of.

Here followeth an account of severall more sufferings of Friends belonging to ye particular meeting of Setle, through the information of ye afforesaid informers and upon warrants given out by some or all of ye afforementioned Justices upon ye afforesaid Statute made agst conventicles and through distress made upon the goods of ye afforesaid persons for their peaceable meeting together."

Then follows a list which shows that Peter Atkinson, "for being at a meeting in Setle, was fined for himself and severall other friends £3 : 3 : 4 for which they made distress of Corne and Hay to ye vallue of £10."

Robert Heaton, fined £2 : 7 : 0. Had seized two cows and a heifer worth £7.

John Kidd fined £1 : 5 : 0., which was "payed by some neighbours without his consent."

Christopher Armistead fined £1 : 15 : 0., "had shooes taken from him worth 15s., and the rest of the fines were laid upon other friends."

John Hall, fined £1 : 5 : 0. Had seized "shooes and an hammer worth £1 : 10 : 0."

John Robinson, of Settle, fined £5 : 5 : 0., "goods distrained to the vallue of £11."

Lawrence Peacocke "fined £3, for which they distreaned Corne of the vallue of £5, the 10th day of ye 8 mo., 1670."

Tho. Chapman, fined £3., Corn and Hay to the value of £5., seized.

John Preston, fined £1 : 13 : 0. Had horse, &c., worth £4., taken.

Robert Cookson, fined £1 : 15 : 0. Corn worth £2 : 10 : 0., seized.

John Armestead, fined £1 : 0 : 0., "payed by a neighbour without his conscent."

. And so on for several more items.

Under the heading of "The Sufferings of Friends within Settle Monthly Meetings for denying to sweare and to marry with the priests, and for some other particular testimonys borne for ye Truth by the people of God commonly called Quakers," the following entry may be quoted:—

1671. Richard Wilson and Ann his wife of Langcliffe in the parish of Gigleswick committed to prison 1671 because they could not conforme to ye Nationall forme of mariag, though maried in a publick assembly of said people and continued prisoners about a yeare and released amongst severall others by the Kings proclamation in the yeare 1672.

GIGGLESWICK RECTORIAL TITHES.

A.D. 1600—1750.

King James the First, by Letters Patent bearing date the 18th day of May, in the 7th year of his reign (A.D. 1610), granted unto Francis Phillips and Richard Moore, their heirs and assigns for ever, all that Rectory and Parsonage of Giggleswick in the County of York, with all rights, members and appurtenances to the same belonging, reserving to himself, his heirs and assigns for ever, the yearly rent of £44.

By indenture bearing date the 24th day of June, in the year aforesaid, the said Francis Phillips and Richard Moore granted and conveyed the said rectory and premises unto Sir Gervase Helwysse and Sir Richard Williamson, their heirs and assigns for ever, to be holden of the King on the same tenour as his manor of East Greenwich.

The said Sir Gervase Helwysse and Sir Richard Williamson by Indenture bearing date the 14th day of December, in the 8th year of the reign of the said King James, did grant bargain and sell unto Thomas Hall, Robert Moorhouse, Thomas Armistead, Adam Brown, and Hugh Iveson, their heirs and assigns for ever, three-fourths of all the Tenths, Tithe and Tithes of Corn, Grain, Sheaves, and Straw, with the appurtenances, in the Township of Settle in the said Parish of Giggleswick, in as ample manner as the same was granted to Sir Gervase Helwysse and Sir Richard Williamson by the said indenture of the 24th of June aforesaid, paying unto the King, his heirs and assigns for ever, towards the fee-farm rent of £44, the yearly sum of four pounds ten shillings.

By indenture of the 14th of December, in the same year, the said Sir Gervase Helwysse and Sir Richard Williamson conveyed unto John Robinson, his heirs and assigns for ever, the moiety of the Tithe Corn in the Township of Rathmell in the Parish of Giggleswick aforesaid, and also several parcels of Glebe Lands in the said indenture particularly mentioned, paying therefor to the King, his heirs and assigns, towards the said feefarm rent of £44, the yearly sum of two pounds five shillings.

The before-named Sir Gervase Helwysse and Sir Richard Williamson sold the Rectory and Parsonage of Giggleswick to Robert Banks for eleven hundred pounds, but reserved thereout the advowson of the Vicarage and certain other rights contracted to be sold to Mr. Nowell. From Robert Banks the rectorial tithes descended to Ann, his only daughter and heiress, who married Roger Pepys. These sold to John and Richard Pepys in 1640, and then various transactions follow up to 1682, when the Pepys family sold to James Benson, who died in 1685, leaving the tithes to his sister, Ann Whitmore.

In 1690 Ann Whitmore granted all the Rectory and Parsonage of Giggleswick, and all the glebe-lands, tithes of corn, grain, hay, lambs, wool, calves, &c., to Stephen Bateman for a term of a thousand years at a peppercorn rent.

Matters were further complicated by sales of portions of the Rectory. The Armisteads bought a moiety, they sold to the Dawsons, and William Dawson sold to the Graysons, but reserved to himself certain space, then vacant, in the Parish Church.

As to another part, the Batemans sold to the Wilsons, through whose hands it passed to the Graysons.

In 1722 Charles Harris purchased from the Graysons, from Richard and Jane Brayshaw, and from William Dawson, "all the Rectory and Parsonage of Giggleswick aforesaid, in the County of York, and all and singular the rights, members, and appurtenances thereunto belonging or in anywise appertaining, sometime parcel of the possession of the Cathedral Church of Durham, and all and singular the glebe-lands, tithes of corn, grain, and hay, lambs, wool, and calves, and all others the tithes whatsoever, as well as great as small, and of what nature and kind whatsoever, and all oblations, offerings, fruits, rents, issues, profits, emoluments, privileges, commodities, advantages, hereditaments, and appurtenances whatsoever, lying and being, coming, increasing, renewing, and growing, or which should thereafter come, increase, renew, and grow within, upon, or out of the said Rectory and Parsonage of Giggleswick."

We have thus traced the tithes so far as they relate to the Township of Giggleswick. Space prevents our dealing *in extenso* with the rectorial tithes of the other townships, suffice it to say that about the year 1750 various portions had become vested in the following persons:—

The tithe corn within the Township of Giggleswick, with the tithes of calf, wool, and lambs, and mortuaries throughout the whole Parish, in Mr. Levitt Harris, son of the above-named Mr. Charles Harris.

The tithes of the Township of Settle were divided into quarters:—Mr. William Dawson, Mr. Josias Dawson, Mr. Thomas Watkinson, and Mr. Henry Airton, each holding one such quarter.

The tithes of Rathmell were also divided, one-half being the property of Mr. Charles Nowell (whose predecessors purchased it in the year 1610), a quarter belonged to William Banks, of Settle, and the remaining quarter to William Banks, of Rathmell.

The tithe of Feizor belonged to William Armistead.

I am unable to say by whom the tithes of Langcliffe and Stainforth were owned at this period, but the owner paid no part of the said Rectory-rent of £44 per annum.

The tithes having, as I have above set out, become split up into portions, it naturally followed that trouble and confusion ensued. The tithe-owners not only claimed certain privileges, which were resisted by various parties, but also repudiated certain responsibilities, and matters reached an acute stage when a member of the Dawson family was refused burial in the chancel, although such right had been admitted and exercised before the sale to the Graysons. Mr. Harris claimed to have the sole right to permit such burials and to allow any monument or tombstone in the chancel, and he reaped all the profit derived from the sale of seats and spaces for monuments erected therein. But whilst claiming these rights he repudiated the liability to repair the chancel, and that part of the fabric eventually fell into such a ruinous condition that is was stated in the course of the legal proceedings which ensued that "of late the Parishioners are now deprived of the benefit of receiving the Holy Sacrament therein." Mr. Harris tried to throw a portion of the liability on to the other owners of the rectorial tithes, notwithstanding the fact that his predecessors, the owners of the tithe corn in Giggleswick and of the "Tithe of Calf, Wool and Lamb" and of the Mortuaries throughout the whole parish had reaped the whole benefit of the chancel and repaired the same at their own expense. Whereupon the parishioners cited Mr. Harris and the other owners of the tithe-corn within the parish (but not the owners of the glebe lands), to appear in the Ecclesiastical Court of York and show cause why monition should not issue against them to repair the said chancel, or in default thereof why the "fruits, rents and profits" of the Great Tithes of the parish of Giggleswick should not be sequestered for the repairs of the chancel.

The parishioners who caused the citation to be issued were Josias Morley, William Bradley, Thomas Brayshaw, Thomas Clapham, John Richardson, Thomas Lister, William Hall, Henry Town, Lawrence Wharfe, Robert Banks, Richard Redmayne, and James Pearson, whilst the suit was brought against William Dawson, Levitt Harris, Charles Nowell, the Rev. Anthony Lister (Vicar), William Banks of Settle, William Armistead of Giggleswick, Henry Airton of Malham, Thomas Watkinson of Skipton, William Dawson (a minor, son of the late Josias Dawson), and Susannah Dawson, his mother.

In the cause of the proceedings the Dawsons and Mr. Harris asked to be dismissed from the suit as they were willing to pay their share, but this was not allowed.

In May, 1751, the Judge of the Ecclesiastical Court decreed that Dawson and the other respondents should "be admonished to repair the chancel according to their respective proportions of the tithe they possess," and condemned them in costs.

Fête at STACKHOUSE.

A dainty little invitation, printed in gold on embossed paper, recalls one of the most memorable entertainments ever held in this locality.

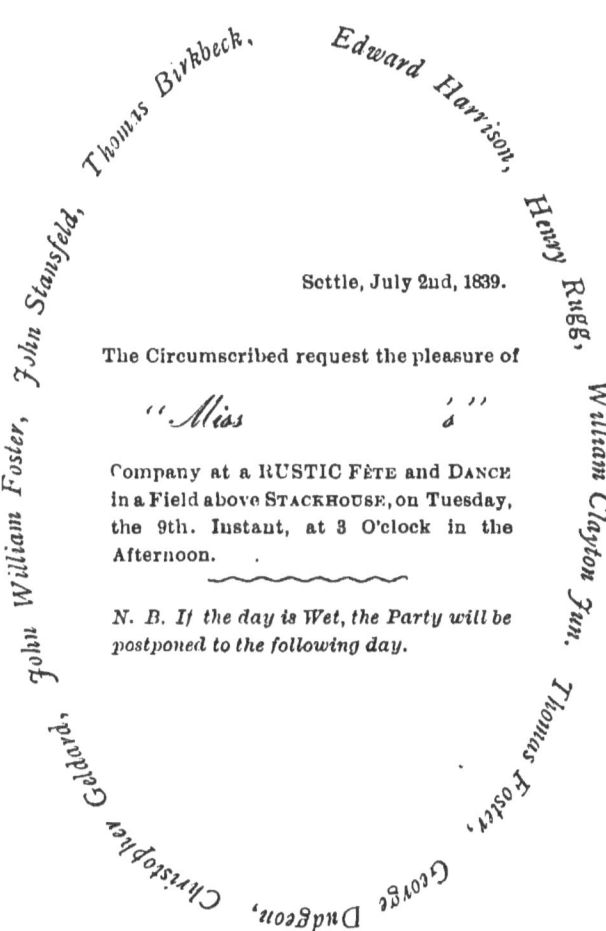

Settle, July 2nd, 1839.

The Circumscribed request the pleasure of

"*Miss*   *'s*"

Company at a RUSTIC FÊTE and DANCE in a Field above STACKHOUSE, on Tuesday, the 9th. Instant, at 3 O'clock in the Afternoon.

N. B. *If the day is Wet, the Party will be postponed to the following day.*

(Surrounding names: Thomas Birkbeck, Edward Harrison, Henry Rugg, William Clayton Jun., Thomas Foster, George Dudgeon, Christopher Geldard, John William Foster, John Stansfeld)

Mr. JOHN HARE.

The people of Settle often mention with pleasure the close associations of Miss Ellen Terry with the locality in times past, and other ties which bind well-known theatrical "stars" to the place; but the fact that the first appearance in public, as an amateur, of Mr. John Hare, the eminent actor, took place in the Mechanics' Hall, is one in which they take especial pride. For further particulars of this appearance I would refer my readers to Mr. Pemberton's biography of Mr. Hare, but I think the programme of the performance, which was given in aid of the Fund for the relief of the distressed Cotton-spinners (who were suffering great privations in consequence of the American Civil War), is well worthy of preservation. I may say that Mr. Hare's pseudonym at this entertainment was "Mr. Rattleton," whilst the names assumed by the other performers were as follows :—Mr. Winbolt (Mr. Brewin), Mr. Bellingham (Mr. Berrington), Mr. Smith (Mr. J. H. Burrow), Mr. Linton (Mr. J. L. Swale), Mr. Rogers (Mr. J. Clark), Mrs. Horton (Mrs. Sanderson), Miss Crofts (Mr. H. E. Stansfeld), and Miss Meadows (Mr. B. R. Stansfeld).

Mr. Hare's histrionic abilities were even then conspicuous, as the *Settle Chronicle*, in reviewing the performance, stated that he and Mr. Brewin "distinguished themselves by a display of dramatic talent of an order which is seldom seen even among professional actors."

RELIEF FUND.

AMATEUR DRAMATIC PERFORMANCES

In aid of the above Fund.

MECHANICS' HALL, SETTLE.

THURSDAY, and FRIDAY, the 29th and 30th of JANUARY, 1863.

PROGRAMME.

BLANCHARD JERROLD'S COMEDIETTA OF
'COOL AS A CUCUMBER'

Characters.

OLD BARKINS	*Mr. Winbolt.*
FRED. BARKINS .... (his son)	*Mr. Bellingham.*
PLUMPER	*Mr. Rattleton.*
MISS JESSY HONITON	*Mrs. Horton.*
MARY WIGGINS .... (her servant)	*Miss Meadows.*

SCENE.—DRAWING ROOM IN MR. BARKINS' LONDON RESIDENCE.
TIME.—THE PRESENT DAY.

THE *VERY LATEST* EDITION OF
'THE LADY OF LYONS'

The new and elegant Scenery by H Palmer, Esq The Overture and the whole of the Music composed and arranged by Mr. W. H. Montgomery.

Characters.

BEAUSEANT (a decidedly "bad lot," who being of considerable weight in Lyons, may, with justice, be termed a heavy villain) ....*Mr. Rattleton*

COLONEL DAMAS (a veteran of the old school, an advocate for military moustachios, and a strict dicipline-hairy'un) *Mr. Bellingham*

DESCHAPELLES (Wholesale Grocer, Tea Dealer, and Italian Warehouseman. N.B.—"*The Trade supplied,*" &c)....*Mr. Smith*

CLAUDE MELNOTTE (a youth of imaginative temperament, who, from the fact of never doing anything for his living, is looked upon by his comrades as a genius, and who, although he commits a fraud which in modern times would result in unlimited horse-whippings, &c., is nevertheless considered by a British audience an object of sympathy and regard)....................................*Mr. Linton*

GASPAR (a virtuous peasant, who offers himself as a go-between, and gets, as usual, more pedal applications than small coin of the realm) ....*Mr. Rogers*

LANDLORD OF THE "GOLDEN LION" (a re-publican)...*Mr. Rogers*
THE FAMILY PORTER (who, unlike the "Family Porter" of the advertisements, is always up) ...*Mr. Winbolt*
MADAME DESCHAPELLES (M. Deschapelles' "good lady") ...*Miss Crofts*
PAULINE (her only child, so highly polished that she may be said to take the shine out of every rival,—proud, but eventually penitent) ...*Mrs. Horton*
JANET (barmaid at the "Golden Lion")...*Miss Meadows*
THE WIDOW MELNOTTE ("a lorne lorn creature")...*Mr. Winbolt*

TO CONCLUDE WITH THE
LAUGHABLE FARCE
By J. M. Morton, Esq., of
'BOX AND COX'

Characters:

BOX.................. (a journeyman printer) ....*Mr. Rattleton*
COX.................. ..(a journeyman hatter)..............*Mr. Winbolt*
MRS. BOUNCER......(a lodging-house keeper) ....*Mrs. Horton*

ADMISSION.

Reserved Seats (numbered), 4s.; Second Seats, 2s.; Gallery, 1s.;—may be secured at Mr. Wildman's, Bookseller, or at the door.

It is requested that Tickets be taken in advance to avoid delay on entering.

Doors open each evening at half-past SIX, to commence at SEVEN o'clock.

Carriages may be ordered for half-past ten.

THOS. BRAYSHAW.

LOCAL FRAGMENTS.

(Reprinted from the Settle Household Almanack for 1899.)

Compiled by Thos. Brayshaw.

SETTLE:
THE CRAVEN PRINTING AND STATIONERY COMPANY, LIMITED.

LOCAL FRAGMENTS.

SETTLE FAIRS.

In the year 1708 the right of the Earl of Burlington to hold at Settle "an antient weekly market on Tuesday" and a fair at Lawrencemass, as well as several new fairs, was confirmed.

As I have already printed a copy of this grant of confirmation in No. 8 of my "Stackhouse Series of Local Tracts" I do not propose to recapitulate it here, but the following supplementary proclamations, &c., are of interest :—

The first is a table of
    TOLLS TO BE TAKEN AT SETTLE FAIRS.
Agreed upon by Sir Chas. Ingleby }
        Aug. 5th 1708.

New Ffairs.

Beasts.	For every Beast. Two pence	2
Horse, &c.	For every Horse, Mare, Gelding, and ffoal. Ffour pence	4
Old Sheep, &c.	For every Score of Old Sheep. Eight pence	8
Lambs Suck^{ng}.	For every Score of Lambs. Ffour pence	4
Wool.	For every Pack of Wool sold. Two pence	2
Leather and Stalls.	{ For every Pack of Leather sold. Two pence	2
	Stallage for every Man's Parcel of Leather. Two pence	2

Booth, &c.	For every Stall or Booth the usual Toll of Two pence.	2
Goods, &c. except Butter, &c.	For every Stall, Booth, or other Goods laid down in the ffair Except Butter and Cheese. Two pence	2
Penny Toll.	That all Sorts of Goods bought in any of the Great ffairs and Carried out of Town except Meal, Corn, Grain, and Victuals shall be tollable at One penny if sold at or above the value of Thirteenpence half-penny	1
Raw Hides.	For every Tenn Raw Hides. Six pence	6
Single Hide.	For every Single Hide. One penny	1

AT LAWRENCEMASS.

The Tolls as usual.

Persons ffree. The Inhabitants of the Town and Township of Settle to be ffree from the Tolls above other than such as Buy Cattle to sell again.

Matters however did not run very smoothly, and in May, 1715, it became necessary, in order to protect the Earl's interests, to issue the following proclamation against illegal trading in Cattle at Settle Market :—

A PROCLAMATION PUBLISHED AT SETTLE.

𝔚𝔥𝔢𝔯𝔢𝔞𝔰 A pattent was lately granted to the Rt. Honble Rich^d. Earle of Burlington and Corke for the holding of severall ffaires in the towne of Settle, at severall days and times mentioned therein, As also ffortnight ffairs, to be held on the ffridays beginning on the ffriday before Easter and soe to continue every ffortnight for some time as the said pattent directs, wherein Beasts and Cattle may be sold, And also a Markett to be held in the said towne on every Tuesday ffor such wares and comodities as are allowed to be sold there,

And whereas Complaint hath been made that many of the Inhabitants and Country people not regarding the Direction of the said pattent tho' the same hath been openly and publickly read at the Markett Crosse, in the hearing and presence of very many persons, **Yet** in opposition to the said pattent and of the Authority by which the same was granted and contrary to the Directions therein given severall Goods & Chattels have been brought into Settle aforesaid to bee sold there on the Markett days, which are not to be sold there on those days But on ffair days as appointed by the said pattent, to the damage of the sd Earle And great disappointment of Chapmen that have come many miles to the said ffairs to buy Cattle, And are yet willing to come to buy goods at the said ffairs in case the Country people will take care for the future to observe the same and to bring in such Cattle as they have to sell on the ffair days appointed for the same and not on Markett Days.

These are therefore to give Notice unto All persons whatsoever for the time to come, to forbear to bring in or Expose to Sale any Beastes or Cattle whatsoever in the said towne of Settle on the Markett day unlesse that some ffair shall happen to ffall on a Markett day there that the same are allowed to be sold there att that time by vertue of the said pattent, On payne of fforfeiting of the Beasts and Cattle so sold or Exposed to Sale within the Limitts of the ffair on any Markett day other than as aforesaid, and on payne of being ffin'd, prosecuted and proceeded against as the Law Directs.

Not the least interesting however is the
PROCLAMATION
made from the Settle Market Cross at the time of commencement of each fair.

The Most Noble William, Duke of Devonshire, Chief Lord
    of this ffair, In his Majesty's Name doth strictly charge
    and command

FIRST   *That* All and every Person and Persons that shall repair resort and come into this Fair and Markett do well and dutifully observe and keep his Majesty's Peace, upon pain of Imprisonment, and to be ffined for their contempt According to the Laws and Statutes made for Breach of the Peace in ffairs and Marketts.

SECONDLY   *That* No Person or Persons attempt or presume to Ride or go armed, or to carry wear or Bear any Armour or Weapons within the precint and during the time of the ffair and Markett here holden, contrary to the said Laws (except such as be attending on the Steward of the said ffair) upon pain of fforfeiting such Armour or Weapons and further to be Imprisoned and punished according to the Laws and Statutes in that case made and provided.

THIRDLY   *That* all and every Person and Persons Do Bargain and sell Sound and Lawful Goods and Chattels, Wares and Merchandizes, And use Lawful and Allowed Weights and Measures, without ffraud or Deceit, upon pain of fforfeiting the same Goods and Chattels, Wares and Merchandizes or the value thereof.

FFOURTHLY   *That* No Person or Persons Bargain for or Buy any Horses, Mares, or Geldings, within or during the time of the ffair aforesaid, before true Testament be given of the Lawful Owners; and thereupon be entered in the Toll Book kept for the ffair according to the Statute in that case provided, Nor take or withdraw any such Horses Mares or Geldings or any other Goods, Chattels, Wares and Merchandizes Sold and Bought during the time of this ffair and Markett before due Toll be paid for the same to the Officer or Officers appointed for the Receipt thereof, upon the like pain of fforfeit-

	ing the same Horses, Mares, Geldings, Goods, Chattels, Wares and Merchandizes or the value thereof.
FIFTHLY	*And Lastly* If any Person or Persons have any Wrong or Injustice done to them by reason of any Contract or Bargain made within and during the time of this ffair and Markett let them repair to the Steward thereof at the Court Chamber or Toll Booth and inforce their Cause in course of Law, And the same shall be heard and tryed according to Law, Justice, and Equity.

God Save the King and the Most Noble William Spencer Duke of Devonshire, The Steward, and Gentlemen attending him.

Miss TURNER'S ABDUCTION.

One of the sensations of the year 1826 was the abduction of Miss Ellen Turner, an heiress, by Edward and William Wakefield and others, which is also noteworthy as being one of the last of the "Gretna-Green Marriages." The case was tried at Lancaster in March, 1827, and the Wakefields were each sentenced to three years imprisonment. As the parties passed through Settle in their flight the following local evidence is interesting.—

Ann Bradley, sworn. Examined by Mr. Parke.

I keep the "Devonshire Arms" at Skipton, and recollect two gentlemen and a lady coming to my house in a carriage and four. They arrived about ten o'clock on the evening of the 7th March, 1826. I was at the door and saw them by the light of a lantern. Four horses were then ordered for Settle. I ordered my maid servant to take out some gingerbread and two glasses of water to them—the gingerbread was placed on the lady's lap. I saw they were two gentlemen and a lady in the carriage, but I could not swear to them again.

As they were going away did you make any request to them?—I said I should be glad to see them on their return.

What induced you to make that observation?—I thought it was a runaway match.

What did they say?—I don't know. I cannot speak to what they said; they were very cheerful. The lady was in good spirits and I heard her laughing with the gentlemen. I was then in the bar and the chaise was at the outside of the house.

Where did they go to from Skipton?—To Settle.

Cross-examined by Mr. Sergeant Cross.

My friend has asked you every question but whether the gingerbread was good,—was it good?—Very good.

Re-examined by Mr. Scarlett.

It seemed to please the lady, did it not?—Yes.

Mr. Hartley, sworn. Examined by Mr. Pattison.

You are the landlord, I believe, of the "Golden Lion," at Settle?—Yes.

Do you remember a party coming there on the morning of the 8th March?—Yes.

About what time?—Half-past one.

Who were the party?—Two gentlemen and a lady.

Did they change horses there?—Yes.

Four horses?—Yes.

And went on where?—To Kirkby Lonsdale.

Sarah Colman, sworn. Examined by Mr. Scarlett.

Do you live at the "Rose and Crown," at Kirkby Lonsdale?—I do.

Do you remember early in the morning of the 8th of March, two gentlemen and a lady coming with a carriage-and-four?—Yes.

What time in the morning did they arrive?—Between three and four.

COUNTY RATE IN A.D. 1602.

In the 44th year of Queen Elizabeth's reign it was ordered that of every £100 which had to be raised by the West Riding of Yorkshire, the following proportions had to be given by the townships in this locality:—

	s.	d.
Settle	10	0
Giggleswick	10	0
Long Preston	10	0
Rathmell	5	5
Wigglesworth	6	8
Stainforth	8	4
Langcliffe	3	4

When we compare these figures with the amount paid by other places in the Riding, the result is startling, as we find that Leeds only had to pay 16s. 8d., Bradford 8s. 4d., whilst Sheffield got off for 3s. 9d. Thus it appears that Settle, Giggleswick, and Long Preston actually had to contribute more between them than had Leeds, Bradford, and Sheffield together.

Dr. JOHN WINDSOR.

JOHN WINDSOR, F.R.C.S.E., was born at Settle in the year 1787 and died at Manchester on the 1st of September 1868. At an early period of his life he manifested an ardent taste for botany and showed such zeal in the study of the science that Sir James Smith, in 1810, mentioned his name in that author's "English Botany" as that of an "assiduous young botanist," and although for many years his favorite studies were interrupted by the imperative demands of a very extensive medical practice he resumed the pursuits of them in later years with great ardour and added largely to his herbarium of British plants.

He contributed several papers to the "Phytologist," and one or two to the "Journal" of the Linnean Society, of which he was a Fellow for 55 years. He is best known by his work "Flora Cravonensis, or a Flora of the vicinity of Settle," the publication of which he did not live to see, but which, as it was ready for the press, was issued for private circulation by his representatives.

This work was dedicated "To the Memory of his old friends and fellow-botanists, William Kenyon of Settle, Thomas Williams Simmonds of Settle, John Carr of Stackhouse, and John Howson of Giggleswick."

In addition to these Botanical works DR. WINDSOR was the author of several papers in various medical periodicals, and was at one time the editor of the "Ophthalmic Review."

JOHN OVEREND.

This worthy Quaker, founder of a well-known house, is deserving of mention amongst our local notabilities. The following account of him is extracted from a book relating to the Society of Friends.

JOHN OVEREND, son of John and Isabel Overend, was born at Settle, Yorkshire, on 2nd of 6th month, 1769. This Friend, who became alike one of the shrewdest and wealthiest of London money-lenders, came originally from the North, and, it is said, with so little means of his own, as to have worked his way up to London by driving the horses of the waggons while their waggoners slept inside. He soon entered the services of Smith & Holt, Woollen Factors and Bankers. Here his knowledge of the road and his trustworthiness led to his being sent to and fro to Norwich with valuable banker's parcels, which brought him into acquaintance with John Gurney of that city. To this friend he communicated a plan that had occurred to him of greatly simplifying the then existing system of discount, which was to charge two commissions on all transactions, one to the lender and one to the borrower. JOHN OVEREND thought that a sufficient profit could be made if but one commission were charged, and that on the party borrowing the money. It gained the approval of John Gurney, and in consequence through his support, JOHN OVEREND, leaving the Banking house, commenced business as a discount and bill-broker on this one commission system, in a small office upstairs in a house in Finch Lane, Cornhill. He induced Thomas Richardson, who was then a clerk at Smith, Wright & Gray's to become associated with them in this enterprise, and the rapid success that attended it induced John Gurney to allow his son Samuel, then very young, to enter the concern, which moved to larger premises, and became famous in commercial circles as the firm of Overend, Gurney & Co. JOHN OVEREND married Mary Kitching, but left no family. He lived during his latter years in a beautiful park-like estate, situate at Clutts Hill near Southgate, where he died on the 17th of 1st month, 1832, and where his widow, who survived him more than 30 years, died at the age of 79 on the 20th of 8th month, 1862. Her delicate health had prevented her mixing much in society, but the suffering and afflicted often had substantial proof of the good use she made of the abundant means at her disposal.

JOHN OVEREND'S portrait is in the London "Friend's Institute."

SONNET ON "STACKHOUSE."

The Rev. H. J. Bulkeley was formerly a Master at Giggleswick School and Assistant Curate of Settle. He has published several volumes of charming verse, and many of his poetical effusions relate to this locality.

I content myself by simply quoting his beautiful sonnet on

"STACKHOUSE."

Stackhouse, low nestling in thy wooded niche
   Five hundred feet below me, as I stand
   Out-gazing on the glories of this land
Of crag and meadow, thou art very rich
   In what should make life beautiful, these grand
Grey scars that curve and break the misty sky
Purpled in sunset, sheep and cows that lie
   Deep in the pasture, hand that graspeth hand.
Brave natural beauty, wealth of life, and home—
   All these thou hast. Has even God a blessing,
God of the mountains, richer than these three?
Yon scarlet spray of cherry blends the dome
   Of heaven with rock and grass in its caressing.
So may sweet piety bless all in thee!

Oct. 1st, 1889.

"CAMMOCK" AND "THE DRUID'S CIRCLE."

The following extract is from a letter, dated November 11th, 1847, addressed to Capt. Yolland of the Ordnance Survey.

"I beg to acknowledge the receipt of your note of the the 5th inst., relating to the "Cammock." It is a difficult matter to say what is its real origin. In the year 1842 Dr. Buckland and Mr. T. Sopwith (author of "Economic Geology") visited Settle and gave it as their opinion that to glacier formation is due the *Cam ock* (or "little hill," from "Cam," Danish, and "ock" the Saxon diminutive, as we have it in "hillock"), which I think is most likely both as to origin and name. The Cammock is situated in the centre of a natural basin, or rather the bottom of a lake, about a mile in diameter, open to the south, through which runs the River Ribble which washes the west side of the hill. With regard to the earth-works they seem to me natural formations, as the same appearance occurs on the east and west side of the valley, about half a mile distant, and about the same level, indeed the same form of lines, steps, terraces,—or by what other name they are called,—are quite common in this neighbourhood, some having only a slight covering of soil, being rock nearly to the surface.

I suppose the circle of stones in Cleatop High Park to be aboriginal British or Druidical remains from the following appearances :—The circle is complete and the large stones are set *on end*, some of them several tons weight. The stones are twelve in number now standing, besides several others that seem to be rolled a short distance, as it is placed on the ascent of a steep hill and commands a beautiful and extensive prospect (more so than any given point of the same altitude in the vicinity). The circle is 36 feet in diameter."

I was particularly pleased to come across the latter part of the above letter, as I well remember how, when I delivered the first of my lectures on "Local Jottings" in Feb. 1883, many of my audience seemed very sceptical when I described the few stones remaining at Cleatop as part of a Druidical Circle. At that date the study of the antiquities of this locality was entirely neglected, and the numerous historical guides to this district, which now help the student, were as yet unwritten.

My remarks on that occasion were as follows :—

"About a mile to the south of Settle, close to Cleatop Wood, there is marked on the Ordnance Map an "Ancient Stone Circle." Within the memory of man this circle was very perfect; indeed it was so regular and well defined that one or two gaps caused by the removal of stones could easily be noted. The circle is supposed to have been a Druid's Temple, and strongly resembled similar erections in various parts of the country, and it is a curious circumstance that the hill at the back of it is known as "Druid's Hill" to this day. The site was a well chosen one, as in ancient times the hills behind were covered with forests, whilst in front spread a beautiful landscape. In the foreground there would be Giggleswick Tarn, on the right hand the valley of the Ribble, with Penyghent keeping guard at the top, and at the left the valley running towards Clapham, with the mighty mass of Ingleborough in the background. As in the case of the old graves, known as "The Giants' Graves," on Penyghent, considerations of utility caused the removal of the old stones, which were broken up by the aid of fires built on them, and they were used to build walls. Few traces of the circle now remain."

SETTLE CHURCH.

In order that due credit may be given to those persons by whose efforts Settle Church was built, I venture to print a copy of a circular issued in 1835.

PROPOSED CHURCH AT SETTLE.

In consequence of the very liberal offer made by MR. WILKINSON of Hellifield and MR. TENNANT of Riddings, and their Sisters, to contribute five hundred pounds towards building and endowing a Church at Settle, and of the further kind offer of MR. WILKINSON to give a Site for the same in Upper-Settle (if approved of):—a public Meeting was holden, pursuant to notice, at the Golden Lion Inn, on TUESDAY the 17th of FEBRUARY 1835, to consult upon the measures proper to be adopted for enabling the Inhabitants to avail themselves of those munificent offers without delay.

The REV. ROWLAND INGRAM B.D. having been called to the Chair the cordial thanks of the Meeting were unanimously voted to MR. WILKINSON, MR. TENNANT, and their Sisters, for the very generous offers above-mentioned.

A Subscription was then commenced, for carrying the objects of the Meeting into effect : and a Committee was appointed, to solicit and collect further subscriptions, and to take the subject of a Site into consideration : and it was resolved that MR. WILKINSON and MR. TENNANT should be Honorary Members of the Committee, whenever they might think proper to act.

At the close of the Meeting, the List of Subscriptions was as follows :—

	£	s	d
Mr. Wilkinson, Mr. Tennant, and their respective families...	500	0	0
The Miss Dawsons, Marshfield... ...	200	0	0
The Rev. John Clapham...	100	0	0
Thomas Clapham	100	0	0
John Peart	100	0	0
The Craven Bank...	100	0	0
Wm. Bolland	50	0	0
John Moffatt	50	0	0
John Preston	50	0	0
H. J. Swale	20	0	0
A. Stackhouse, Settle	10	0	0
E. Hardacre & Son	5	5	0
Wm. Robinson	50	0	0
Rowland Ingram	10	0	0
John Howson	5	5	0
A. Stackhouse, Stainforth	30	0	0

BY ORDER OF THE COMMITTEE.

ROWLAND INGRAM, Jun. } Secretaries.
WM. ROBINSON,

Further Subscriptions will be received by the Secretaries, and at the Craven Bank.

SALE OF CASTLEBERG.

The question as to when the Lease of Castleberg expired is one that has often been asked. The following is a copy of an old poster, which will serve to answer the query.

SETTLE IN CRAVEN.

To be
SOLD BY AUCTION,
by Mr. Merryweather,
at the house of
Mr. R. Hartley, the Golden Lion Inn, at Settle,
in the County of York,
Between the hours of Six and Eight o'clock in the evening, of Wednesday, the 13th day of January, Instant, subject to such conditions as will be then and there produced:
The Reversionary Interest
In all that Romantic and Picturesque Plot,
Piece, or Parcel, of
LAND & ROCK,
Situate in the Town of Settle aforesaid, called
CASTLEBAR OR CASTLEBERG ROCK,
Now set out and used as a Pleasure Ground, subject to a Lease thereof for 99 years, at the Yearly reserved Rent of 6d., about 52 years whereof are yet to come and unexpired therein.

Mr. Hartley, of the Golden Lion, will show the premises, and further particulars may be had on application to Messrs. Smith, Weir and Smith, Solicitors, Cooper's Hall, London; or at the Office of

Mr. Alcock, Solicitor, Skipton,
January, 6, 1830.

See another Hand Bill of certain other premises adjoining the above, which will be Sold at the same time and place.

Garnett, Printer, Stationer, and Bookbinder, Market Place, Skipton.

VOLUNTEERS, 1794.

A hundred years ago the nation was in great fear of a French Invasion, and steps were taken to raise a local regiment of Volunteer Cavalry, which formed the nucleus of the "Craven Legion." In No. 6 of my "Stackhouse Tracts" I re-printed a poem by Mr. R. Kidd on a Meeting of these Volunteers at Settle in August 1794, and the following copy of an old circular will show us the part taken by Settle in the widespread movement to safeguard the national honour.

Settle, 14th June, 1794.

Enrolment and Subscription for raising Volunteer Corps of Cavalry within the West Riding of this County, for internal defence.

At an adjourned Meeting for the Wapentake of Staincliff and Ewecross, held at this town, for the purposes above-mentioned, a liberal Subscription was entered into, and several gentlemen enroled themselves for Personal Service.

To afford persons who are desirous of coming forward a further opportunity of entering their names, this Meeting is adjourned to Kighley, at the *Golden Fleece*, on Wednesday the 25th day of June Instant, at 12 o'clock at noon.

That the thanks of this Meeting be given to the Chairman for his conduct on this occasion.

Thomas Garforth, Chairman.

The Subscription at Settle is as follows :—

		£	s.
Michael Mitchell	Stainton ...	5	5
Abraham Chamberlain	Skipton ...	10	10
Thomas Salmon	Settle ...	5	5
Anthony Lister	Giggleswick ...	10	10
Edward Clayton	Settle ...	10	10
Thomas York	Halton Place ...	21	0
Thomas Ingilby	Austwick ...	10	0

			£	s.
C. Ingilby	Austwick	...	21	0
Thomas Backhouse	Giggleswick	...	10	10
Thomas Barlow	Ingleton	...	3	3
Thomas Clapham	Giggleswick	...	10	10
John Clapham, Clerk	Giggleswick	...	10	10
William Clapham	Stackhouse	...	10	10
Bryan Waller	Mason Gill	...	5	5
Thomas Toulman	Ingleton	...	5	5
Hartley and Swale	Settle	...	10	10
Thomas Starkie and Son	Gisburn	...	10	10
Rev. Richard Dawson	Bolton	...	21	0
Thomas Ingilby	Clapham	...	10	10
William Carr	Stackhouse	...	5	5
John Baynes	Skipton	...	40	0
Thomas Foster	Clapham	...	5	5
William Lawson	Giggleswick	...	5	5
Revd. William Paley	Giggleswick	...	10	10
Mrs. Foster	Settle	...	10	10
John Peart	Settle	...	5	5

The Subscription at Skipton is as follows :—

			£	s.
Thomas Lister, Esq.	Gisburn Park	...	200	0
High Sheriff of the County of York.				
Thomas Paley	Langcliff	...	10	10
David Swale	Settle	...	10	10
C. Clapham, Clerk	Clapham	...	10	10
&c.	&c.			

Jackson, Printer, Settle.

THOS. BRAYSHAW.

ITEMS

OF

LOCAL INTEREST,

RELATING TO

SETTLE AND NEIGHBOURHOOD,

CONTAINED IN THE

"GENTLEMAN'S MAGAZINE,"

From its commencement in 1731 to A.D. 1800.

WITH ILLUSTRATIONS.

COMPILED BY

THOS. BRAYSHAW.

* *

STACKHOUSE,

NEAR SETTLE,

JUNE 10TH, 1884.

Some three years since I compiled an Index to the Items relating to Yorkshire contained in the "*Gentleman's Magazine*," and the first part of this Index, consisting of about 1600 entries, was published in the "*Leeds Mercury Weekly Supplements*" from December 17th, 1881, to September 9th, 1882,

In compiling this Index I found several articles relating to this neighbourhood, and as sets of the Magazine are scarce, and not easily accessible, (perhaps the reason of such scarcity is not difficult to find when I state that my own set takes up about twenty-eight feet of shelving,) I thought a reprint of such local items would be of interest to persons residing in this locality. I therefore decided they should form the second of my series of " Local Tracts."

THOS. BRAYSHAW.

Twelve large and one hundred small paper copies printed for private circulation.

EXTRACTS

FROM THE

"GENTLEMAN'S MAGAZINE" RELATING TO SETTLE AND NEIGHBOURHOOD.

To the Author, &c.,

Settle, in Yorkshire, April, 13th, 1749.

Sir,

Till the 7th instant we were, for anything we know, at least 20 miles distant on all sides from the contagious distemper among the cattle; neither is it suspected that any herd or beast have been drove from any infected place to us, which makes us strongly suspect, what does not seem to have been much attended to, that the infection may, and often is, carried many miles in clouds by strong winds, such as we have had for many days past from the east, and at last falls in form of a dew or mist agreeable to the doctrine of the great Frederick Hoffman, who, in his chapter *de temporibus anni insalubritus*, says "For it appears from experience that many corrosive salts are generated in the air itself which chiefly shew themselves in a very corrosive dew, which falling upon vegetables, not only corrupts, but even eats them up, and stains with variety of colours the leaves of trees and plants, whence it is observed that the fruits and grass on which this dew falls have been highly pernicious both to man and beast. For which reason many skilful physicians not injudiciously attribute the death or even plague that rages among the cattle, swine, sheep, &c., not only to a moist rotting season, but to a very corrosive dew. Thus, in the years 1693 and 1694, in the principality of Hesse, the vegetables were infected with a kind of corrosive dew from whence oxen and cows fell down dead by heaps of a consumption of the lungs."

Altho' the above distemper does not appear to be the same which now rages with us, yet there is the same reason for the propogation of the one as the other, viz., the currency of the air; and we are the more confirmed in that opinion from the concurrent testimony of many people who were near the infected place on the 7th instant, the day the cattle were first seized, who say that there was that day a most intolerable stench in the air, which made them sick and otherwise disordered them. The place where it now rages is a farm called Cleatop, about a mile from this town, where the farmer has already 18 dead, and all others about the house are now ill in the same distemper, three or four of which, however 'tis thought will recover. Gentlemen who have seen cattle ill in different parts say this distemper appears to be the most violent of any.

Yesterday we saw one of the carcasses opened.

Here follows a long account of the symptoms, which, I think, are better omitted.

P.S.—Other accounts say that the distemper was brought to Settle by a tanner's buying some hides of infected cattle, which he laid in water, that afterwards running through the above farmer's grounds, occasioned "the intolerable stench" and infected the beasts.

In connection with this outbreak I thought an extract from a communication immediately following the above letter would not be out of place, as it gives a curious bit of Yorkshire folk-lore.—T. B.

An angel (so says the legend) descended lately into Yorkshire and there set a large tree on fire, the strange appearance of which, or else the savour of the smoke, incited the cattle around (some of which were infected with the distemper,) to draw near, where they all either received an immemediate cure or an absolute prevention of the disorder. It is not affirmed that the angel staid to speak to any body, but only that he left a written direction for the neighbouring people to catch this supernatural fire, and to communicate it from one to another with all possible speed throughout the country; and in case that, by any unhappy means it should be extinguished and utterly lost, that then new fire of equal virtue may be obtained, not by any common method, but rubbing two pieces of wood together till they burn. Upon what foundation this story stands we shall not be at the pains to enquire, but so much is certain, that it has gained sufficient credit to have put the farmers actually into a hurry of communicating flame and smoke from one house to another over the whole country.

Wakefield, 1760.

MR. URBAN,
Travelling lately thro' Craven, in Yorkshire, I was informed of a very remarkable well near Settle which ebbs and flows four or fives times in an hour to the height of near six inches. It arises at the bottom of a prodigious ledge of rocks, runs with a plentiful stream, is enclosed in a quadrangle of stone flags of about two foot square, and had formerly proper outlets for the current, to enable the spectator to distinguish the degrees of its rise and fall with more exactness. But it is now much neglected and out of order, which is a little surprizing, as it is the capital curiosity of the country, and is close by the high road side.

Springs of this sort are said to be in many parts of England. That at Tideswell I have seen, and its rise is barely perceptible, and, by description, the others are very far short of this, which is the only one unnoticed by naturalists. And I cannot omit mentioning that the *Fells* (as they are called) in that neighbourhood, will amply repay the fatigue of a speculative man in viewing some openings in the ground of terrible appearance and unknown depth. Indeed, the chief reason of giving you this trouble, is to induce some of your correspondents in that part of the world to give a particular account of those uncommon curiosities which are in the environs of Ingleborough, which, in my opinion, far surpass those of the Peak, in Derbyshire, and want nothing but a Buxton to solicit the traveller to a thorough examination of them. And methinks, gentlemen, who frequent those parts in quest of moor game, might spare one hour in their rambles to survey these almost unknown wonders.

Those who have taken a very cursory view of them are apt to conclude that some of Squire Buncle's most extraordinary adventures are not so romantic and ill-founded as many have supposed, and 'tis a pity they did not fall within his knowledge, for his pen would have done them justice.

In the list of deaths for July, 1762, is the following:—

William Dawson, of Llancliff Hall, near Settle, Yorkshire, Esquire, aged 87.

In the list of deaths for the year 1766, we find:—

January 16th, the Countess of Gyllenborg, at Settle, Yorkshire. She was so created by the late Queen of Sweden, her mother being married to his Excellency Count Gyllenborg, sometime ambassador at this court, and afterwards Prime Minister of Sweden. By his Excellency Baron Sparre (who served under Charles XII, in all his campaigns, and was taken prisoner with him at the battle of Pultowa), her ladyship has left issue one daughter, the Hon. Amelia Melifina Sparre.

In an article (in 1781,) on Count Gyllenborg, Prime Minister of Sweden, is the following:—

After the Count's death the younger Countess Gyllenborg, a very accomplished lady, returned to England, having a pension both from Sweden and Hesse Cassel, and resided several years in London. In the latter part of her life she retired into Yorkshire where she died at Settle, January 16th, 1766. Her only daughter, the Hon. Amelia Wilhelmina Melifina Sparre, born in 1733, to whom Frederick, Prince of Wales, was godfather, died unmarried at Thirske, in Yorkshire, October 5th, 1778.

Settle, Yorkshire, March 14th, 1784.

Mr. Urban,

If the following account of some antiquities, &c., found in this neighbourhood, merits a place amongst the curious accounts, &c., in the *Gentleman's Magazine*, you will oblige me by inserting it. W. F.

Some workmen digging for stones, about a year ago, in a quarry by the road side at Craven Bank, (the boundary of that extensive country called Craven), above Giggleswick, found in a crevice between two rocks, about the depth of two yards, a large quantity of Roman coins, chiefly of the two Constantines, as appeared very plain by the reverse and the legend GLORIA EXERCTVS still very legible. Some appeared also to be Denarii of Gratianus. There are likewise three or four which, upon examination, I found to have on one side the figure of Romulus, and round the head the letters ROMVL. very plain. On the reverse the figure of the wolf with Romulus and Remus sucking, with the words VRBS FVN., which I suppose means the founder of the city, but the other parts are rendered by that enemy to antiquaries, Time, illegible. I should be glad of an explanation of the above coin, as I apprehend it must have been struck long after Romulus' time and probably in honour of him.*

Not long since the old cross at Settle, being found ruinous, was taken down, in the inside of which was the appearance of another cross or pillar, rudely designed, upon which were found two or three silver coins, which are now unhappily lost, but I have in my possession a curious antique which was also found in the inside, which I conjecture to be Saxon ; a representation of it I have sent, if it is fit to be seen in the corner of a plate.

As to its antiquity it is undoubted, as it was carried to be shewn to an honourable court, when a great cause was depending to prove the antiquity of Settle as a market town, &c. For an explanation of this I shall also be obliged to any learned correspondent.

At High-hill, above Settle, are still visible the remains of two Roman fortifications. The first takes up an immense tract of ground, in the middle of which is a noble spring, artificially surrounded with an earthen bank. The second is small, of an oblong form, exactly like that described at Mani Tor, by Mr. Bray, in his tour through Derbyshire. At Craven Bank, where the above coins were found, is an artificial tumulus, or mount of earth, raised in the form of a cylindrical cone, with a neat cut path-way and flat top, with a raised bank above the summit. On this has probably been a watch tower.

* These are very common in Roman stations, particularly Reculver which makes it probable that they are of the lower Empire.

It may just suffice to observe that a branch of the Roman military way passes over the moors by Sunderland,* and in view of Craven Bank. At Bracewell, near Thornton, is a curious old ruinous castle or monastry, of which, if required, I will give a more particular description at a future period, but would just request an account, from any correspondent, by whom it was founded or built, and who dwelt there, as a report goes that one of the King Henry's or Edward's resided there for a few days on an excursion to the North, and there is still shown his chamber; also a curious castellated mansion known by the name of *Hellefield Cocheni*. An explanation of the word "Cocheni" is requested. As no author has yet gratified the publick with an account of the above antiquities, they lying remote from the road, it will be agreeable if some antiquary will explain the above particulars. W. F.

Mr. Urban, June, 1784.

The coins enquired after in p. 259, by the author of the very curious communication from Settle, are some of those common ones struck during the reign of Constantine the Great, and if attentively examined will be found to read on the side V R B S. R O M A with the head of the city of Rome, the letters upon the exergue of the other side, with the figures of Romulus and Remus sucking the wolf, I should suspect not to be as described in the letter, but others denoting the place where the coins were minted; and these were exceedingly numerous almost to a degree of incredibility to those not versed in these matters. Their varieties may be seen in Banduri's Numism. Imperatorum, &c. It is most natural to suppose that the quarry wherein these coins were found bore the marks of having been heretofore worked, although this gentleman has not expressly said so.—Yours, S. E.

Mr. Urban, Settle, July 28th, 1784.

Emboldened by the general and ready admission you give to all the branches of useful correspondence, I once more send an account of some trivial antiquities in this neighbourhood, and which I apprehend have never yet been noticed by any author, they lying too remote from the road, and I hope they will meet with the approbation of the literati. The first (see plate,) is a curious antique cross, now standing near the

* In a later letter the writer says this is a misprint for "Saukland," but this latter word again is probably a misprint for "Laukland" (or Lawkland as it is now spelt.)—T. B.

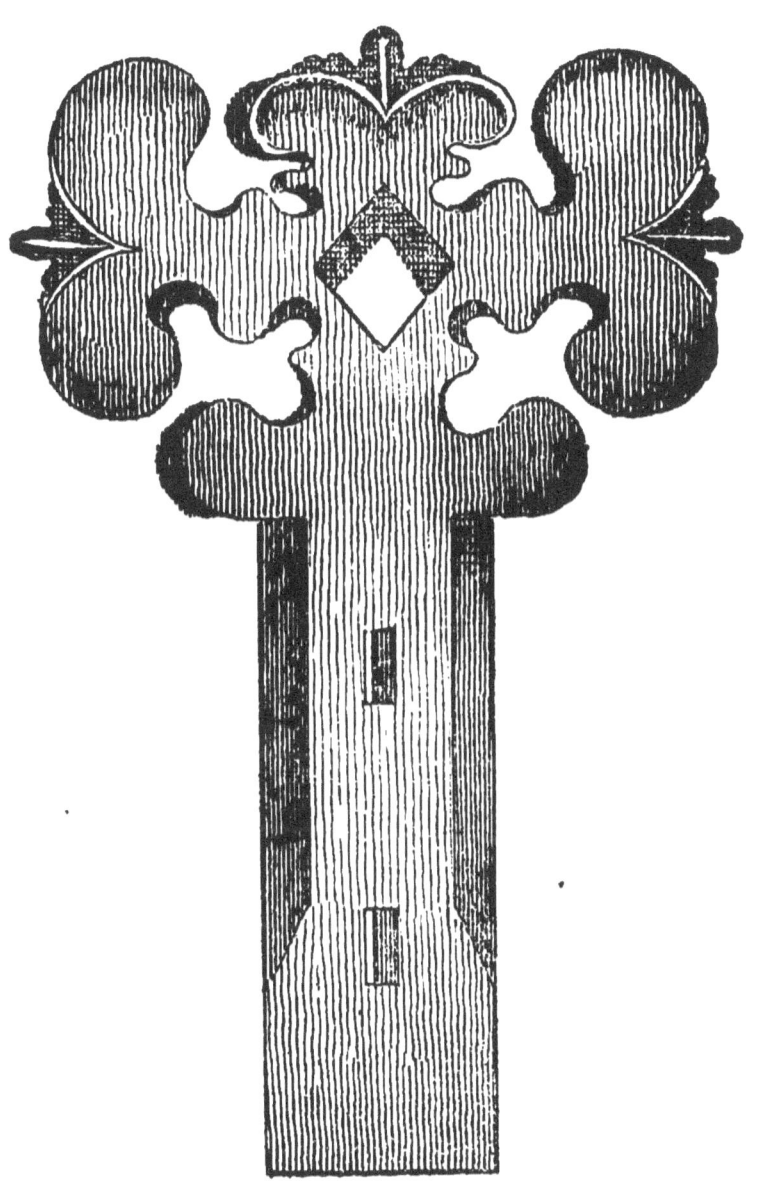

OLD MARKET CROSS AT GIGGLESWICK.

church in the town of Giggleswick, but of what æra is left to the learned to determine, however, its antiquity is undoubted, being used many years before its erection as a threshold in an old house, and its beautiful Gothic head walled in. The house itself was ancient and is now pulled down. It might probably belong to some monastry (though neither author nor tradition informs us of any being here), or might perhaps be set up in days of monastic splendour, amongst the numerous ones at those times in being.

Tradition, through the channel of the inhabitants of Settle, informs us that some of the Giggleswick residents stole it from the base of the old cross at Settle, in order to prejudice the trial (see previous extract on page 10) concerning the antiquity of the market, but this is partial, and as it is an interested tale the inhabitants of Giggleswick deny the assertion. This pillar is about five yards high, two yards are stuck in the ground and walled up as a pedestal. I dare not assert whether it is Saxon or not. The other figure is a coin, I suppose also inedited, the legends and characters are very much defaced, however, it appears to be of the Edwards.* An explanation as to the age, antiquity, &c., of the above articles, will oblige yours. W. F.

Settle, Yorkshire, November 23, 1784.

Mr. Urban,

It is much to be regretted that the great protoparent of antiquaries did not visit in his extensive excursions this part of Craven, in which are many curious antiquities that are yet buried in oblivion, especially some of them, which it must be acknowledged are so recluse as to admit of no speculation from our modern tourists. I therefore once more give your readers what may excite the attention of an abler pen. The Sepulchral Barrow has upon all occasions awakened the curiosity of the antiquary and public in general, which may be witnessed from the many spectators present upon opening those venerable reliques. A kind of respectable veneration naturally inspires even the most ignorant rustic during the operation. The Rev. Mr. Hutchins, in his history of Dorsetshire, pleasingly remarks, Thus we see, all nations, however

* The coin is of Edward IV. Legend on the obverse, EDWARD DI G R. ANG. & FRANC. Reverse, POSUI DEUM ADJUTOREM MEUM. CIVITAS EBORACI. See the coins published by the Society of Antiquaries, Tab V. (some varieties in the inscriptions excepted.)—EDIT.

differing in language, customs, or manners, showed a religious regard for their dead. The venerable Druid, the civilised Roman, the barbarous Dane alike observed the rites of sepulture, whether deposited under the lofty pyramid, mixed with their mother earth, or reduced to a handful of ashes covered with a heap of turf, the deceased alike employed the pious care of their surviving friends, who wept over and buried them. And these rites, founded in nature, were supported for the encouragement of the living, not with a view of benefiting the dead." But the Sepulchral Tumuli frequently when searched and examined with the nicest accuracy, rather confuse and embarrass the searchers, unless the appearance of coins, instruments, trinkets, or other national appurtenances clear the difficulty. This evidently proceeds from the exact similitude between those of the four early nations. Indeed, it has, with some degree of propriety been urged, that the two latter, the Danes and Saxons, left off the custom of burning their dead immediately after leaving their own countries; and, were it not asserted by such reputable and judicious authors, it appears rather improbable, on considering that domestic or national customs are so riveted and unalterable, that, though they may appear evidently ridiculous, it is impossible for many ages to root them out. It hath also been observed, that the Romans and Britons always burnt their dead ; but it is certain that they did not always (though they might in general,) since it is beyond dispute that entire skeletons, and perfect bones, of Roman generals have been found. Though these reasons may go far to resolve the many confused opinions and doubts formed, yet they will not altogether suffice. An ingenious author, speaking upon this subject remarks, " That this way of burying under tumuli was so universal, that it is not easy to decide by what particular nation any barrow was erected, unless some criterion within it determine the uncertainty. Thus, we may form some conjecture from the materials and workmanship of the urn, the cell that contains it, or from coins, or instruments of war, or domestic life, which may accompany the bones ; but where these, or such like matters, are wanting, conjectures are vain." He then argues with the similar reasons that have been given concerning the Danes and Saxons, and are also originally hinted by Camden on his learned annotator, and if I mistake not, by a correspondent of some of the early publications in the *Gentleman's Magazine*, that universal Antiquarian Repertory.

Though the descriptive part of this letter may appear long in introducing, and the above subject be considered as tedious, yet I thought it proper to give some brief reasons respecting its real attention, which is no other than to request the opinion of some of the literati upon this head, before I proceed to describe the tumulus, which, I must acknowledge, puzzles this neighbourhood with respect to its original erection, and to what peculiar people it owed its existence. This barrow or tumulus, (see plate,) stands in an elevated situation upon a mountain, above the hamlet of Stackhouse,* and may be discerned at a great distance. It is known in the country by the name of The Apron full of Stones, from a ridiculous tradition that the devil flying over the hill to build a bridge near Kirkby Lonsdale, in Westmoreland, his apron string broke, and he dropped this vast heap. Some other curious legendary tales are told on this occasion.

The form of this vast mass is circular, or rather orbicular; the height, by computation on the spot, about nine or ten feet. It is composed of an incredible quantity of stones, piled in such a manner as to rest upon each other's basis, and strengthened by its conic form; it rises upwards in this curious shape. Those stones that form the outside of the work are so small that a soldier could carry them; and since it has been argued that such a monstrous work as this would not be attempted by any nation, but was natural, the largeness of the tumulus may easily be accounted for, since they were annually increased out of reverence, as Mason evinces in his " Caractacus," where he introduces him soliloquizing on his son Arviragus's body.

> Posterity
> Shall to thy tomb with annual reverence bring
> Sepulchral stones, and pile them to the clouds.

This barrow hath been opened many years ago, and it is represented in the plate in the state in which it hath appeared till lately. Some old people in the neighbourhood remember it being entirely complete, and having a very flat top. It was usual, in finishing these works, to lay a flat stone on the top. The people that opened it left their intention unfinished, only throwing down the lid of the stone coffer, and one or two of the sides, and, meeting with nothing worth digging for they left it. Upon examining it in this state, before its being entirely disfigured in the last attempt, I found several human bones scattered up and down therein, amongst which I

* Stackhouse was originally an appendage to Furness Abbey, Co. Lanc.

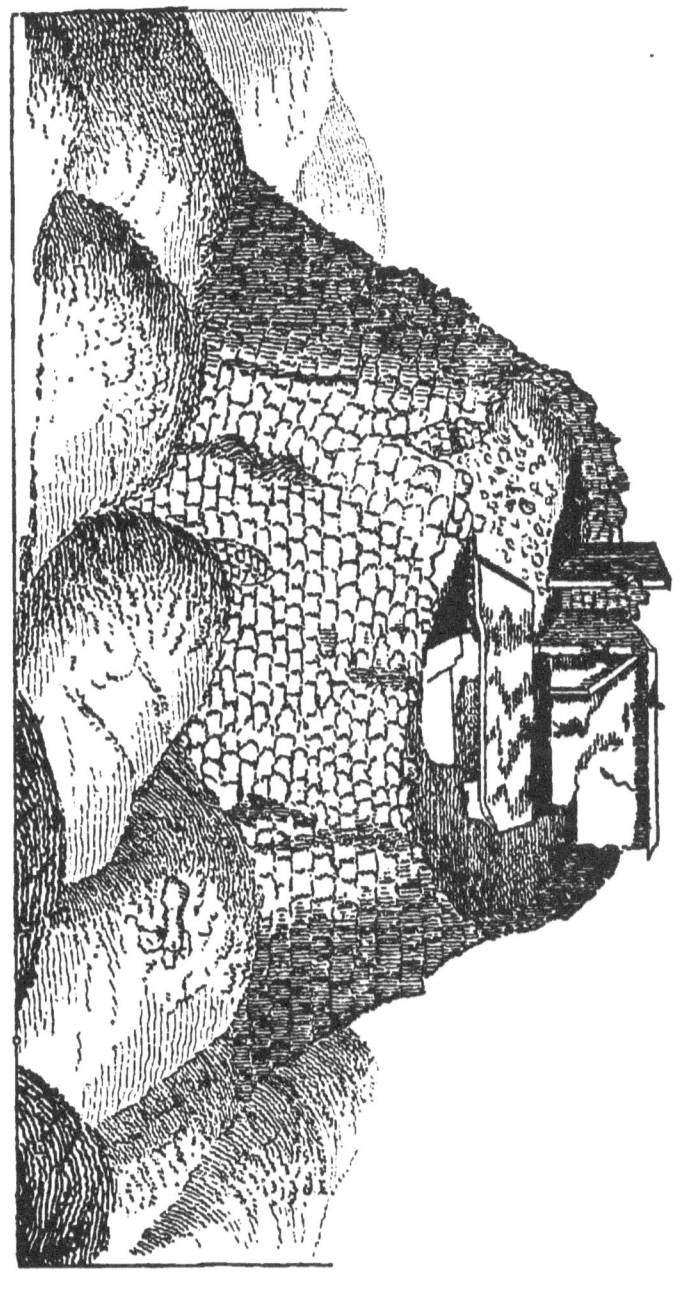

TUMULUS AT STACKHOUSE.

collected the patellæ of the knee, the vertebræ of the spine, part of the jaw, and several teeth. Round the area is a wall or rampart, of the same material as the outside, its height from the interior part about two feet, irregularly ranged with fissured remnants. In the centre of the cavity or area is the above chest, consisting of several huge stones of vast magnitude and density, fixed firmly into the ground, which supported a lid of equal size, though it is now thrown off the top. In this chest are partitions, for what purpose is not known, unless each space was allotted to its particular relique or body. In the partitions and sides of the coffin is a kind of hole in the edge, with a rude mold. Not many weeks ago the curiosity of some of the neigbourhood was excited to investigate this stupendous work of art, and accordingly labourers were hired, when, upon searching a day, (yet not half the work done), a human skeleton was found, in due proportion, and in a fine state of preservation, excepting the skull and one of the limbs, which were moved out of their place by the workmen's tools. A small circular piece of ivory, and the tusk of an nnknown beast, supposed to be of the hog genus, was also found; but no ashes, urns, coins, or instruments were discovered. There is a tradition, (if mere tradition may be relied upon,) that this was raised over the body of some of the Danes slain in the general massacre of that nation. However, from collecting all circumstances, as there is no appearance of ashes, it is supposed to belong to them or the Saxons. This is, however, what I wish to be acquainted with. Such a conspicuous work must certainly be erected to the manes of some chiefs; though there is no ground to support its origin but a mere tradition. The tumuli of the Romans and Britons have frequently a black friable earth round their foundations, but this has not, neither is there any appearance of the operation of fire in its cavity. In the Archæologia, vol. III. art. xxviii., an extract of a letter from the Rev. George Low, mentions the opening of one of the numerous tumuli in the Links of Shail, in the Orkney Isles, in which was found a well preserved skeleton, within a coffin or chest composed of four stones covered by a fifth. He observes, "Little can be said as the antiquity of this tumulus, only that it was made before the introduction of Christianity." The insertion of this extract is only meant to compare it with this, and to assert the original reasons. And as the present century can honestly boast of a greater fund of antiquarian knowledge than any of the preceding ones, and this noble science, which, in the days of ignorance and superstition, used to be considered as despicable and ridiculous, is now esteemed, not only honourable, but altogether useful and necessary, being ornamented by the labours of genius, thence, in this enlightened age, may the adepts in antiquity have their doubts resolved, and the ignorant meet not only satisfaction, but pleasure and instruction.

P.S.—In a former letter of mine Saukland has been misprinted Sunderland.* Upon an excursion to Old Ford, near London, not long ago, I saw the remains of an old palace said to have been built by King John. An account of this, or a drawing would be gratefully received, since no authors mentions it. W. F.

Mr. Urban, 1785.

Had I happened to have seen your supplement sooner, I should have been glad to have given an answer to W. F. time enough for insertion in this month; as I think the facility of an early reply is one considerable advantage in publications like yours. Being myself only of the humble order of fireside naturalists and antiquaries, I am always thankful when the business, pleasure, or locality of gentlemen of another turn, concurs with their disposition to oblige, in giving us good descriptions of things rare or uncommon in nature or art. And they should the rather be encouraged to do so, from the consideration that many have the talent of describing in an higher degree of perfection than many others, who can better account for and explain. Of this I lately saw a curious instance in a foreign journal, a gentleman described minutely a very large, but damaged piece of tapestry, but without pretending to know the history represented, the discovery of which he requested from others. An answer was immediately given by one who declared that he had seen the tapestry over and over again, but without ever attempting to make out its meaning, so confused and perplexed it always appeared to him, but that from the description it certainly was, &c., &c. Here we have an instance of a person's not being able to make out a story from the reality, tho' he could readily do it from the representation of another, who was himself perfectly unacquainted with the subject. How many gentlemen saw, and bestowed vast profusion of learning upon the few letters that compose the Greek inscription

* (See page 10.) This is evidently a misprint for Laukland. T. B.

to Astarte, which Mr. Tyrwhitt made out so clearly in his study, that there was no occasion to say a single word more about it! Let therefore gentlemen be so kind as to give accurate descriptions and representations, and it is probable that some one will be found able and willing to explain them, not that anything perfect is pretended to be said on the present occasion, as the want of historical information must for ever leave us often in the dark, as to many surprising monuments of a rude and illiterate race of predecessors, which provoke, without satisfying, our curiosity. One could wish, however, to have a few more particulars given of this extraordinary barrow, as nothing like it seems to be mentioned by Mr. Collinson in his " Beauties of British Antiquities," 1779, 8vo., p. 9 and 13. The dimensions most wished for are the diameter of the flat part at top, the circumference of the base, and whether the present height being said to be 8 or 9 feet, be not a false print, as not suiting very well with " vast mass," and taken " by computation on the spot," as one should think so small an height might easily be measured; nor is the meaning very clear of " stones piled in such a manner as to rest upon each other's basis." Were I to judge from the engraving, I should conclude that it was made like other barrows, by accumulating a large quantity of earth, and then casing, coating, or facing the whole with stones. I should imagine too, that, when perfect, its summit rose in an oval form considerably above the top of the tumulus as represented, so as to cover with a considerable quantity of earth, and stone-casing, the part where the bodies were deposited; as they usually lie on the ground, and all the earth is heaped on them. As to what is called the wall surrounding the present flat top, that appears to me plainly to be the outer stone casing, which stands up a little higher than the internal soft materials, which have been stirred and thrown away, partly in the attempt to bare the stone coffin work, and partly by the weather since, so that the whole, to use a familiar image, looks like a poached egg held in one's hand and broken atop, with some of the soft contents run out, so that the shell rises a little above them all round. Perhaps so much would not have been said on the present subject but from a fancied resemblance between it and that of King Gyges, mentioned by Herodotus, and which Dr. Chandler informs us still subsists; as indeed what works of mens' hands seem so likely to endure, the end certainly aimed at by all builders? I forgot to mention that the idea of increasing the heap by stones thrown on by passengers, though often practised in other places, seems out of the question, on a spot, where few visitors could reasonably be expected, nor could so large a mass be thus increased any more than the Tower of London, by throwing stones at it. A. BARROWIST.

Settle, May 25th, 1785.

Mr. Urban,

Permit me to return thanks to the Barrowist for his seasonable advice, with respect to accuracy in descriptions of antiques, which would be of much greater utility to the world were they more generally attended to. I cannot but acknowledge that the computation of the dimensions of the barrow was in some degree inaccurate, as it mentioned 9 or 10 feet instead of 9 or 10 yards, which was certainly erroneous, though a mistake easily committed. The circumference of the base is 210 feet; and the diameter of the top of the present wall or coating, or what he pleases to call it, 45 feet. But as the summit of the coating is much broken and very irregular, and great part dislodged by the workmen, the present actual altitude is only 7 yards. The stones which compose the coffer are 6 feet 9 inches long, and 3 feet broad, some more and some less, according to their situation in composing the cell. The meaning of " stones piled in such a manner as to rest upon each other's basis " is very evident that they are to each other a solid prop, foundation, or support, as the barrow is formed in an inclined position, or conic shape. The barrow is delineated as accurately as possible with respect to the appearance before its late investigation, except with regard to the oval form, which was certainly too circular for its extent; but this was my fault, not the engraver's, who has, much to his credit, made an excellent and true copy of the original sketch. After allowing myself to blame in those two oversights, which are rather the effect of chance than inaccuracy, let me put a few reasonable queries to the Barrowist, and answer some of his objections, which are equally faulty in their turn. Mr. Collinson, it is true, in his " Beauties of British Antiquities," gives the world a pleasing account of several monumental reliques in the barrow line; but there is an innumerable quantity of barrows in Britain, and in those quantities different species, which·have, in a general sense, their various peculiarities, of which this may be one. The judicious and accurate Captain Grose, in the second addition of his " Antiquities " in his treatise upon the subject, coincides in this point, as well as Camden, Weever, and many other authors who have written upon this head. Mr. Collinson, no doubt, described with accuracy many different species ; but let me ask the Barrowist if he could reasonably expect to find every barrow minutely described, with its peculiar appendages, either opened or unopened ? In different situations considerable variations may be discovered in investigating tumuli, where stones were most convenient to form the whole, they were used ; and many barrows are almost entirely composed of earth, where earth was rich and stones few. I would recommend to the Barrowist to satisfy himself with personal observation, and then he will find this argument indisputably true, as description and expression will not convince his delicate sensibility. I have a shrewd suspicion that this gentleman disputes the validity of my correspondence, or at least has an idea of a glaring extension, magnified beyond the bounds of truth or reason, by comparing it injudiciously with Dr. Chandler's curious description of Herodotus's mausoleum of King Gyges. I have a hope, at least, that the present account of the dimensions will satisfy his incredulity. I should deem it the highest ingratitude to transmit to so valuable a publication accounts of things unexisting, or at least supposed to be stretched beyond the line of probability. The Barrowist must be a person of extraordinary discernment if he can judge, from the engraving, of what sort of internal materials the barrow is formed. The internal materials are composed of stones, some much larger than the external coating, and, as the barrow is situated near a considerable quantity of stones, rocks, &c., they have undoubtedly been more convenient to collect than the earth from a barren rocky moor. The summit of the barrow was certainly originally above the coffer ; is it said in the description it was not ? Though this barrow is much exposed, yet the weather could not discompose the internal parts, as it required the force of several men, with iron handspikes, to remove them ; and it would be a work of many days to explore this " vast mass." I am of opinion that it has been a general burial place for the Danes or Pagan-Saxons, so large a quantity of bones having been found, that were they collected together they would form several bodies. Had the Barrowist a proper knowledge of ancient customs, he would have found that it was our ancient forefathers, (not the moderns,) who, out of a superstitious veneration, increased the sepulchral tumuli. I am sorry he disputes the opinion of the great Mason, one of the first historians of the age, who supports this just idea. But how comes he to compare the barrow with the Tower of London? He must have seen neither of those places, or his ideas must be very capacious indeed; and I should be afraid of drawing upon myself the ridicule of all the cooks in England were I to introduce the scheme of poaching an egg with the shell on. I should have been glad of hearing the Barrowist's opinion respecting the origin of this tumulus. His sentences are so copious in strictures that I expected something extraordinary to be the result of his letter; but I was greatly disappointed in not finding one single opinion in favour of my request, except the old repetition, want of historical information, which cannot withhold opinion. I am afraid he runs into the same error himself, as the gentleman who described the tapestry. The tapestry was minutely described, but without pretending to know the history represented. Was this the case with me? I cannot take the hint, as my description was only faulty in two trifling mistakes. An opinion was formed, every circumstance was described, and only a civil request for the opinion of others, in conjunction with my own. I should have contemplated his remarks with a contemptuous silence, but I was roused and uncommonly struck with his erroneous ideas, which could have originated from nothing short of a fire-side observation, and not from an experienced personal investigation of barrows. Hasty opinions are not always just. And, as an apology for my egregious inaccuraries, permit me to plead a juvenile antiquary; in short, I should not have replied, but with regard to the words of the poet, let me tell the Barrowist he forces

"As it were in spite,
Of nature and my stars to write."

W. F

From the list of deaths for 1785.

August 17th, Mr. William Hoole, an eminent tanner, near Sheffield. Going to Settle fair his horse unfortunately ran away with him near Bradford, and threw him, by which he was bruised in so terrible a manner that he expired soon after.

Mr. Urban, August 8th, 1786.

As I have been informed that the school, (see plate,) at Giggleswick, near Settle-in-Craven, is shortly to be pulled down, to be rebuilt in a more elegant and commodious manner; I thought it a pity that the memory of the old one should drop with the stones. As it is a structure which can boast of some antiquity, no doubt my intentions will meet the approbation of those who are zealous for the preservation of venerable reliques.

The building is low, small, and irregular, consisting of two stages, the lower for reading, the higher for writing, &c. On the north side is a small projecting building in which was once a tolerable collection of books, now dispersed.

Upon the front wall, almost over the door, is an ornamental vacant niche, under which is the following inscription in old characters (see the plate,) " Alma Dei Mater defende " malis Jacobum Carr, presbyteris quoque clericulis. Hoc " domus fit in anno millen' quingen' duoden' nostri miserere " Deus. Senes cum juvenibus laudate nomen Dei." * By the above inscription it appears that this building was originally a chantry, and on searching Browne Willis † I find " Egleswick, Virgin Mary's Chauntry, an annuity of £3 12s. to Richard Summerskale, incumbent." This must certainly mean Giggleswick, which was anciently spelt Gegleswick. There are some old cups preserved, upon which it is spelt Ygleswick. The initial G or Y is probably left out by an erratum in Willis, there being no such place as Egleswick in those parts. This then fixes, in conjunction with the stone, the date, &c., of the foundation of this chauntry, and, we may conjecture, the nich was filled up by the effigies of the Virgin Mary. This building stands on the north side of the Church yard; and I find authors remark that Chauntries were as frequently placed without as within the Church. The school was founded May 26th, 7th Edward VI., and in the grant is styled " The Free Grammar School of King Edward VI. of

* The correct inscription, according to Whittaker's History of Craven, should be

Alma Dei Mater defende malis Jacobum Carr
Presbyteris quoq. clericulis hoc domus fit. In anno
Mil. quint. Cent. d'no D'e J. B. A. Pater miserere
Senes cum jubenibus laudate nomen Dei.

† History of Abbeys, Vol. II., p. 290.

FIRST GRAMMAR SCHOOL AT GIGGLESWICK.

Giggleswick,,' and was endowed by several rents and services (amongst which was twelve pence and two chickens annually), with the appropriations of the tithes of the collegiate church of St. Andrew the apostle, of Nether Acaster, in Yorkshire, which lands so appropriated were situated in North Cave, Brampton, and North and South Kelthorpe. Also the appropriation of the lands belonging to the Chauntry of the Blessed Virgin Mary, founded in the Parish Church of Rise and Aldborough, in Yorkshire; those possessions to be held of the Crown as of its Manor of East Greenwich, in Kent, by fealty only, in free socage, and not 'in capite,' yielding to it £63 annually.

In the grant no mention is made of the building in which it should be held, but I conjecture that the late-dissolved chauntry was thought a proper place for it, in which it hath since been.

It is superintended by eight governors, one of whom is to be the vicar of the parish for the time being. John Nowell, vicar; William Caterall, of Newhall; Henry Tennant, gent., Thomas Proctor, of Cletchop; Hugh Newhouse, of Giggleswick; William Brown, of Settle; Roger Armistead, of Knight Stayneford; and William Bank, of Fesar, were the first governors.

There are two masters, and one occasionally for writing, &c., it is under Christ's College, Cambridge.

I have also heard that it is dependent upon the see of Durham, but this may only arise from its belonging originally to the Church of Giggleswick, which, I apprehend, once belonged to Durham Abbey, and is dedicated to St. Cuthbert.* The Archbishop of York is also to be consulted on the election of a Master or Governor, &c. Since its original foundation its revenues have increased very much, and it is at present well endowed. A person left a certain sum of money to be laid out, upon the 12th day of March annually, in figs, which curious legacy is yet kept up, being styled the Potation-day; and upon the same day a jubilee or fair is kept up at the village, and the governors meet to inspect and regulate their affairs.

Yours, &c.,

INVESTIGATOR C.

* Giggleswick Church, which is dedicated to St. Alkelda, formerly belonged to the Priory of Finchale, which was subservient to Durham.

T. B.

Settle, August 13th, 1793.

MR. URBAN,

I have seen lately several dissertations upon Swallows in your Magazine. I was much pleased this spring in observing a young *white* swallow bred in this neighbourhood. I saw it every day I walked out for about a month, and when I missed seeing it I was, to my mortification, told that it had taken flight into a shoe-maker's shop in Settle, where it was caught and killed. W. C.

Sept. 30th, 1794.

MR. URBAN,

I request the favour of a place in your entertaining and useful Miscellany for the following account of a very curious and remarkable phenomenon, the unexpected appearance of a piece of water at the distance of two miles from Settle-in-Craven, as it may not be familiar to, or unworthy the observation of, a few among your numerous and ingenious readers.

The method I shall pursue, in order to describe it in the most intelligible and satisfactory manner, is first by relating the circumstances attending its rise, continuance, and situation; secondly, by subjoining a delineation of it with the admeasurement. First, this water was first discovered about three years ago, and, as far as I can recollect, did not increase gradually, but was of its perfect magnitude soon after, if not immediately upon, its first appearance. There was not, according to the information I have received, any remarkable fall of rain at the time, nor any visible cause which could account for such a phenomonen; but even if rain could be supposed to be the first cause of its appearance, since it has continued with little alteration for the space of three years, and during the severe drought of the present summer, we may fairly conclude that the supply of water will be regular and permanent. The quantity produced in the course of twenty-four hours must be very considerable, as it furnishes water for sixty large cattle, exclusive of what must necessarily be carried off by evaporation. It is situated on the summit of a high mountain, surrounded on all sides with limestone rock. The ground near it is remarkably dry, nor was there ever before that time known to be any water in the place. The above circumstances are in direct opposition to those which usually attend similar phenomena, as low and swampy ground, with others, generally are sufficient to afford a plain and easy solution. There are no springs in the lands adjoining, except one at the distance of half a mile, and that much below the level of this now under consideration.* Secondly, the axis major A B fo the figure, (see plate,) which is nearly an ellipse, is 30 yards 1-8th; the axis minor C D is 23 yards 1-8th. Consequently the area is nearly 18 perches, 2 yds., 5 feet, 3 inches.

			yds.	ft.	in.
The depth at point W is	...	...	2	2	2
Ditto do. X	...	...	3	0	5
Ditto do. Y	...	...	2	1	7
Ditto do. Z	...	...	3	0	3
The periphery of the figure	...	...	83	1	1

This admeasurement was made after a drought of two months, when the water must be supposed less than at any other season of the year. If any of your ingenious correspondents can give an account of a similar phenomenon, they will much oblige a constant reader.

From the list for deaths of 1796.

July 22nd, in his 85th year, Mr. Thomas Carr, Stackhouse, near Settle-in-Craven, county York, whose family have lived at that place for many generations.

In an account of Edward Parker, Esq., of Browsholm, Yorkshire, who died Dec. 22nd, 1794, there is the following mention of his son:—

"He had only one child, the present representative of the family, John Parker, Esq., of Marshfield, † Yorkshire, late M.P. for the borough of Clithero. This gentleman was educated at Eton, was a gentleman commoner of Christ's College, Cambridge; a member of Bootle's (Club,) and married Breatrix ‡ (whose prophetic baptismal name proved truly indicative of the manner in which she fulfils all the relative duties, and exhibits all the endearing accomplishments), the only daughter of the late, and sister of the present Thomas Lister, Esq., of Gisburn Park and Malham Water House, Yorkshire, proprietary and late representative of the borough above mentioned. By this lady he had issue eight sons, ||

* There are several springs at the foot of the mountain, among which is that remarkable one the ebbing and flowing well, none of which is in the least affected by the appearance of the present water.

† This is Marshfield, Settle, now divided into two houses.—T. B.

‡ Marshfield was rebuilt by Mr. Lister, and was probably part of Beatrix Lister's dowry on her marriage to Mr. Parker.—T. B.

|| All of whom were baptised at Giggleswick church. Septimus and Octavius were also buried there.—T. B.

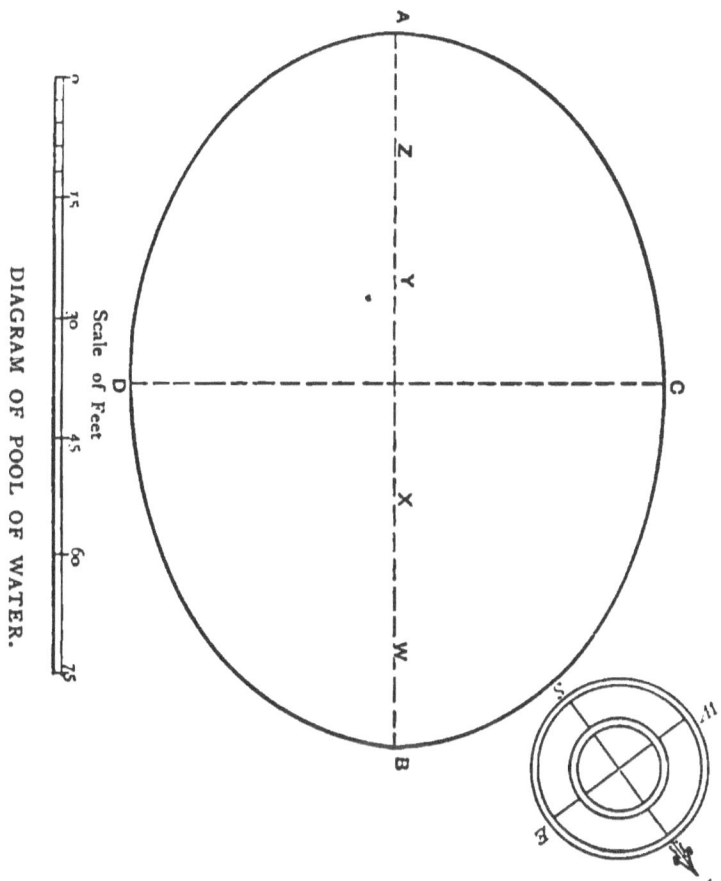

DIAGRAM OF POOL OF WATER.

of these, Septimus and Octavius, the two youngest, are dead. Thomas Lister, the oldest, is a pupil of Dr. James, at Rugby ; whose amiable character and sweet deportment bid fair for an illustrious ornament of that church, for which he has made his election. Edward, the second, and Charles, the fourth son, have been dignified by the appointment of pages of honor to his Majesty. The latter is at St. James's, the former gone in the suite of the vice roy of Ireland. John and William are yet at school in the country. It is but justice here to say that this antient and respectable family has consorted, and continues to live in habits of friendship and intimacy, with some of the most distinguished nobility and eminent characters in the kingdom. And thus, in their descendants, are they remunerated, for their long, warm, and inviolate attachment to their King and Constitution, by the grateful notice of the present sovereign :—by a duplicate of honour, which rarely attaches singly to any but those whose family has been ennobled not merely by the virtue, but by the coronet of their ancestors.

From the list of deaths for 1797.

May 25th, in London, aged 42, John Parker, Esq., of Browsholm and Marshfield, county York, late M.P. for the borough of Clithero, in Lancashire, of whom a particular account shall appear next month.

In accordance with the above promise the following memoir of Mr. Parker was given the following month :—

Mr. Parker was the only son of Edward Parker, Esq., who died at Browsholm, county York, December 22nd, 1794, by his wife Barbara, who survives him, daughter and coheiress of the late Sir Wm. Fleming, Bart., who died in 1736, and was great uncle to the present Sir Michael le Fleming, Bart., of Rydall Hall, county Westmoreland. He married Beatrice, only daughter of the late and sister of the present Thomas Lister, Esq., of Gisburn Park, representative and proprietary of the borough of Clithero, by whom he has six surviving sons, the oldest of which, Thomas Lister, is entered a gentleman-commoner at Cambridge, and will, on his coming of age, succeed to the inheritance of a very large property. The body was carried down into the country, in a manner suitable to the rank of the deceased, and interred in the family vault at Waddington, on the 10th of June last, of which church, together with Bentham, Ingleton, and Ingleton Fells, the family have the patronage. Several further particulars respecting this ancient and illustrious family are recorded in our volume lxv., page 82. (See page 26.) The more immediate subject of this memoir possessed a most retentive memory, and from his education, rank, and habits of life was well known and much respected in the circles of the polite and noble on account of his great hilarity, benevolence, and generosity, not to mention the hereditary characteristic of Browsholm—a boundless hospitality.

From the list of deaths for 1799.

September 29th, in his 89th year, the Rev. Wm. Paley, M.A., head master of the Free Grammar School, at Giggleswick-in-Craven, county York, and father of Dr. Paley, Archdeacon of Carlisle. He was of Christ's College, Cambridge, M.A., 1733.

There are several notes relating to this neighbourhood in the later volumes of the *Gentleman's Magazine*, but I have thought it best to embody them in various articles that I hope to issue in this series of local tracts.—
T. B.

J. W. LAMBERT, PRINTER, CHAPEL-ST., SETTLE.

LOCAL SCRAPS.

(Reprinted from the Settle Household Almanack for 1897.)

Compiled by Thos. Brayshaw.

SETTLE:
THE CRAVEN PRINTING AND STATIONERY COMPANY, LIMITED.

LOCAL SCRAPS.

SETTLE A HUNDRED YEARS AGO.

The following description of Settle is from the account of a tour by a Mr. Housman towards the end of last century.

"Settle is an inconsiderable market town, containing about 900 inhabitants.

It is ancient, and was once famous for its manufacture of, and trade in, leather and hides, which are now in the decline: a fair, however, is still kept here once a fortnight, for the sale of these articles, and also of fat cattle. Its situation with respect to the neighbouring country is low, and the vale before it extensive and pleasant. It stands near the base of a white limestone rock, called Castlebar, which some travellers say resembles that of Gibraltar, and is 300 feet above the level of the town. The inhabitants have lately been at the expence of cutting an easy winding path to the top of it, from whence there is a fine prospect of the vale below, and the long range of craggy hills on each hand, which shew a mixture of grey rock and luxuriant verdure. In cutting stones from this rock fragments of great magnitude have sometimes rolled down, breaking through the garden walls, which stand on a sloping ground at the foot of the hill, forcing their way into the street, and sometimes even damaging houses.

This district enjoys a fine air, and plenty of excellent water. Land is generally applied to the purposes of grazing, to which the soil seems peculiarly adapted, being a fine hazel mould upon a stratum of limestone. On climbing to the top of a high mountain near Settle, we found fat bullocks feeding on remarkably long, rich and thick grass, which we thought the most singular instance of the luxuriance of mountain pasturage. We were told that most of the neighbouring hills have an equal propensity to the production of grass. From a want of trees (stone walls being universally the fences) the country has a naked appearance.

The pleasant village of Giggleswick stands about a mile from Settle, on the road towards Ingleton; it was formerly a market town, while Settle was only a hamlet, and it still contains the parish Church to that place. Giggleswick now principally consists of a few genteel houses."

Dr. POCOCKE'S TOUR.

The following extracts from the account of a tour undertaken in the year 1750, by Bishop Pococke, are interesting as making mention of the Old Sundial on Castleberg.

"Wentworth House in Yorkshire,
August 8th, 1750.

My last was of the 30th of July from Halifax, in which letter I gave you an account of Hornby Castle. In the afternoon of the 26th I travelled eastward along the Wenning, and crossing over it at Bentham, from Lancashire, I came into Yorkshire. We crossed over the heath and came to Clapham and coming to the brow of the hill over the vale in which the Ribble rises, a very romantic and agreeable scene opened of high craggy rocks to the left, almost perpendicular, and a fine uneven, improved country to the south. Out of the foot of these rocks, there come three or four considerable streams, large enough to turn a mill: one of them has been remarkable for ebbing and flowing very suddenly and frequently, but I find cannot be reduced to any certainty, and people have been puzzled to find out the cause of it, which may be that at certain times the water may bring up a great deal of sand, and fill some cavity and stop the rise of the spring, and when that sand subsides it may then again flow plentifully. A little further we came to a most pleasant village, called Giggleswick, under these rocks, and very beautifully situated over the Ribble, it is adorned with trees, and there are many good houses in it, and on the other sides are well improved rising grounds.

Crossing the Ribble a little beyond this place, we came in a quarter of a mile to Settle, a little town situated under a high rocky hill, on the lower part of which four stones being placed they serve as a sun-dial to the country for three or four miles southward, as they know what hour of the morn it is when the shadow comes to them, from nine to twelve. Settle is a pretty great thoroughfare and has a small manufacture of knit stockings. We passed this day near a high hill called Inglebarrow, at the foot of which, near Ingleton, I was informed there was a very curious large cave. On the mountain grow two uncommon plants, the Rosa Radix, and the Ladies' Slipper, on some of the mountains near Settle grows a sort of dwarf bramble, the berry of which they call cloud-berry, and the common people cnute-berry, because they say King. Canute, when he was in exile in these parts, lived on them.

From Settle I went on the 27th up the Ribble about three miles, where below a bridge there is a fine cascade, which in two or three breaks falls down about twenty feet; we then crossed the hills to the south-east, and coming in sight of Malham Ptarne we went up the hills to the south; and came to what they call the Clatering Syke or Rivlet which comes out of the side of the hill towards the pot of it, in which water, that hardly covers the ground, there are abundance of Trochi entrochi, and of the anomiæ shells, as well as masses of them in a thin stone and the water washes them out. These productions do much puzzle naturalists. The Trochi are many of them like shuttles, some are round and plain with little knobs on them like a vegetable shoot, and they are joynted and separate, and some of them when separated appear square, others round, which are called St. Cuthbert's beads; some are an oblong oval, which they call shuttles; the country people call them fairy stones."

ESTABLISHMENT OF THE QUAKERS IN SETTLE.

The following Extracts from the Report of the Monthly Meeting of the Society of Friends, held at Settle in Oct. 1704, give some idea of the troubles which beset the pioneers of the Society in Settle.

"In process of time, in or about the year 1652 or 1653, it was so ordered that one of the servants and messengers of Jesus Christ, namely, William Dewsbury, came to a town called Settle, in the West part of Yorkshire, on a market day, and stood upon the cross, and proclaimed the terrible day of the Lord, which was hastening and coming upon the ungodly and workers of iniquity: but he was soon pulled down, and a great tumult was made, and he was much beaten and abused. But after some time, being taken notice of by a young man whose name was John Armistead (who is yet living), was invited to go with him to his mother's house, whose name was Alice Armistead, being a widow; whither he went and lodged there. And in the evening divers people were gathered to the house, it being in the said town, unto whom he declared fervently againt the fruitless profession of religion which was amongst people at that time, and directed people to the measure of grace and gift of God's Holy Spirit in their own hearts whereby they might be taught how to worship God acceptably in his own Spirit.

And not long ago after this, it was so ordered that another servant and minister of the Lord, called John Camm, came into the said town on a market day, and in the market-place began to preach the doctrine of repentance, and the way of life and salvation unto the people. But they soon fell upon him with violence and did beat and buffet him very much, so that he received many strokes; yet there were some who endeavoured to bear off some blows, and to rid him out of their hands; and after some time he was conducted to the house of John Kidd, in Upper Settle, where there was a meeting in the evening, and then things relating to the kingdom of God were plainly laid down by him.

Also about the year 1652-3, came several of the servants and ministers of Jesus Christ, viz.: William Dewsbury, Richard Farnworth, Thomas Stubbs, Miles Halhead, and James Nayler, and preached the everlasting Gospel, by which many were turned from darkness to light, and from the power of Satan to the power of God."

GRANT OF STOCKDALE TO SAWLEY ABBEY.

In No. 3 of the "Stackhouse Tracts" is set out a grant by Henry de Pudsey of the Church at Giggleswick to the Monks of Durham.

The following is a translation, made in 1620 by Roger Dodsworth the Antiquary, of a grant by the same Henry de Pudsey, nearly seven hundred years ago.

"To all the Sons of the Holy Mother the Church, present and to come, Henry de Pudsey greeting, Know ye that I have granted, and by this my present Charter confirmed, to God and St. Mary of Salley, and the monkes there serveing God, all Stockdale, in free pure and perpetuall Almes, for the health of my Soule and of Adelida de Percy my mother, and Dionisia my wife and all our ancestors and heires as in the Charters of Richard de Morevill and William de Percy more fully appeareth. And it is to be Knowne that so next Alewardest to the great two rockes of Middlehow the monkes shall have whatsoever is betwixt the foresaid Boundaries, yet so that the men of Setel may have passiage to their pasture on the hill towards the North, as it is set out by lawful bounders &c. Wittnesse Marmaduke Darrell, Elias, son of Swenus, then Steward &c.

Rev. ROGER ALTHAM, D.D.

The Rev. Roger Altham, D.D., Prebendary of York and Ripon, was the son of Roger Altham of Settle. He was born about 1648, admitted at Westminster School in 1664 and then elected a student of Christ Church, Oxford, in 1668. He graduated B.A. June 22nd, 1672: M.A. April 29th, 1675: B.D. June 22nd, 1683: and D.D. June 26th, 1694. He was chosen senior Procter in 1682 and Regius Professor of Hebrew in 1691. He was deprived of his chair in 1697, but restored March 12th, 1702-3. Hearne says that he had the professorship conferred on him first of all by the influence that Dr. Radcliffe had with the Earl of Portland, but that either not taking some oath, or not making some subscription in due time, he lost the place, and was succeeded by Hyde. He was collated to the prebend of Trenton in York, October 19th, 1683, and to another at Douthwell, August 1st, 1685. On June 7th, 1688 he was inducted to the Vicarage of Finedon, in Northamptonshire. He was instituted November 6th, 1691 to the Sixth Stall in Christ Church, Oxford: was succeeded by Thomas Hyde, April 30th, 1697, on whose death, February 12th, 1702-3, Roger Altham was restored by the interest of Archbishop Dolben, according to Hearne, who describes him as "a good Scholar and a most excellent preacher." He was also the Archbishop's Chaplain. He died in 1714 and was buried in Christ Church, where are the following inscriptions :—

"Here lieth the body of Roger Altham, Docter of Divinity, Canon of Christ Church, and Hebrew Professor, aged about 66, who departed this life August the 18th, 1714." And "Here lyeth the body of Frances Altham, relict of Roger Altham, D.D., who departed this life Dec. 3rd, 1734, aged 80 years."

QUAKER WEDDING CERTIFICATE, 1774.

The following document, engrossed on parchment and bearing a 5/- stamp, is of interest as showing the wedding-ceremony in the Society of Friends a hundred and twenty years ago.

"Jonathan Hodgson of Settle in the County of York. Cordwainer, and Phebe Beetham of the same place, Widow, Having declared their Intentions of taking each other in Marriage, before several Meetings of the People called Quakers, in the County of York aforesaid, and the proceedings of the said Jonathan Hodgson and Phebe Beetham after due enquiry and deliberate consideration thereof were allowed by the said Meetings, they appearing clear of all others.

Now these are to certify all whom it may concern, that for the accomplishing of their said Marriage, this Sixth day of the First Month, called January, in the year One thousand seven hundred and Seventy four, They the said Jonathan Hodgson and Phebe Beetham appeared in a public Assembly of the aforesaid People and others in their Meeting-House in Settle aforesaid, And he the said Jonathan Hodgson taking the said Phebe Beetham by the Hand did openly and solemnly declare as followeth; Friends; In the fear of the Lord, and before this assembly, I take this my Friend Phebe Beetham to be my Wife, promising through divine Assistance to be unto her a loving and faithful Husband until it shall please the Lord by Death to separate us; or words to this effect. And the said Phebe Beetham did then and there in the said Assembly, in like manner declare as followeth; Friends; In the fear of the Lord and before this Assembly, I take this my Friend Jonathan Hodgson to be my Husband, promising through divine Assistance to be unto him a loving and faithful Wife until it shall please the Lord by

Death to separate us; or words to this effect. And the said Jonathan Hodgson and Phebe Beetham, as a further confirmation thereof and in Testimony thereunto did then and there to these presents set their Hands.

                                  Jonathan Hodgson.
                                  Phebe Beetham.
            Relations :—
                                  James Kendal.
                                  Daniel Hodgson.
                                  Thos. Robinson.
                                  Sarah Robinson.

We whose names are hereunto subscribed, being present among others at the solemnizing of the abovesaid Marriage and subscription in manner aforesaid, as Witnesses have also to these presents subscribed our Names the Day and Year above written.

William Birkbeck, Sam. Sutcliffe, Elihu Varley, James Mill, Joseph Wise, Wm. Hargraves Junr., Eliza. Barlow, Margaret Wilson, Deborah Birkbeck Junr., Wm. Hargreaves Junr., Isabel Atkinson, Deborah Hargraves, Thos. Blackburn, Robt. Wise, John Foster, Mary Thirnbeck, Jno. Birkbeck, Ab. Sutcliffe, Sarah Sutcliffe, Deborah Birkbeck, Barbary Sharpless, Jno. Birkbeck Junr., Robt. Hargraves, Geo. Atkinson, Rachel Wilson Junr."

Rev. GEORGE WOODS.

The Rev. George Woods was born at Settle, and received his early education at the Grammar School, Giggleswick; he was first of Queen's College, Oxford, and afterwards of University College, where he honourably distinguished himself.

Having taken holy orders in 1832, he was appointed assistant curate of St. Mary's, Barnsley. Afterwards he obtained the curacy of Tankersley, and was employed as private tutor in the family of the Hon. J. S. Wortley, through whose influence he was appointed chaplain to the English Embassy at Vienna. In 1828 he published at Barnsley a small volume consisting principally of sacred poetry, which he dedicated to the Rev. Rowland Ingram, B.D., his former Schoolmaster.

REMINISCENCES OF GIGGLESWICK SCHOOL.

The Rev. W. Thornber, who was a pupil at Giggleswick School in the early part of this century, published a History of Blackpool in 1837, and in that work he writes (after describing a wreck):—

"The bodies of the Captain and his brother were found some weeks after between the points of Ayr, Isle of Man, and the Isles of Whithorn and Coll in the Solway Firth; that of my class-mate and friend, Harry Trelfall, was taken from the retreating tide by the family of a clergyman who respectably interred him at Glasserton, in a distant land, far away from the scenes of his childhood and the home of his youth. Farewell, friend of my youthful days, and companion of my rambles; I can tell of thy worth, and can still find pleasure in retracing our wanderings among the romantic hills of Craven, our bold adventures o'er the mountain steeps and fastnesses of the Scars of Giggleswick, the rugged falls of Gordale, and the wild heights of Malham; one while climbing to the highest peak in search of the haunts of the hawk; at another time resting and cooling our wearied limbs in the caves of Attermire, or quenching our thirst in the ebbing and flowing spring of Bucker Brow; and even now the dear remembrance of these by-gone days has not been effaced by the rough hand of the world, but oft bedews my cheek with the tear of tender regret. Nor do I lament, in thy fatal end, the only bereavements that ultimately death has wrought among my class-mates. One fell in India's wars, his forehead pierced with a leaden messenger of death; another died a victim to that scourge of heaven, the cholera, when, after ten years of service in a foreign clime, the ship, that was to convey the soldier to his friends, was awaiting a prosperous wind; a third administered to himself the cup of suicide; a fourth and fifth were hurried to an early grave by the bane of youth, consumption. May the dust be light upon you, till the peal of the last trump shall summon us all to that abode of happiness, where ties of friendship shall no more be severed by the hand of death or rudely torn asunder."

"May I but meet you on that peaceful shore
The parting words shall pass my lips no more."

"TERRIER" 1684.

The following is a "terrier" or particulars of the property belonging to the Vicarage of Giggleswick, A.D. 1684, and is from the Answers given by the Churchwardens for that year to a series of questions by the Archbishop of York.

> "An Answer to the Seventh Paragraph of the first Title in the Archbishops Articles of Enquiry at his Metropolitical Visitation 1684 by the then Churchwardens of the Parish of Giggleswick.
>
> We have no such perfect "Terrier" as is inquired after in the said paragraph but upon our utmost Inquiry we find these particulars hereafter mentioned belonging to the Vicarage of Giggleswick and does not know or can inform ourselves of any thing more belonging the same.
>
> First we find one House standing and adjoining to the Churchyard of Giggleswick aforesaid belonging the said Vicarage.
>
> We also find another House in the said Giggleswick called the Vicarage. Kitchen three Gardens and one Croft thereto adjoining belonging to the said Vicarage.
>
> We also find that all the Tythes of Corn and Grain of the several Towns of Langcliffe and Stainforth being of the yearly value of £38 belongeth to the said Vicarage.
>
> As also one Dale or parcel of Ground lying in the Hall Ing within the Grounds of William Tatham Gent. belonging to Cleatop containing by Estimation about one acre the same being yearly worth 20s.
>
> As also one other Dale or Parcel of Ground lying within the Carr within the Grounds of the said William Tatham being by Estimation one acre the same being yearly worth 10s.
>
> We also find that all the Easter Reckonings in the said parish belong to the Vicarage the same being yearly worth £12.
>
> We also find that all small Tythes and Surplice Fees within the said Parish belong the said Vicarage."

Anth. Lister, Vic.

C. Dawson }
R. Preston } Churchwardens.
Jo. Lister }

Jonas Dawson }
William Paley }
John Cookson } Parishioners.
Tho. Carr }
Richard Armistead }

GRAY, THE POET, AT SETTLE.

In the year 1769 Mr. Gray made a tour of this district, and thus recorded his impressions of Settle :—

Oct. 12th—" The nipping air, though the afternoon was growing very bright, now taught us we were in Craven; the road was all up and down, though no-where very steep : to the left were mountain tops, to the right a wide valley, all inclosed ground, and beyond it the high hills again. In approaching Settle, the crags on the left drew nearer to our way, till we decended Brunton-Brow into a cheerful valley (though thin of trees) to Giggleswick, a village with a small piece of water by its side, covered with cots : near it a Church which belongs also to Settle; and, half a mile further, having passed the Ribble over a bridge, I arrived there; it is a small market town standing directly under a rocky fell; there are not in it above a dozen good looking houses, the rest are old and low, with little wooden porticos in front. My inn pleased me much (though small) for the neatness and civility of the good woman that kept it ; so I lay there two nights and went (Oct. 13th) to visit the Gordale-Scar, which lay six miles from Settle; but that way was directly over a fell, and as the weather was not to be depended on, I went round in a chaise, the only way one could get near it in a carriage, which made it full thirteen miles, half of it such a road ! but I got safe over it, so there is an end, and came to Malham (pronounced Maum), a village in the bosom of the mountains, seated in a wild and dreary valley."

MALE SERVANTS, 1780.

In the year 1780 the tax or licence for having a male servant was 21s. At that time only one Gentleman in Settle, and three in the Township of Giggleswick, indulged in the luxury, the former being Mr. Parker of Marshfield (who kept four men), the Giggleswick ones being the Rev. Anty. Lister, Mr. Jos. Morney, and Mr. Roger Pickering, who had one servant each.

STREET LIGHTING IN 1896.

Owing to a dispute between the Settle Gas Co. and the first Parish Council of Settle the latter body caused the supply of Gas to all the lamps for street-lighting to be cut off, and substituted oil lamps! These were first lit on Dec. 5th, 1895 but proved a miserable failure. The Gas Company having obtained the Royal Assent to the Provisional Order sought for by them, and a new Parish Council having come into office, amicable arrangements were come to between the Company and the Council, and the streets were re-lit with Gas in Sept. 1896.

BIBLIOGRAPHICAL SCRAPS.

A portrait of the late John Birkbeck, senr. appears in the frontispiece to Hudson & Kennedy's "Mont Blanc and Mont Rosa."—The view of Settle from "the Mains" has appeared in "Travel," the "Midland Railway Guide," and the "British Printer" during 1896.—James Carr published a poem in praise of Settle.—The late John Tatham issued a pamphlet on "Popish Idolatry."—Bulmer's "Architectural Studies in Yorkshire" contains a full-page etching of Giggleswick Church Pulpit.—Geo. Dudgeon of Settle wrote a work on "The Duties of Overseers," 1838.—The late John Cowburn issued a "County Court Guide" in 1847.—Miss Thackeray's "Old Kensington" has several local allusions.—The late J. D. Watson prepared for the publication of a book called "The Picturesque Beauties of Craven," only two plates were issued.—One number of "The Settle Chronicle" had to be re-printed on account of its giving a long unauthorised report of Mr. Carr's lecture.

—A full-page view of the market-place appeared in Cassell's "Pictorial England and Wales" Oct. 1896.—Mr. J. Jackson published a series of twelve lectures delivered by him at Settle in 1824.—In Ogilby's "Britannia Depicta" (A.D. 1720) it is stated "Giggleswick was noted formerly for several small springs, ebbing and flowing almost every quarter of an hour."

LOCAL ODDS AND ENDS.

Spurious Coins, probably of Settle manufacture, have been found at Whitefriars, Batty Croft Gardens, and other places in the locality.—The "Ribblesdale" Lodge of Good Templars was established at Settle in Dec. 1871, and the "Scaleber" Lodge in Dec. 1872.—Settle Agricultural Show was not held from 1866 to 1877 inclusive, the cause of its suspension in the first place being the Cattle-plague.—Two ancient Urns have been found at Anley.—The old Masonic Lodge at Settle was held at the "Black Bull" Inn.—In olden times a beacon stood on "Beacon Hill" near Attermire.—"Queen's Rock" on the river, was formerly known as "King's Rock." It is rapidly breaking up.—Bulls used to be baited in Settle market-place.—A "Mayor" of Giggleswick used to be elected annually. Usually some notorious character was chosen.—The word "Settle" means the seat or station of a tribe.—Two of the houses at Stackhouse enjoy the reputation of having a "ghost" each.—Giggleswick and Settle used to be considered a great recruiting-ground for musicians for travelling shows.—An antique Coin or Ornament was found inside Settle Old Cross.—There was a great storm at Settle on Xmas Day, 1852.—The Reversion of Castleberg, subject to a Lease expiring in 1882, was sold in 1830.

THOS. BRAYSHAW.

www.ingramcontent.com/pod-product-compliance
Lightning Source LLC
Chambersburg PA
CBHW030743250426
43672CB00028B/385